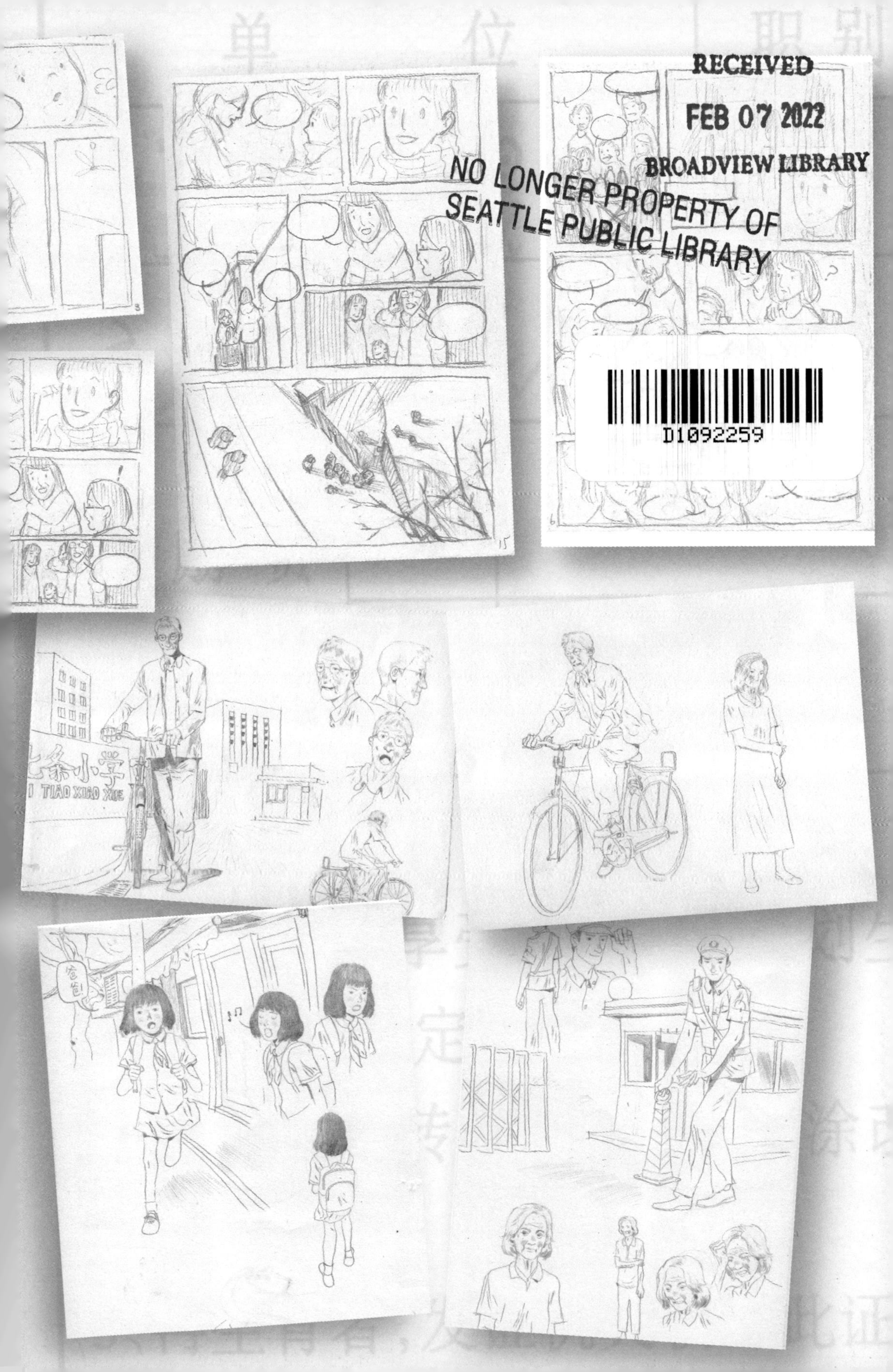
条小学
TIAO XIAO XUE
爸爸

LICAF & FANFARE PRESENTS

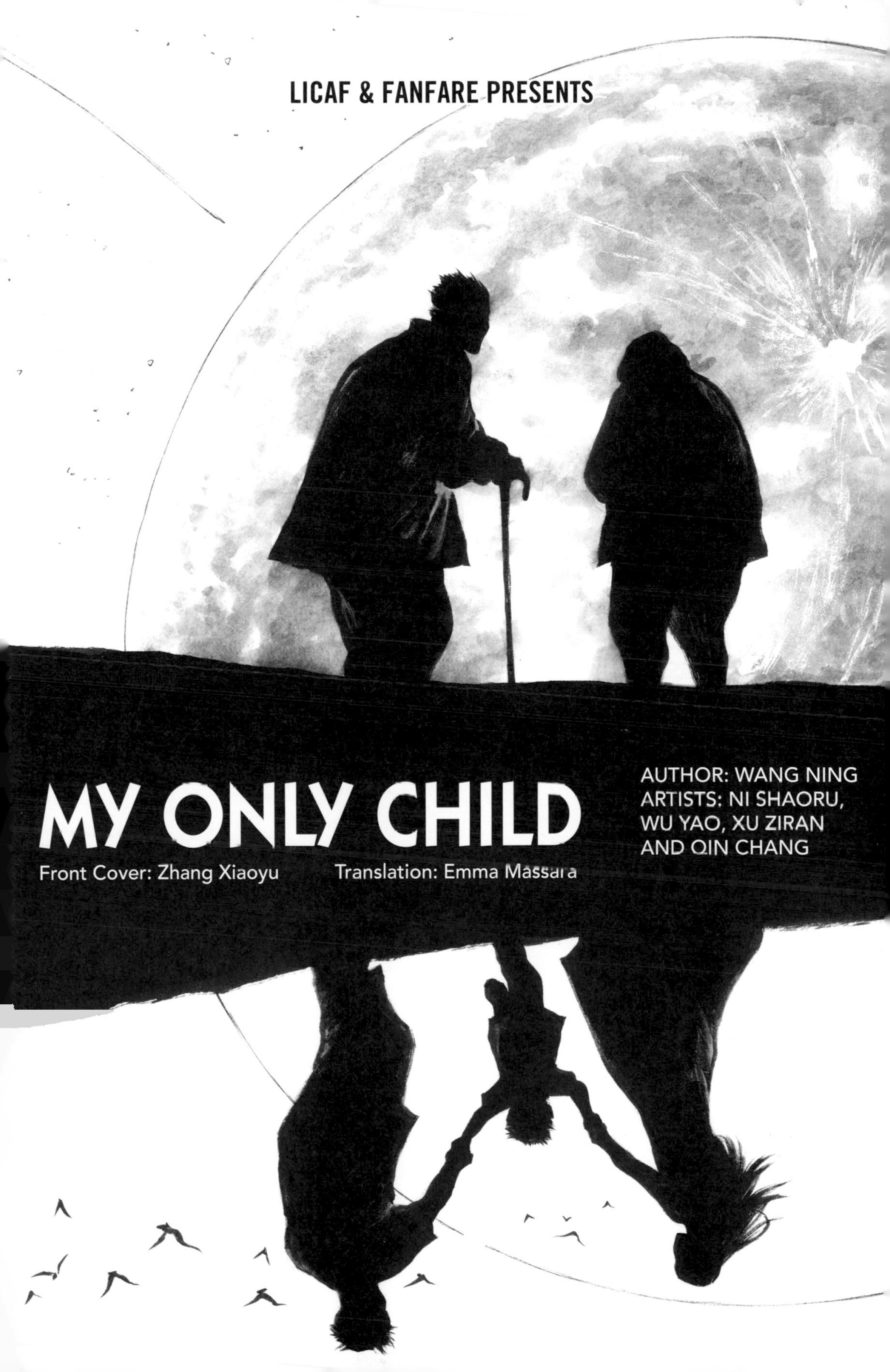

MY ONLY CHILD

Front Cover: Zhang Xiaoyu

Translation: Emma Massara

AUTHOR: WANG NING
ARTISTS: NI SHAORU, WU YAO, XU ZIRAN AND QIN CHANG

One Lonely World
© 2020, story by WANG Ning, illustrated by NI Shaoru, WU Yao, XU Ziran, QIN Chang
All Rights Reserved
English translation rights arranged with WANG Ning of BEIJING TOTAL VISION CULTURE SPREADS CO. LTD.

© Fanfare Presents, 2021 for the English language edition published in association with
The Lakes International Comic Art Festival 2021

English title My Only Child inspired by Nico

www.fanfareuk.com

Translation: Emma Massara
Graphic adaptation and layout: RG E Hijas S.C.P.
ISBN: 978-0-9932112-4-9
Printed and bound by Spauda in Lithuania

Contents:

北京市城镇居民副食补贴证明
№ 1174334
职工姓名
发放补贴单位名称
享受补贴居民情况
姓名
民族
补贴金额
与职工关系
居民类别
居民所在单位
街道办事处盖章（乡镇政府）
（公章）
经办人
年 月 日
制发单位
住址
所属街道
区（县）
办事处（乡镇）
居委会
补贴人数
补贴总金额
¥：
人民币（大写）
拾 元 角
第二联 由代领补贴职工交发放单位作为补贴的依据
说明：居民类别栏分为无业、待业知青、中小学生、学龄前儿童、个体经营者、自由职业者、临时工。

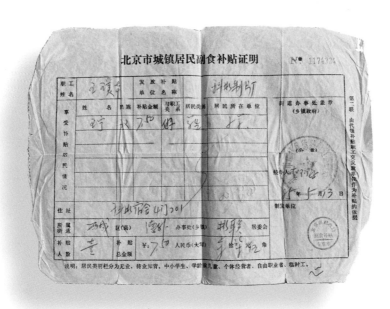

Certificate of Subsidy of Non-Staple Food for Urban Residents in Beijing

I am from a lucky generation

I was born in 1971. At that time, Chinese people could have as many children as they liked, so around me the overwhelming majority of my contemporaries all had brothers and sisters. I remember one friend the most vividly, his mother had 12 children. There was only a year's gap between each of them and, what's more, all 12 were born in sequence: boy, girl, boy, girl...

When I was little, I really didn't have a very clear concept of what being an only child meant. At that time, I didn't envy people with siblings at all, because I didn't have anyone stealing my food or snatching my drink. Later, as I grew older, I started to envy them. I started to feel lonely; there was nobody to chase boisterously, there was nobody to compete with for affection, there was nobody to protect me and, also, nobody for me to protect. Moreover, there was nobody with whom I could share happiness, let alone share sorrow.

I was probably 8 or 9 the first time I saw a One Child Certificate. Only then did I realize that being an only child could actually still have certain advantages. For example, because our family had this small red booklet, every month we could receive a 7.5 yuan food subsidy as well as a specific amount of food coupons from the neighborhood committee until I was 14 years old. Although 7.5 yuan is not a lot, in that era when you needed coupons to buy anything and an ordinary beginner apprentice earned 16 yuan a month, this could be half a month's salary. According to my mother, in 1985 when I turned 14 years old, they didn't receive the food allowance of 7.5 yuan that month. That's why I was able to see this subsidy certificate, as it should otherwise have been taken away by the neighborhood committee.

When I grew up, I had already long forgotten those joys and worries of childhood, so much so that I never even thought about the question of the only-child again. I felt very far removed from the issue until the January of 2010. When I was attending the Comic Arts Festival in Angouleme, my wife's 27-year-old cousin passed away due to illness. She was the family's only child, just like all the children born under this one-child policy. After she died it was the first time I saw and, moreover, personally experienced an issue that I had not paid attention to before: families bereaved of their only child.

Over the next few years, I wanted to make a comic on the subject of the only child. However,

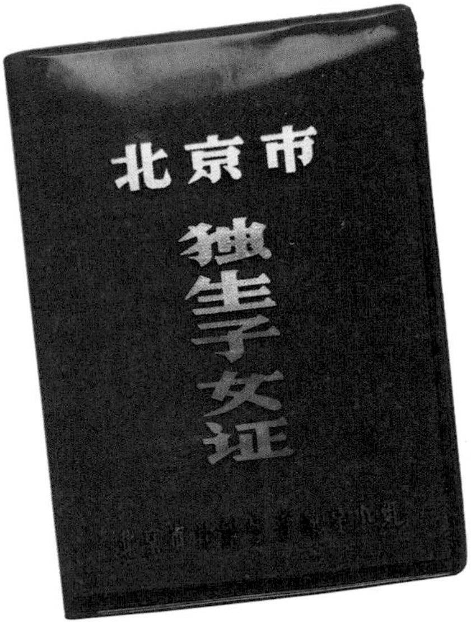
北京市
独生子女证

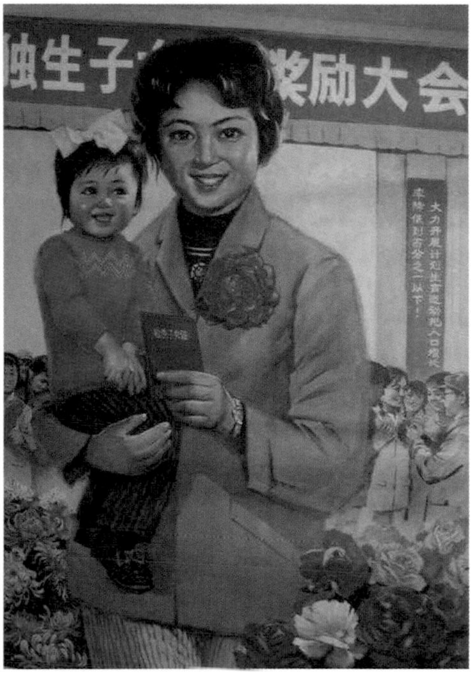
独生子
奖励大会

because I could not figure out how to do it and from what angle, I gradually forgot about it. On the 1st January 2016 the subject of the only child caught my attention afresh. From that day onwards, every family in China could have a second child.

I once again considered making a comic on this theme. However, at that time I thought that the comics I could make were still the type of stories that depict how lonely and driven only-children are. But what's the point of making such stories? They are so familiar to everyone and even I don't feel passionate about them. I had already found several comic authors but, in the end, because I was not satisfied, I shelved the project again.

After this, I continued to pay attention to conversations about only-children. Having consulted a large amount of material I discovered many true stories, all of them with the emerging phenomenon of the only child as the central issue. For example, on 20th September 1994, there was the mass shooting in the Jianguomen area of the capital, Beijing, perpetrated by Tian Mingjian. Also on 7th September 2011, in Nanchang in Jiangxi a legal request was made for "1 yuan compensation for the death of an only child", as well as many more actual legal cases. One phrase kept coming up: "a family bereaved of its only child". Now it was already half way through 2018.

As a result the idea for the comic grew ever stronger. Why not use some real stories set in China to tell people that, living all around us, there are still many families who have lost their only child? Whether responding to a call to action, or on impulse, or because of the former one-child policy; voluntarily or by force; they gave up a basic right. When tragedy happened, they had no choice but to face the brutal reality of society again. Every year, some 76,000 families, aged over 50 on average, are bereaved of their only child.

When I first started to work on this subject, my wife was firmly opposed. In fact, she still does not agree with me making this book now because her cousin's death was too painful for her uncle's family to talk about. I asked several of the family's older generation, as well as family members of the same age. Opinions differed, but the older family members were all opposed. At that time, I had already had a meeting about the project but once again the preparation was short-lived.

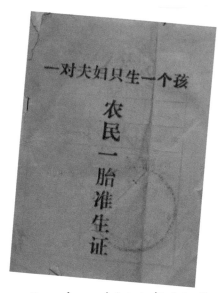

Soon afterwards I started to intentionally contact families who had lost their only child. I wanted to understand what they were thinking. After joining the over 500-member chat group, "Families Bereaved Of Their Only Child", I met some older parents. They had all had the same terrible experience: they had all lost their child; whether from injury or illness or an accident, they had all become "families bereaved of their only child".

When I mentioned to them that I wanted to make a comic to reflect the situation of families who had lost their only child, there were two opinions; one group refused, one group agreed. For the people who refused, it was because they were not ready to discuss distressing memories again. Even if several years or several decades have passed, this is still an horrendous scar, hidden deeply in their hearts, which they can't, and they don't want to, uncover. However, there were many people who agreed. Among them was a mother who said to me, "I am willing if, because of my child's passing, more people are made aware of families who have lost their only child, then his death has some meaning. I am willing to let him leave something meaningful for the world." Her words encouraged me and as a result we have this book.

The sorrow caused by the death of a loved one, especially an only child, is utterly devastating. I deeply understand, from the bottom of my heart, the helplessness and despair this brings. I cried writing these stories. I absolutely do not wish to see more families suffer this kind of pain; still less do I want to expose scars which have been deeply hidden and have never healed. My only wish is to use my one small ability, to tell the world that there may be families around us who have lost their child - love and take care of them, treat them kindly, understand them, help them through their cloud of suffering!

Compared to my peers born in the family planning era, compared to those children who left this world too soon, compared to those parents who are struggling on the edge of pain, I am from a lucky generation.

Lastly, I would also like to thank the four co-creators of this comic who have similarly endured much sorrow: Ni Shaoru, Wu Yao, Xu Ziran, and Qin Chang. I'd also like to thank our editor-in-chief Mr Wang Saili who, with falling tears, coordinated our authors' scripts.

Wang Ning
28th April 2020–

Waiting

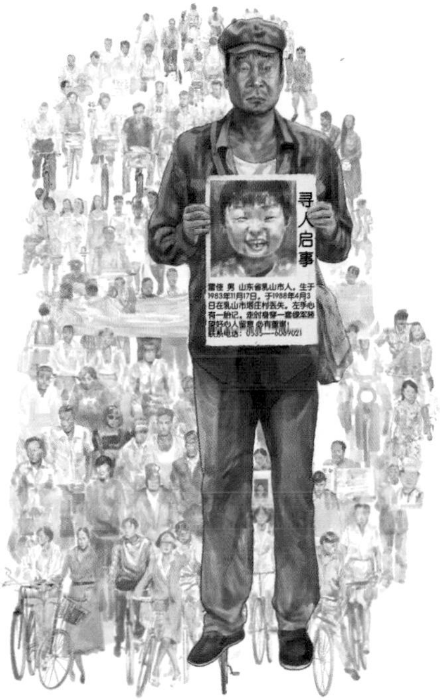
寻人启事

AUTHOR: WANG NING ARTIST: NI SHAORU

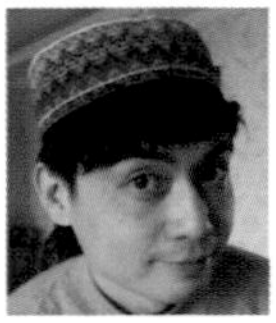

Ni Shaoru (artist)
Independent animation director, storyboard artist and animated film project consultant Ni Shaoru graduated from the French Gobelin Animation Academy and studied plastic art at the Central Academy of Fine Arts for four years. He has experience and skills in modeling design, visual development, storyboards and screen writing.

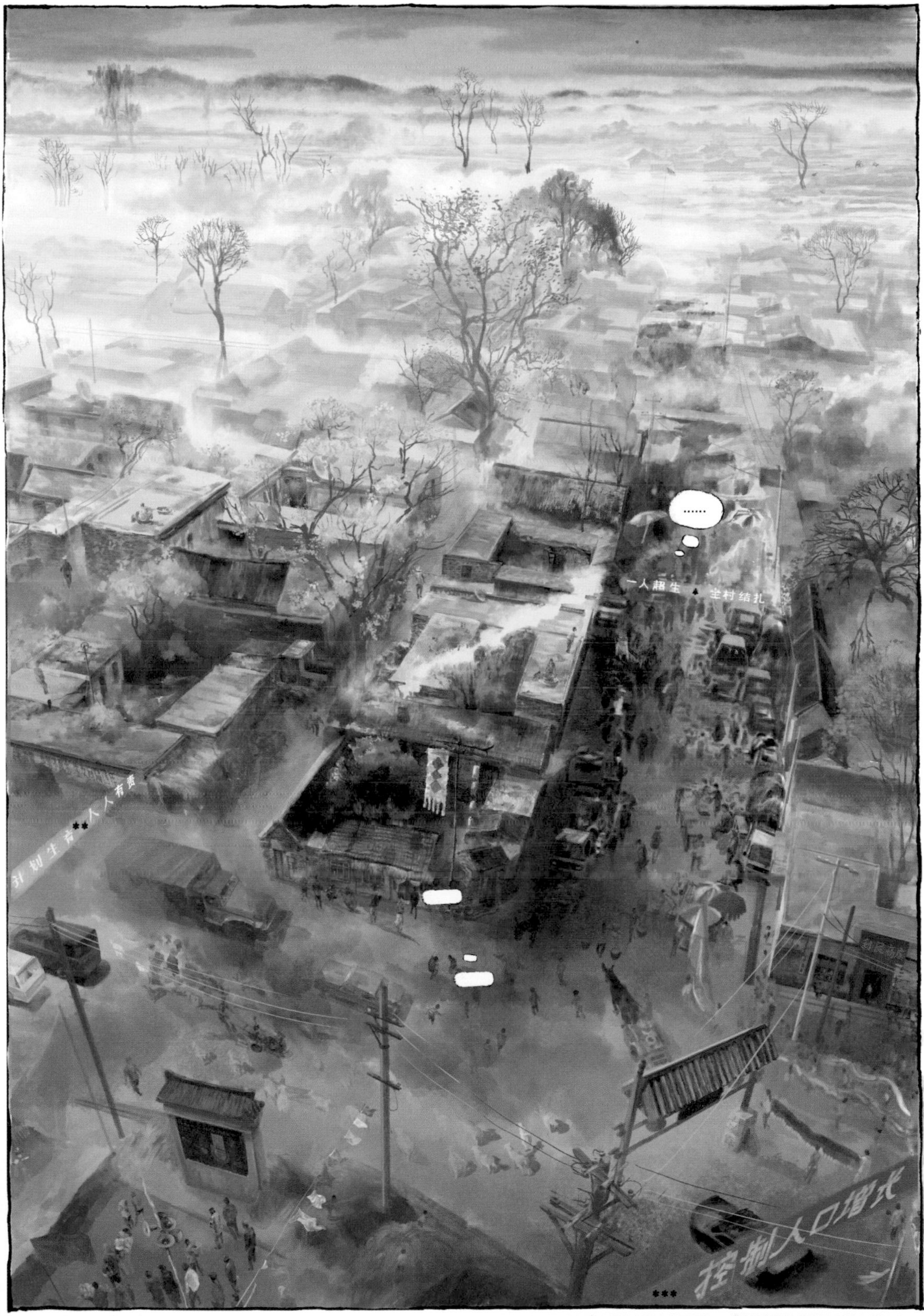
......
一人超生*全村结扎
计划生育**人人有责
控制人口增长***

*DO NOT BREAK THE ONE-CHILD POLICY OR EVERYONE WILL BE STERILIZED **WE ARE ALL RESPONSIBLE FOR POPULATION CONTROL ***CONTROL POPULATION GROWTH

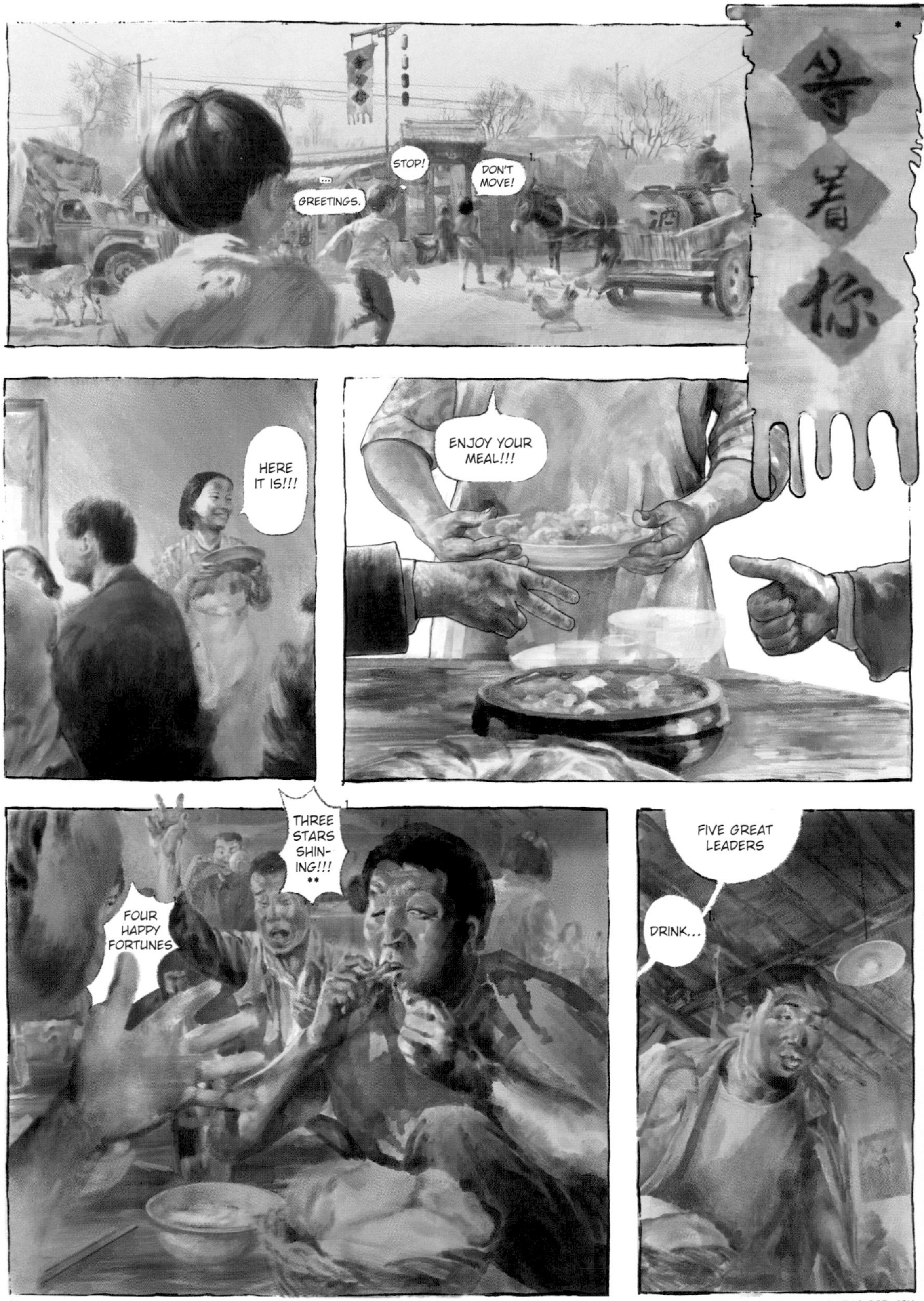
...
GREETINGS.
STOP!
DON'T MOVE!
酒
等着你 *
HERE IT IS!!!
ENJOY YOUR MEAL!!!
THREE STARS SHINING!!! **
FOUR HAPPY FORTUNES
FIVE GREAT LEADERS
DRINK...

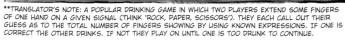

**TRANSLATOR'S NOTE: A POPULAR DRINKING GAME IN WHICH TWO PLAYERS EXTEND SOME FINGERS OF ONE HAND ON A GIVEN SIGNAL (THINK 'ROCK, PAPER, SCISSORS'). THEY EACH CALL OUT THEIR GUESS AS TO THE TOTAL NUMBER OF FINGERS SHOWING BY USING KNOWN EXPRESSIONS. IF ONE IS CORRECT THE OTHER DRINKS. IF NOT THEY PLAY ON UNTIL ONE IS TOO DRUNK TO CONTINUE.

*WAITING FOR YOU

POW!

HALT!!!

STICK YOUR HANDS UP. SURRENDER OR DIE!!

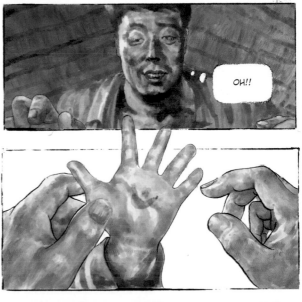

OH!!

HEY LANDLADY, YOUR KID'S GOT A LUCKY GOLD INGOT ON THE PALM OF HIS HAND! GUESS HE'S GOING TO BE A BIG BOSS LIKE HIS DADDY, HA HA ......

OH DEAR, PLEASE DON'T OVER EXCITE HIM TOO MUCH!

I'M BACK!!!

YOU'VE BEEN PLAYING OUTSIDE ALL DAY. YOUR DAD'S BEEN WORRIED SICK!

OH! MY PRE-CIOUS SON'S COME BACK AT LONG LAST!

*LUCKY

LOOK WHAT DADDY'S GOT! I'LL LIGHT IT FOR YOU! HA!

BLOW IT OUT!!!

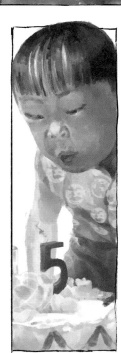

LET'S DRINK TO THAT!!!

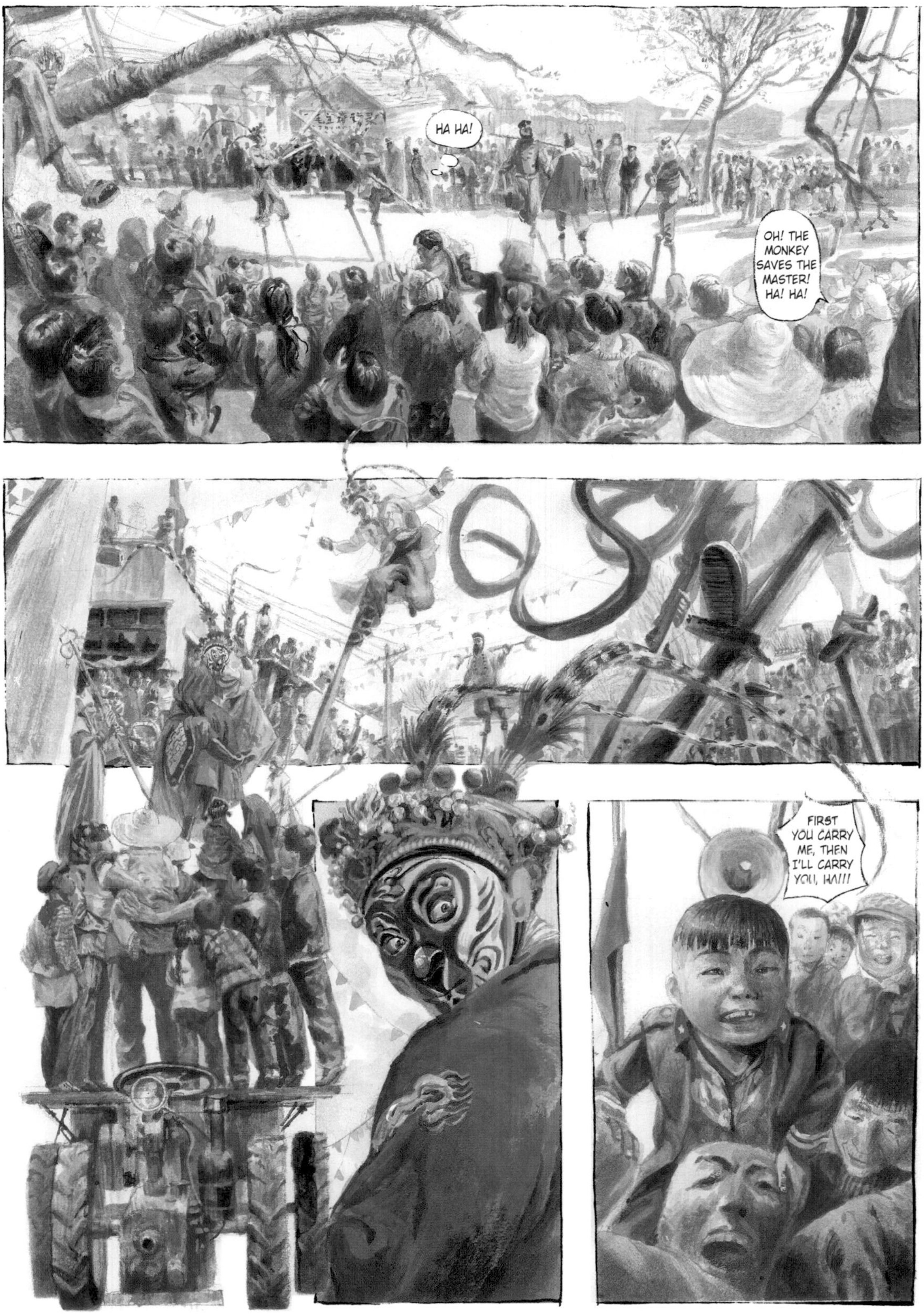
HA HA!
OH! THE MONKEY SAVES THE MASTER! HA! HA!
FIRST YOU CARRY ME, THEN I'LL CARRY YOU, HA!!!

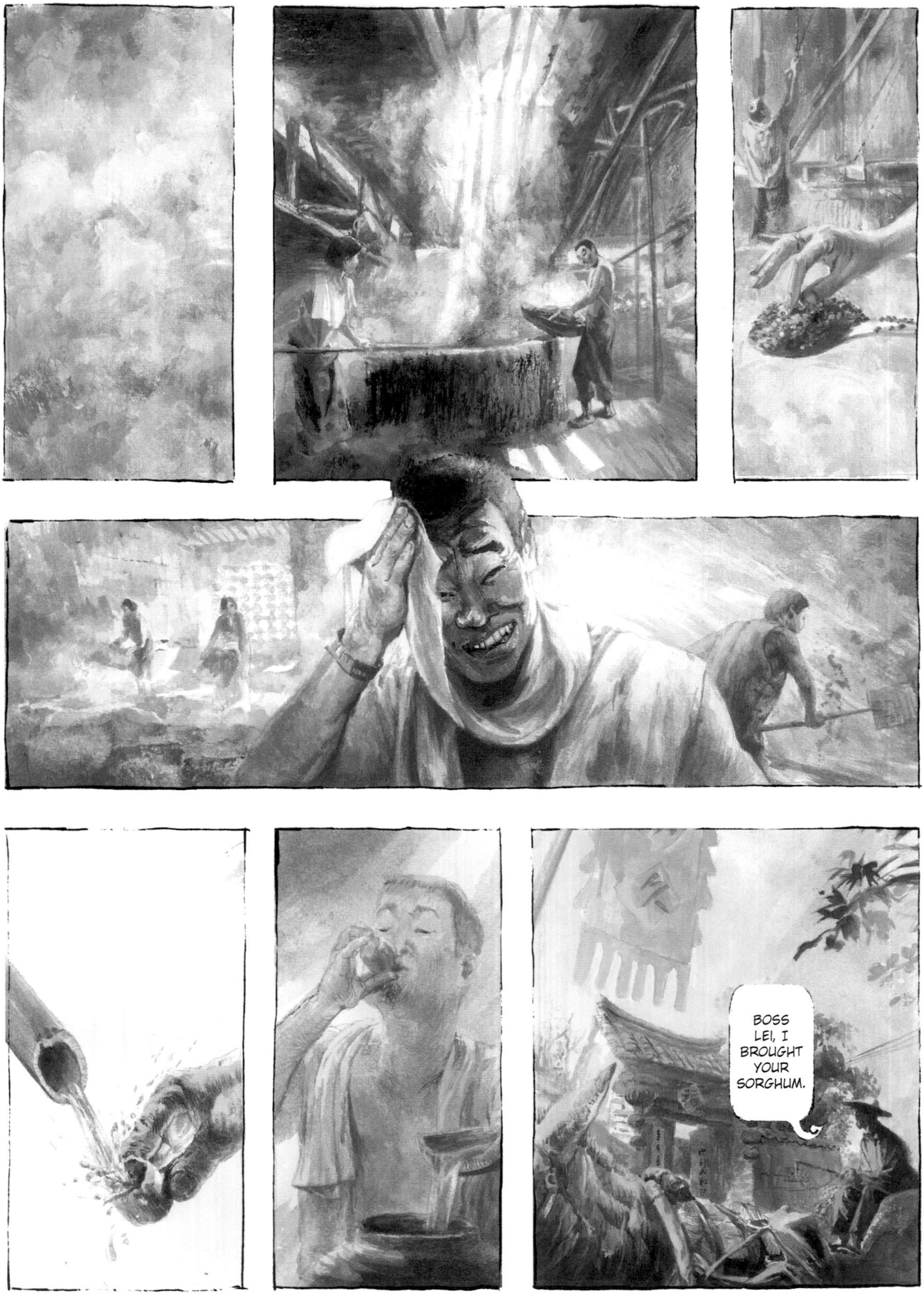
BOSS LEI, I BROUGHT YOUR SORGHUM.

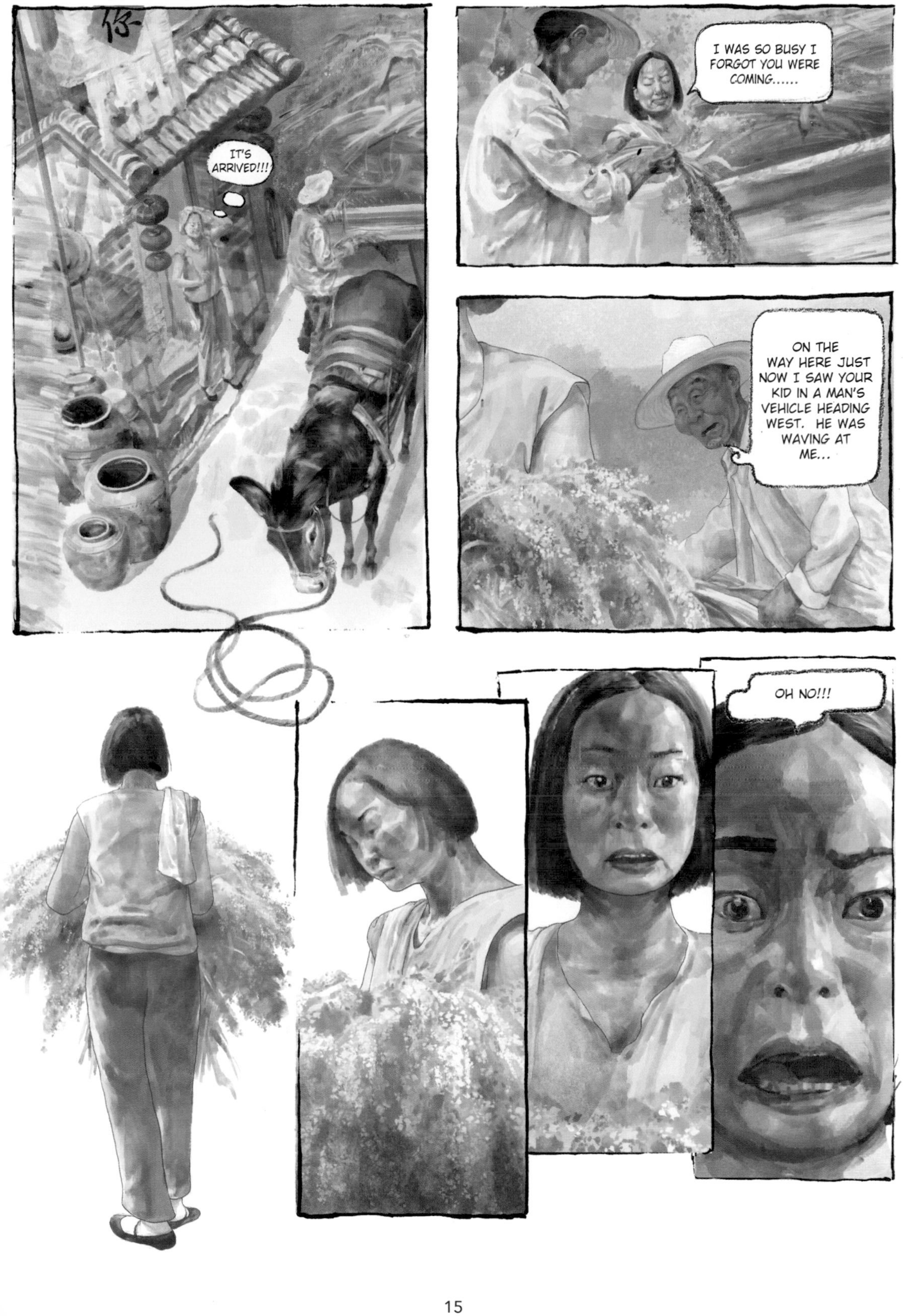
IT'S ARRIVED!!!
I WAS SO BUSY I FORGOT YOU WERE COMING......
ON THE WAY HERE JUST NOW I SAW YOUR KID IN A MAN'S VEHICLE HEADING WEST. HE WAS WAVING AT ME...
OH NO!!!

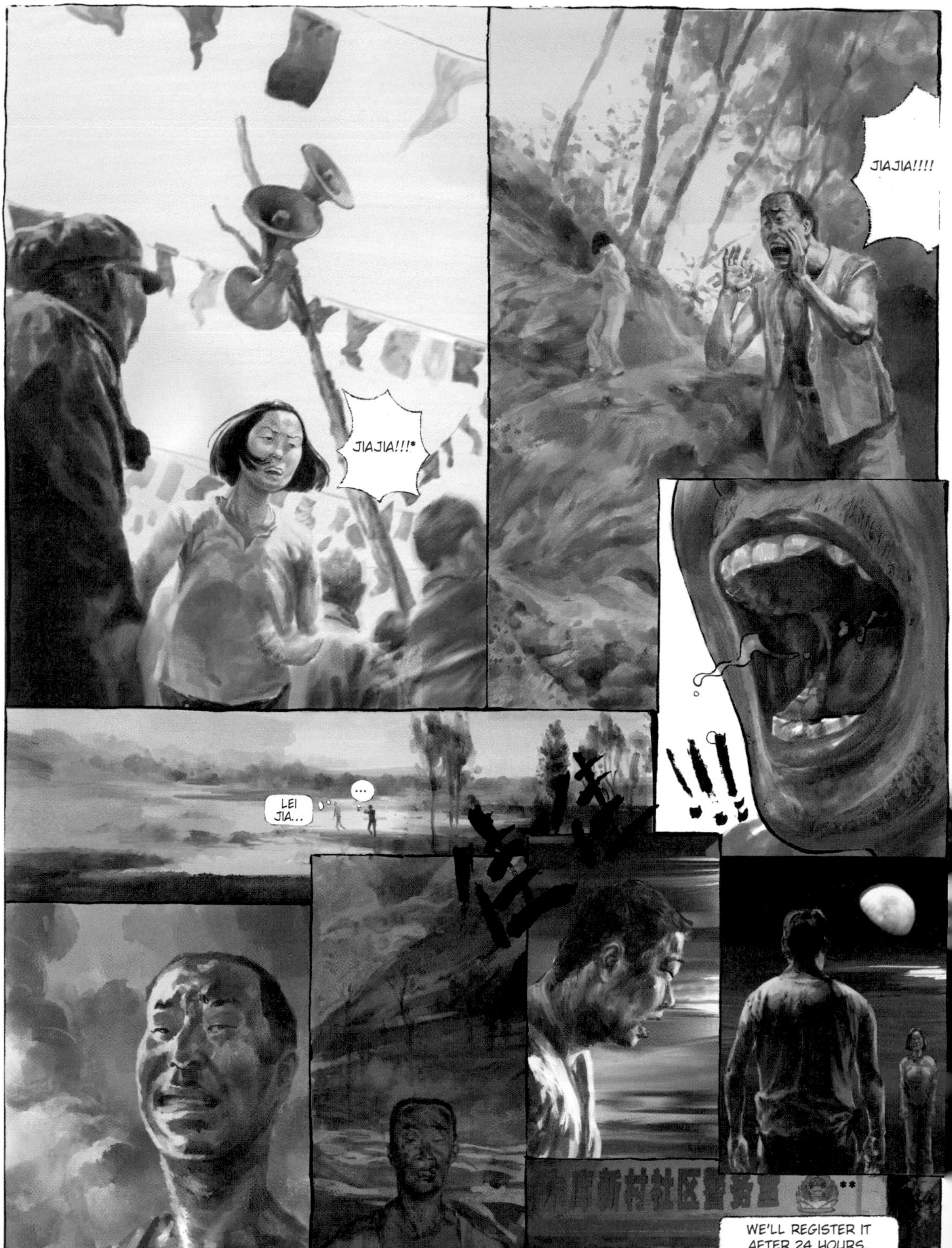
JIAJIA!!!*
JIAJIA!!!!
!!!
LEI JIA...
...
**
WE'LL REGISTER IT AFTER 24 HOURS. FIRST, YOU'LL NEED TO LOOK YOURSELVES....

* THE NAME MEANS: GOOD, FINE, THE BEST

** SHUIKU XINCUN COMMUNITY POLICE DEPARTMENT

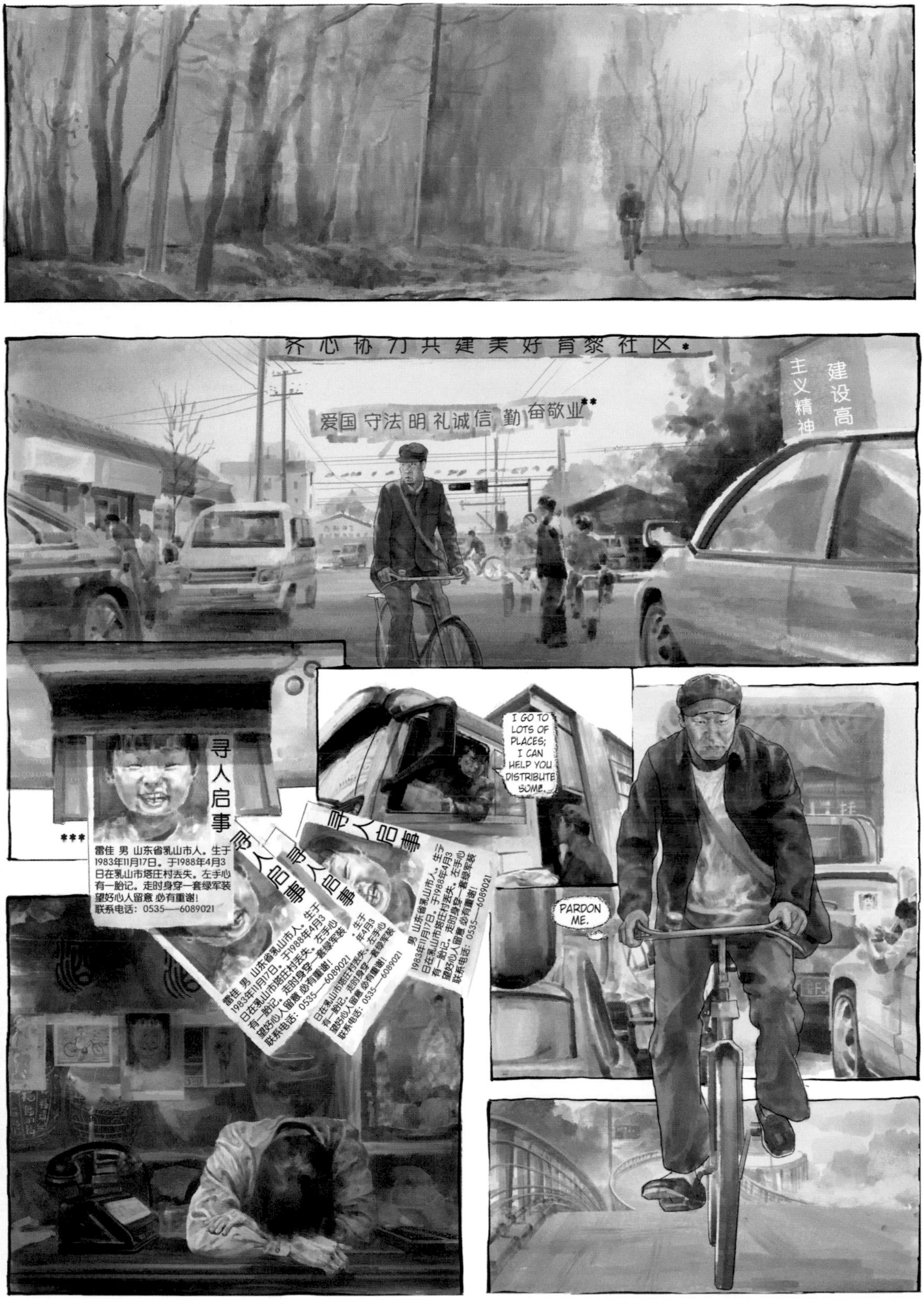
齐心协力共建美好育黎社区*
爱国守法明礼诚信勤奋敬业**
建设高
主义精神
寻人启事
***
雷佳 男 山东省乳山市人。生于1983年11月17日。于1988年4月3日在乳山市塔庄村去失。左手心有一胎记。走时身穿一套绿军装 望好心人留意 必有重谢！
联系电话：0535—-6089021
I GO TO LOTS OF PLACES; I CAN HELP YOU DISTRIBUTE SOME.
PARDON ME.

* MAKE CONCERTED EFFORTS TO COOPERATE FOR A GLORIOUS YULI COMMUNITY

** PATRIOTIC, LAW-ABIDING, COURTEOUS, HONEST, DILIGENT, DEDICATED

***MISSING PERSON ANNOUNCEMENT. LEI JIA. MALE. CITIZEN OF RUSHAN IN SHANDONG PROVINCE. BORN 11.17.1983. HE WENT MISSING FROM TAZHUANCUN IN RUSHAN ON 4.3.1988. THERE IS A BIRTHMARK ON THE PALM OF HIS LEFT HAND. AT THE TIME OF HIS DISAPPEARANCE, HE WAS WEARING A GREEN MILITARY-STYLE OUTFIT. IT IS HOPED THAT KIND-HEARTED PEOPLE WILL KEEP THEIR EYES OPEN FOR HIM, WE WILL BE VERY GRATEFUL. CONTACT TELEPHONE NUMBER: 0535 - - 6089021

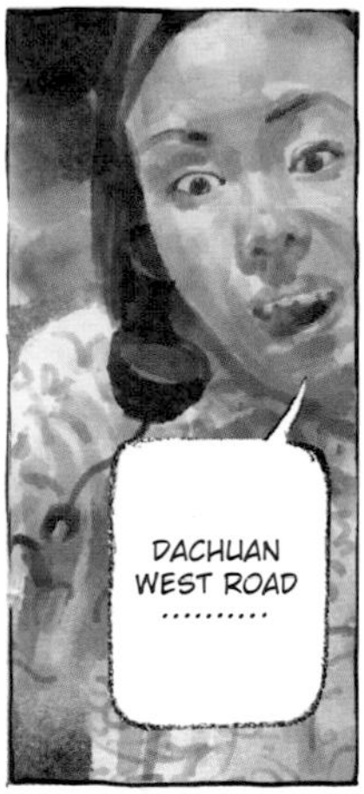
DACHUAN WEST ROAD ....

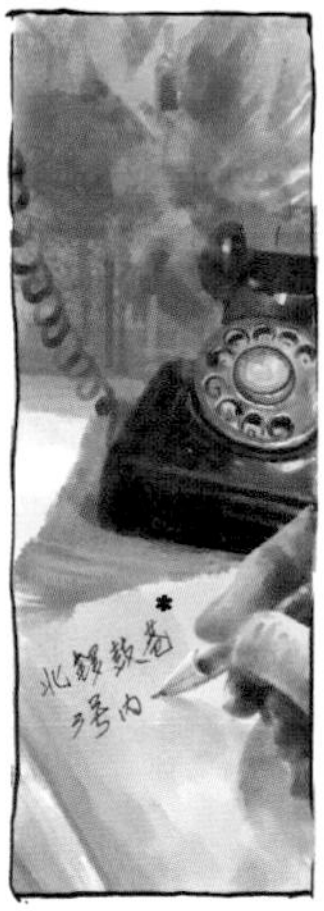
北鑼鼓巷 *
3号内

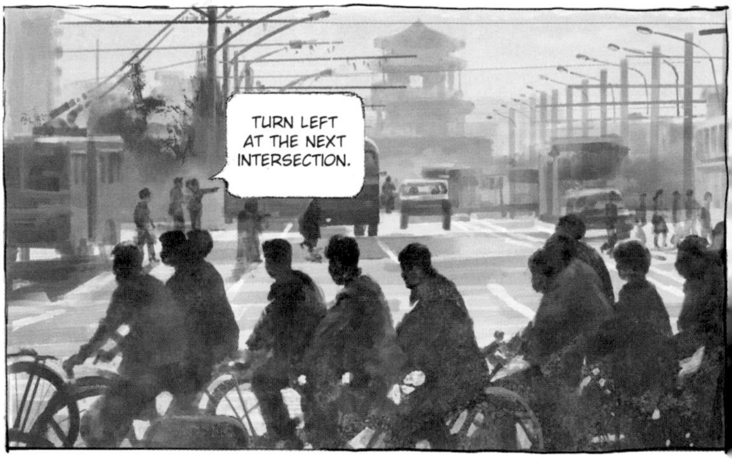
TURN LEFT AT THE NEXT INTERSECTION.

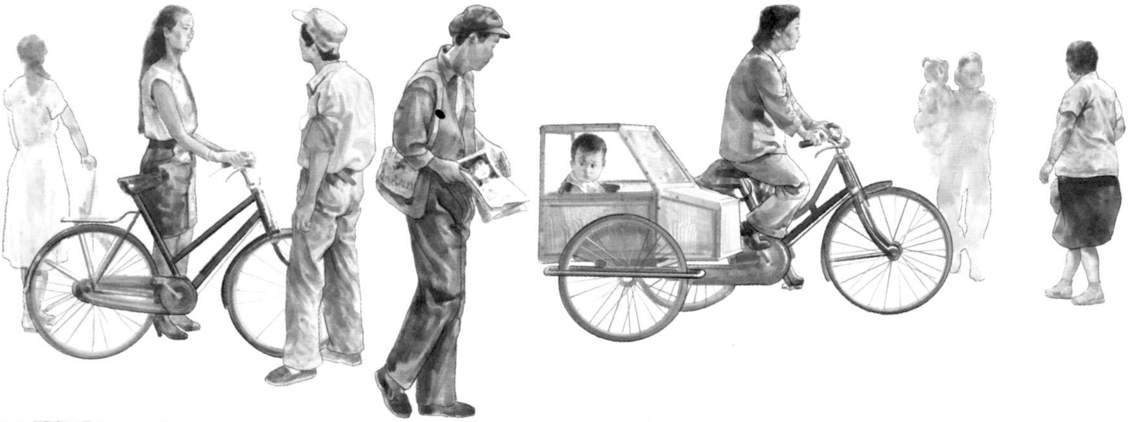

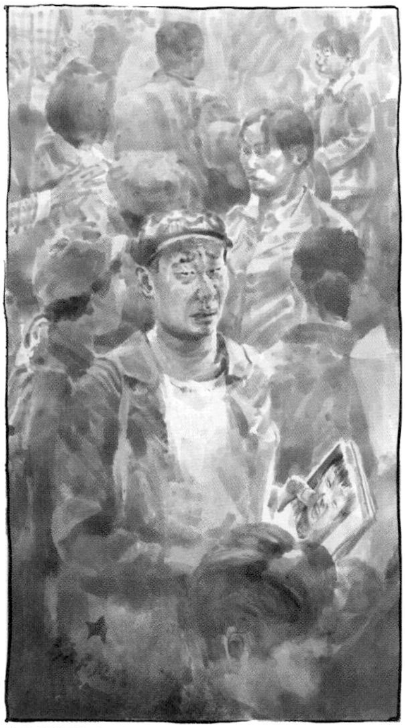

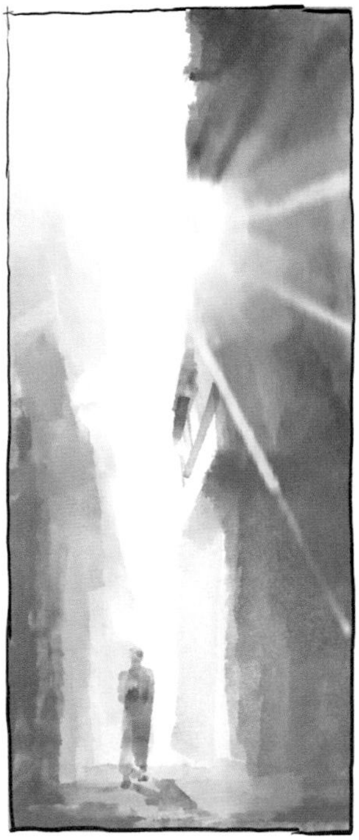

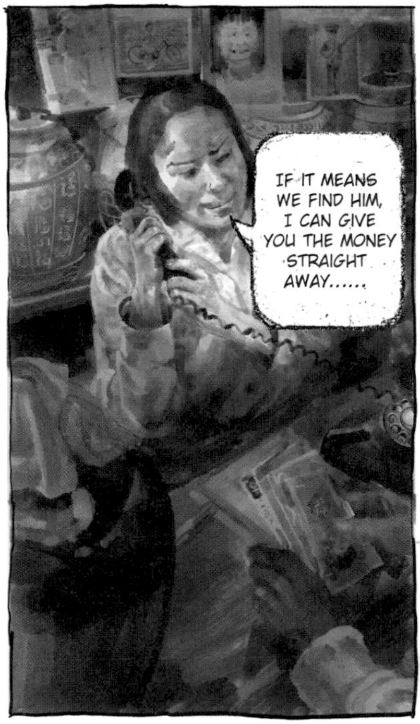
IF IT MEANS WE FIND HIM, I CAN GIVE YOU THE MONEY STRAIGHT AWAY......

* 3 BEILUO GUXIANG

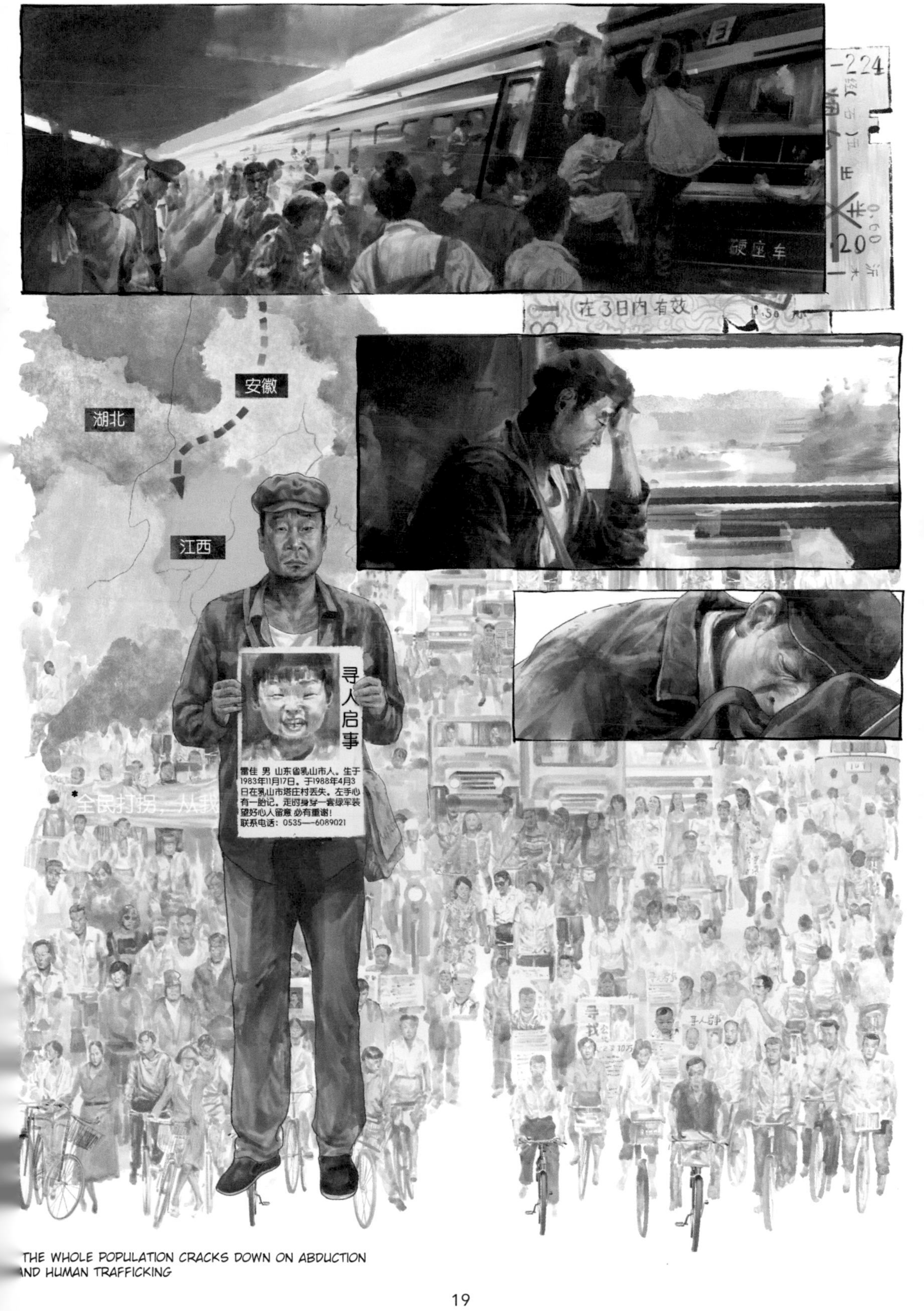
-224
硬座车
在3日内有效
安徽
湖北
江西
寻人启事
雷佳 男 山东省乳山市人。生于1983年11月17日。于1988年4月3日在乳山市塔庄村丢失。左手心有一胎记。走时身穿一套绿军装望好心人留意 必有重谢！
联系电话：0535——6089021
* 全民打拐，从我

* THE WHOLE POPULATION CRACKS DOWN ON ABDUCTION AND HUMAN TRAFFICKING

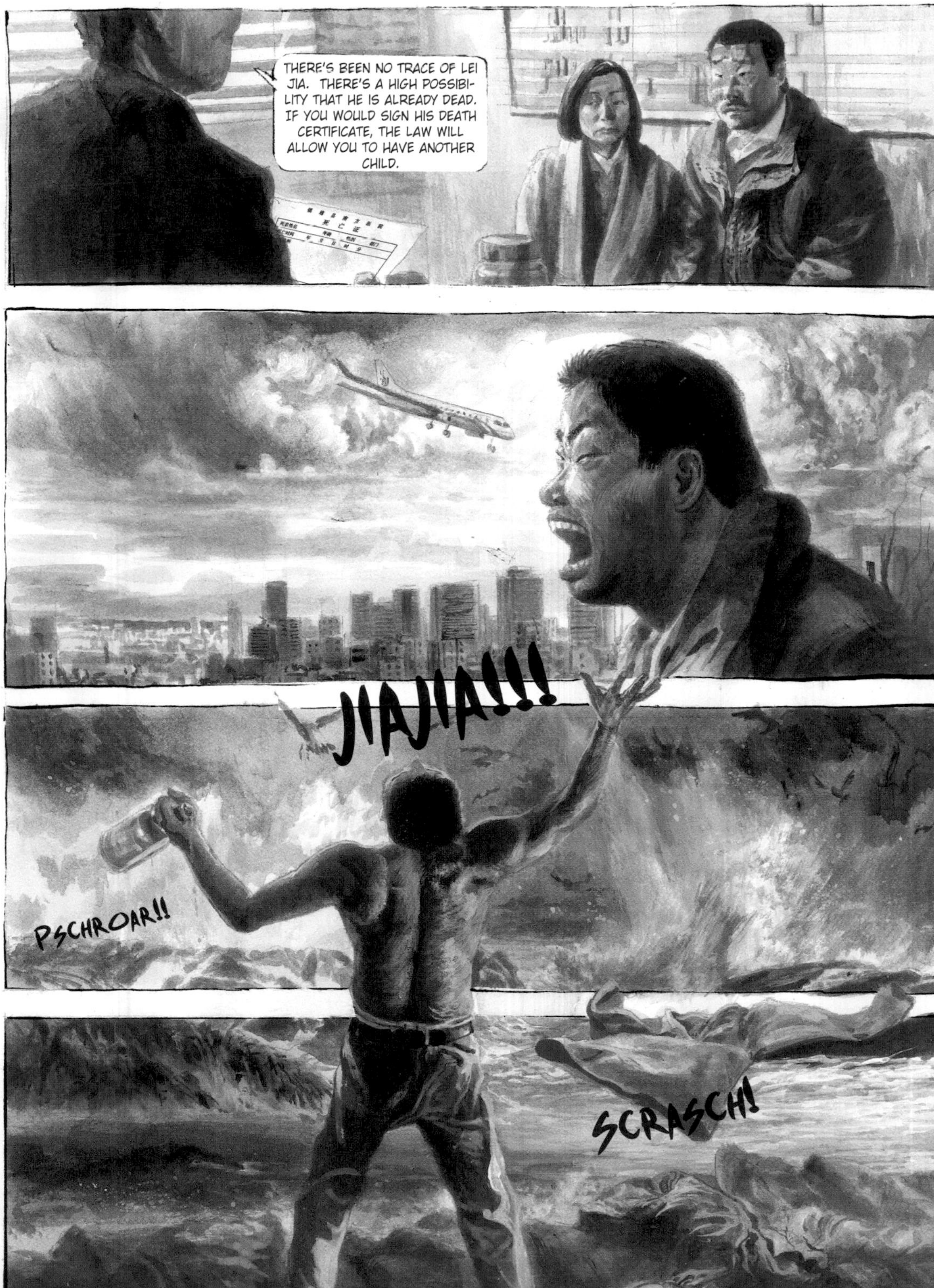
THERE'S BEEN NO TRACE OF LEI JIA. THERE'S A HIGH POSSIBILITY THAT HE IS ALREADY DEAD. IF YOU WOULD SIGN HIS DEATH CERTIFICATE, THE LAW WILL ALLOW YOU TO HAVE ANOTHER CHILD.
JIAJIA!!!
PSCHROAR!!
SCRASCH!

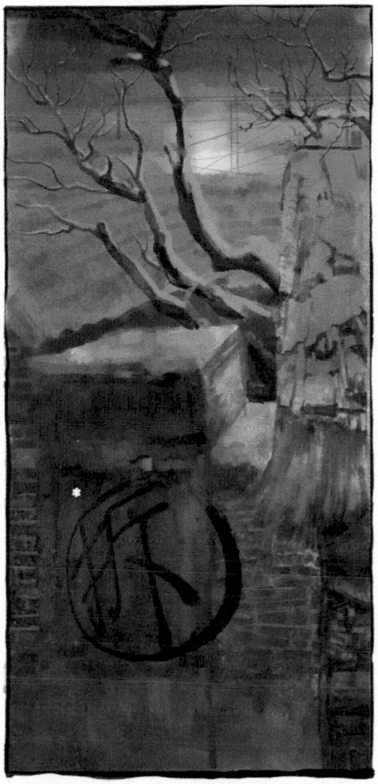
拆*

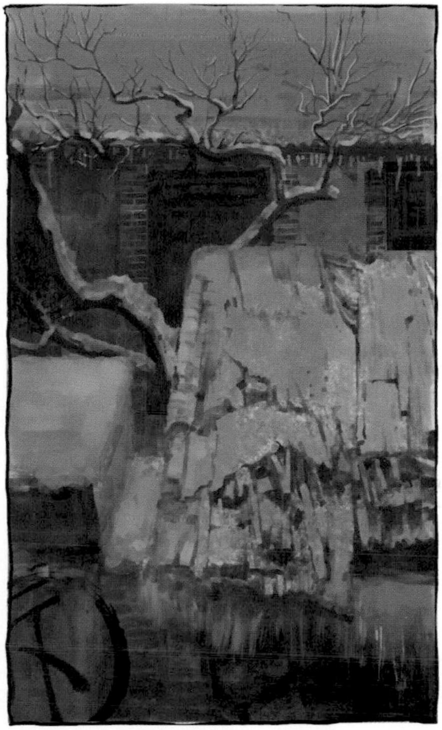

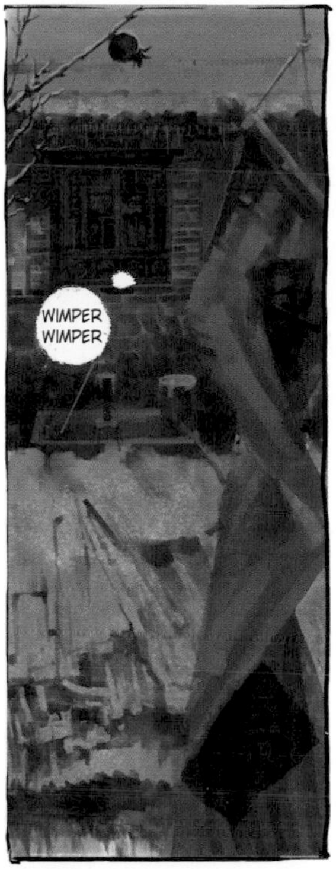
WIMPER
WIMPER

* DEMOLISH

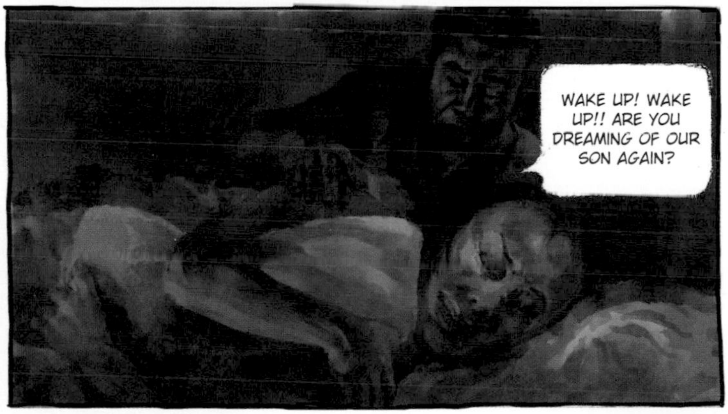
WAKE UP! WAKE UP!! ARE YOU DREAMING OF OUR SON AGAIN?

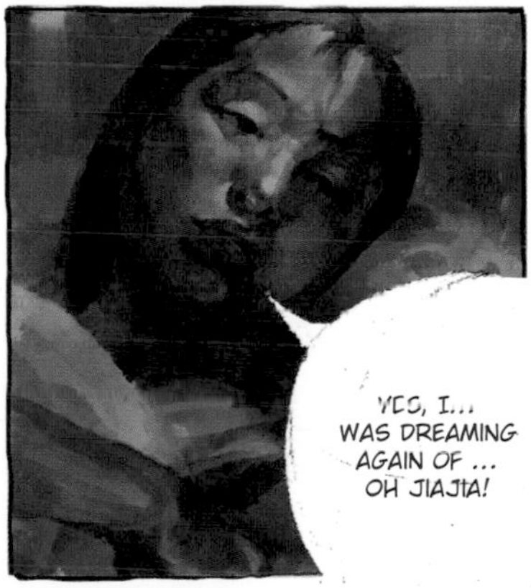
YES, I... WAS DREAMING AGAIN OF ... OH JIAJIA!

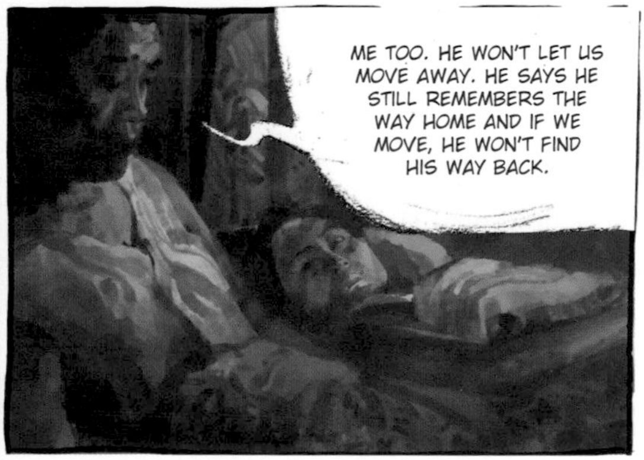
ME TOO. HE WON'T LET US MOVE AWAY. HE SAYS HE STILL REMEMBERS THE WAY HOME AND IF WE MOVE, HE WON'T FIND HIS WAY BACK.

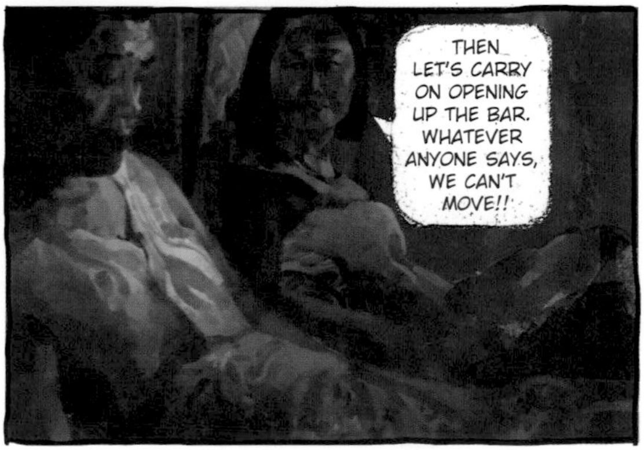
THEN LET'S CARRY ON OPENING UP THE BAR. WHATEVER ANYONE SAYS, WE CAN'T MOVE!!

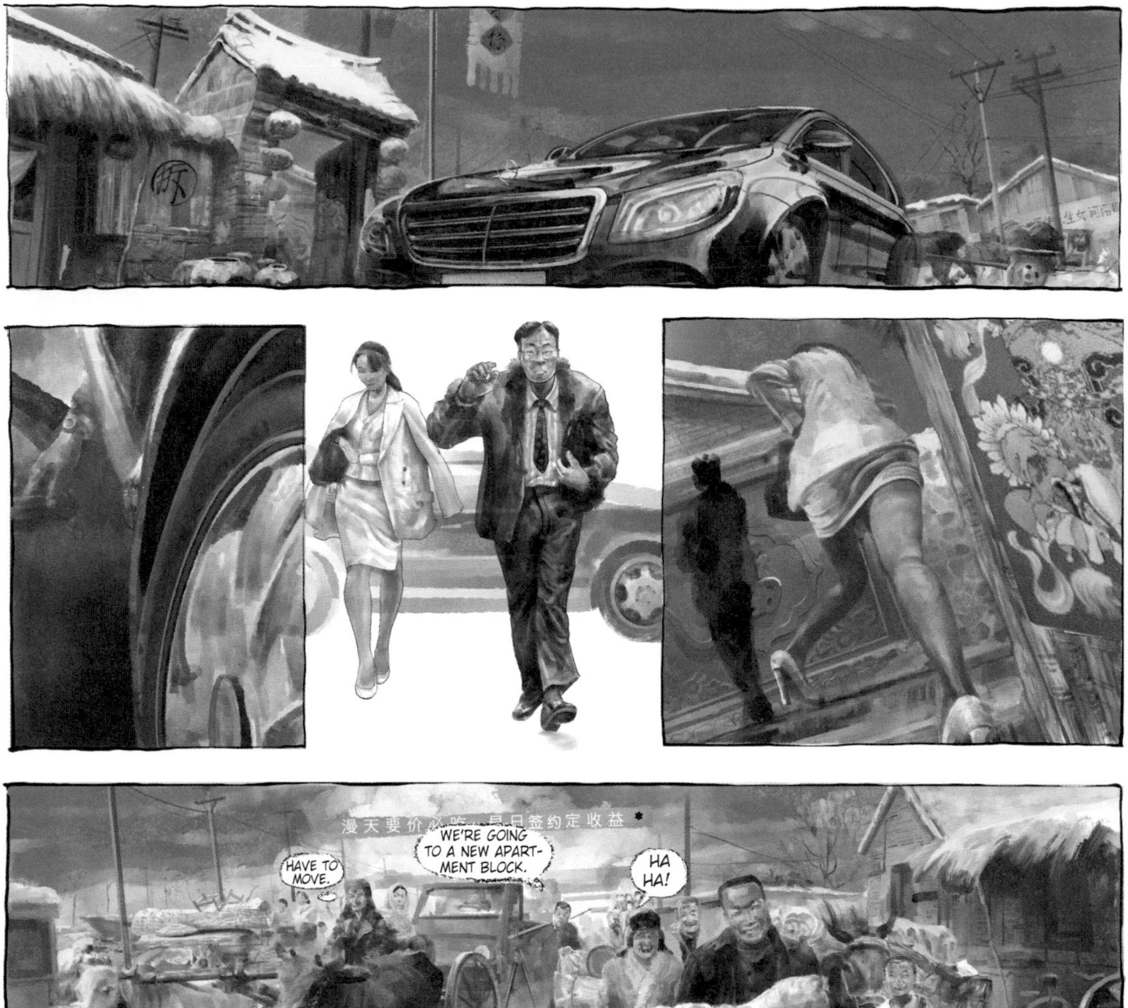
漫天要价必 签约定收益 *
HAVE TO MOVE.
WE'RE GOING TO A NEW APART-MENT BLOCK.
HA HA!

* SIGN NOW FOR A BETTER DEAL.

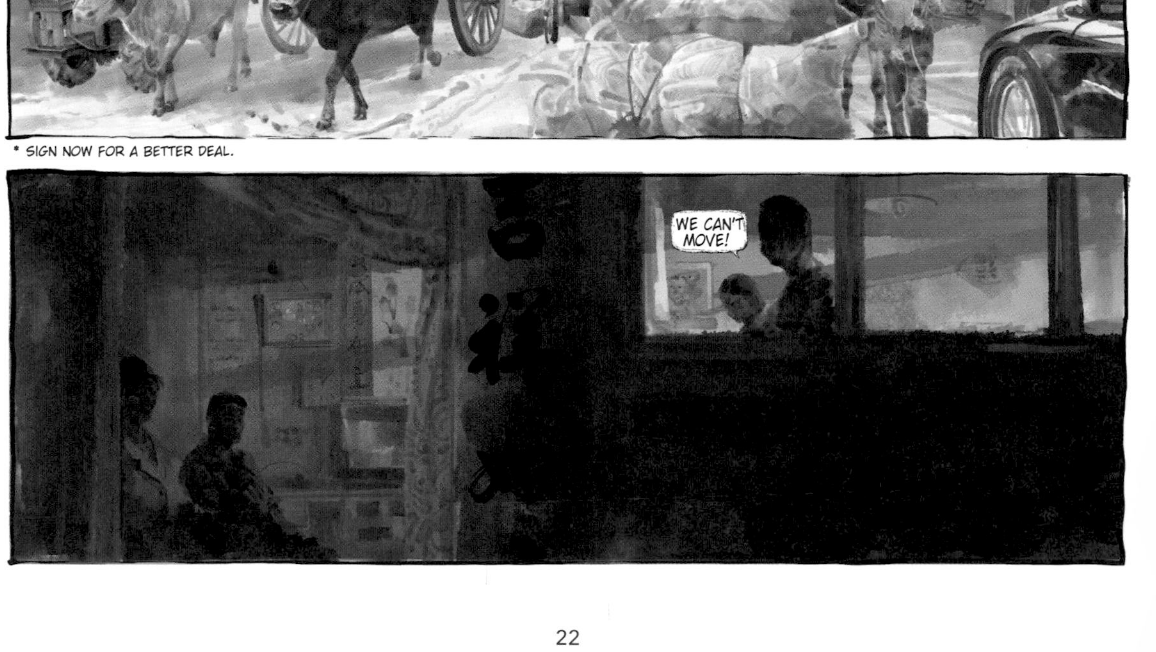
WE CAN'T MOVE!

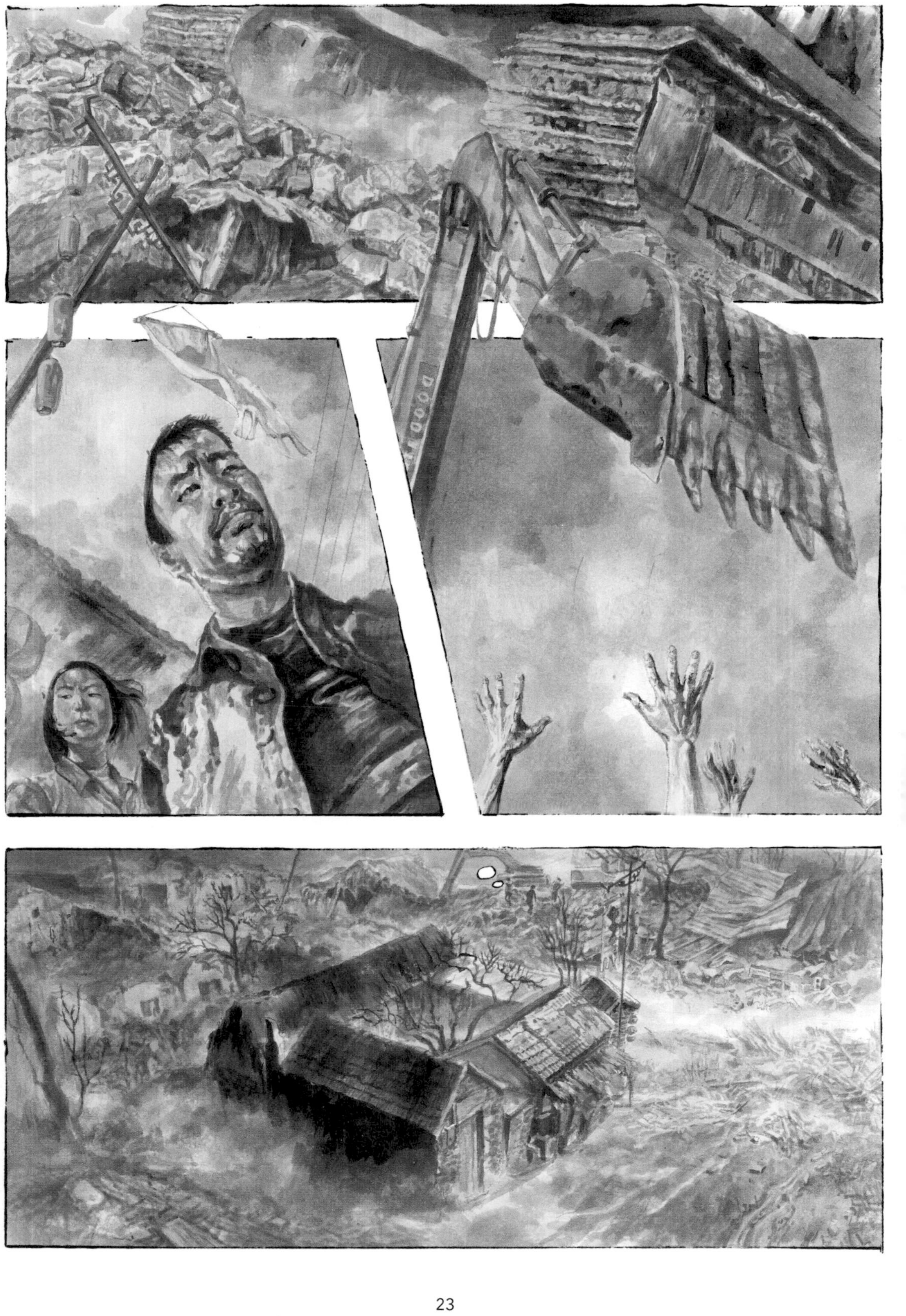

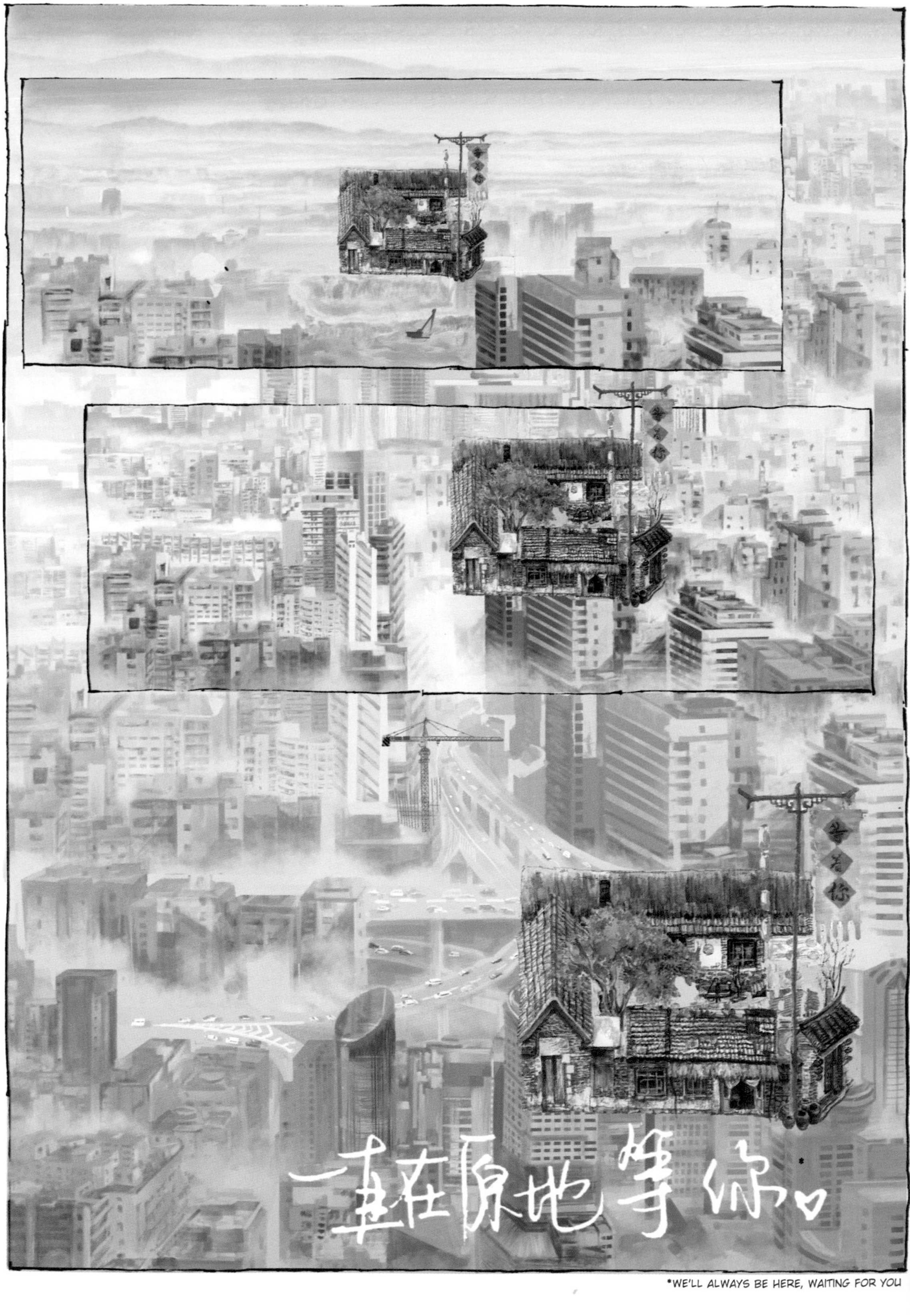
一直在原地等你*♡

*WE'LL ALWAYS BE HERE, WAITING FOR YOU

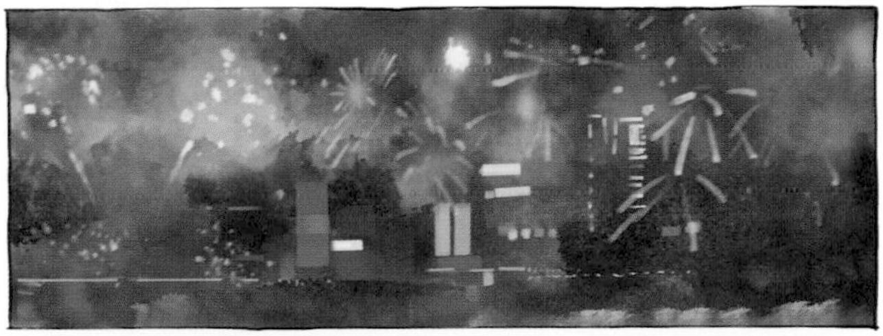

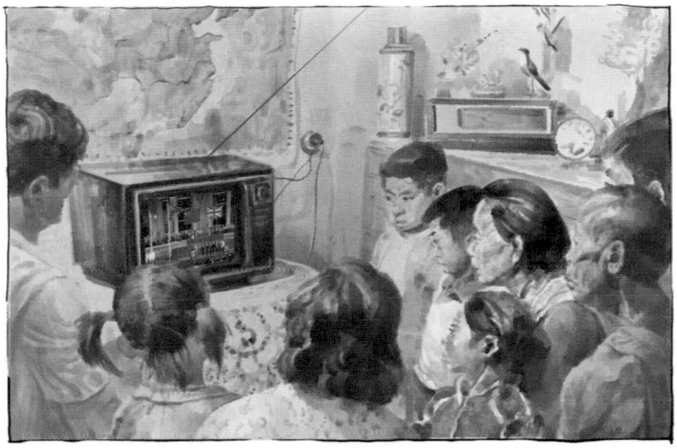

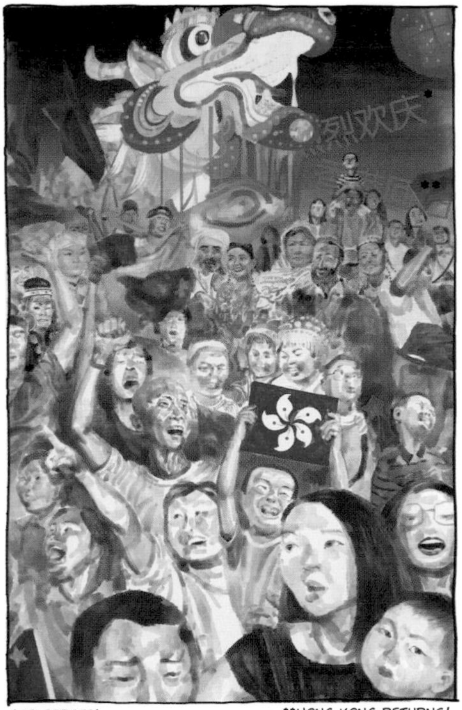
烈欢庆*
**

*CELEBRATE!　**HONG KONG RETURNS!

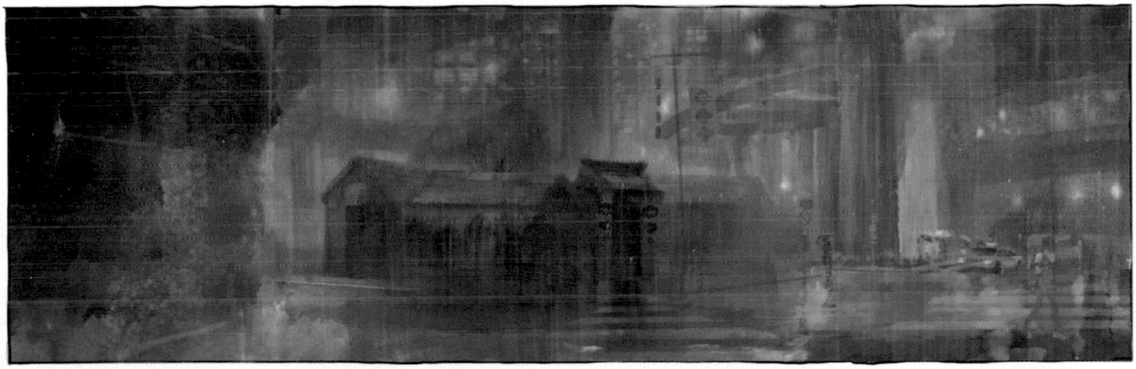

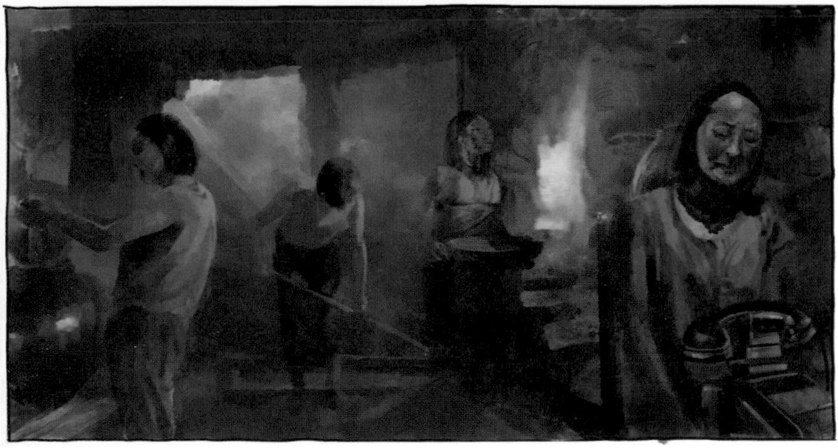

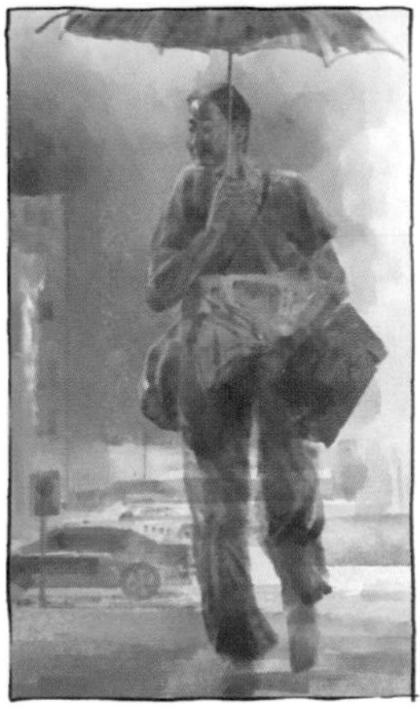

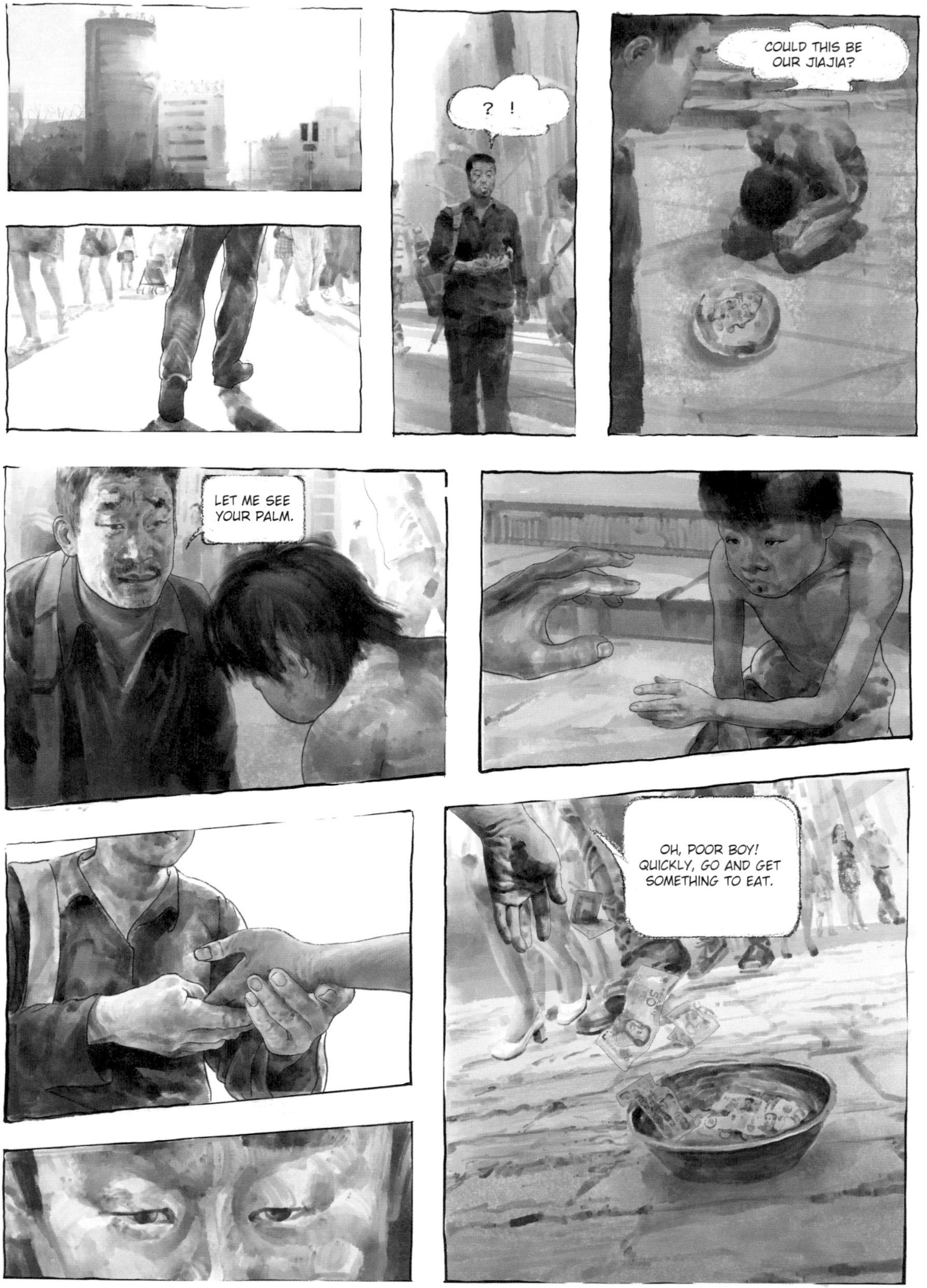
? !
COULD THIS BE OUR JIAJIA?
LET ME SEE YOUR PALM.
OH, POOR BOY! QUICKLY, GO AND GET SOMETHING TO EAT.

OH QUICK, LOOK! RE-PORTERS ARE COMING!

......

CLICK!

CLICK!

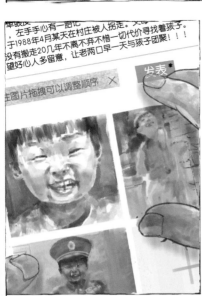

发表*

图片拖拽可以调整顺序 ✕

于1988年4月某天在村庄被人拐走。父母
没有搬走20几年不弃不离不惜一切代价找着孩子。
望好心人多留意，让老两口早一天与孩子团聚！！！

WHEN JIAJIA WENT MISSING HIS MEMORIES WERE ALREADY FORMED. IF THERE IS A DAY WHEN HE IS PERHAPS ABLE TO LOOK FOR HIS WAY BACK, WE WILL ALWAYS BE HERE, WAITING FOR HIM!

* PUBLISH

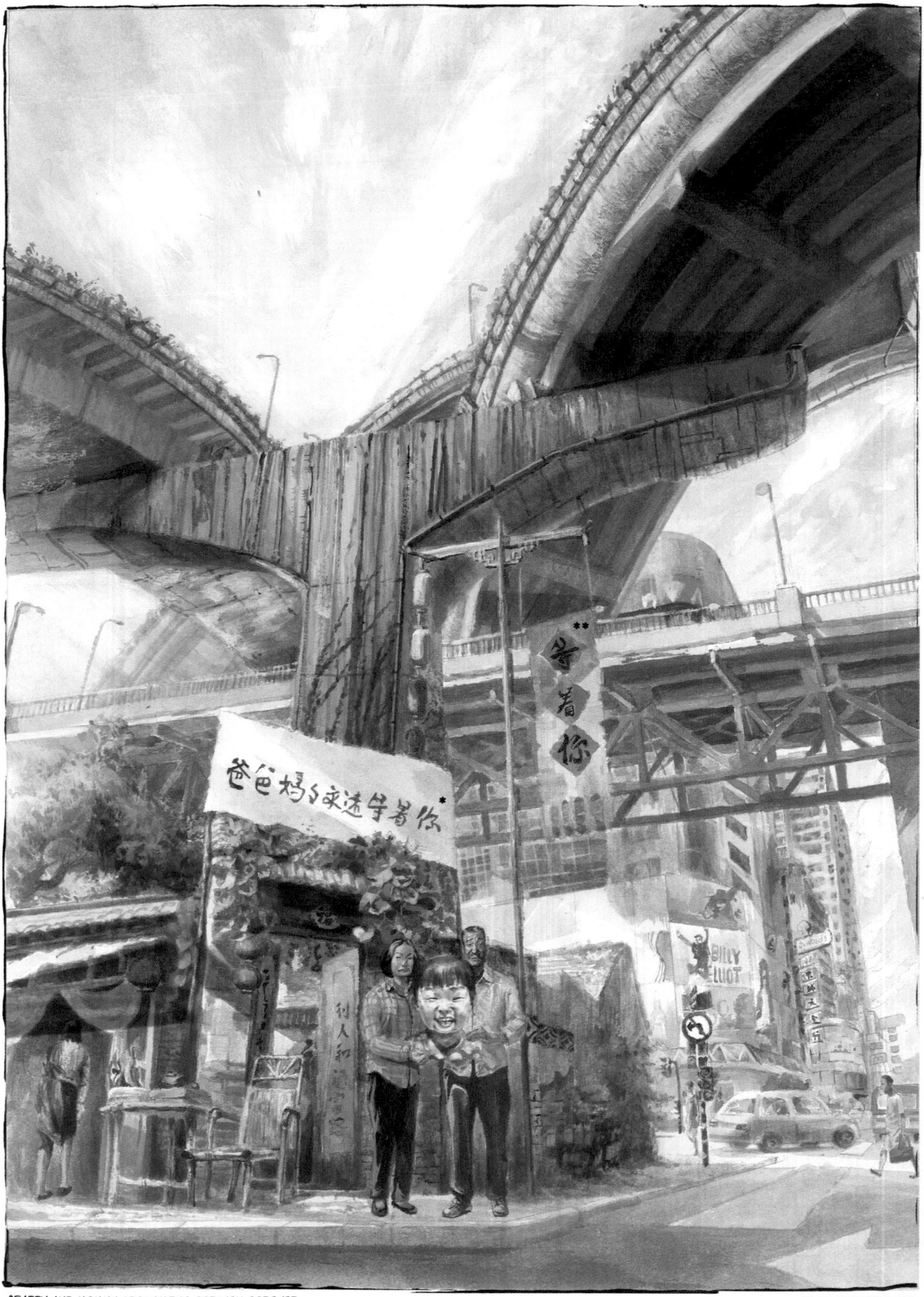
爸爸妈々永远等着你*
**等着你
BILLY ELLIOT

*DADDY AND MOMMY ARE WAITING FOR YOU FOREVER.

** WAITING FOR YOU

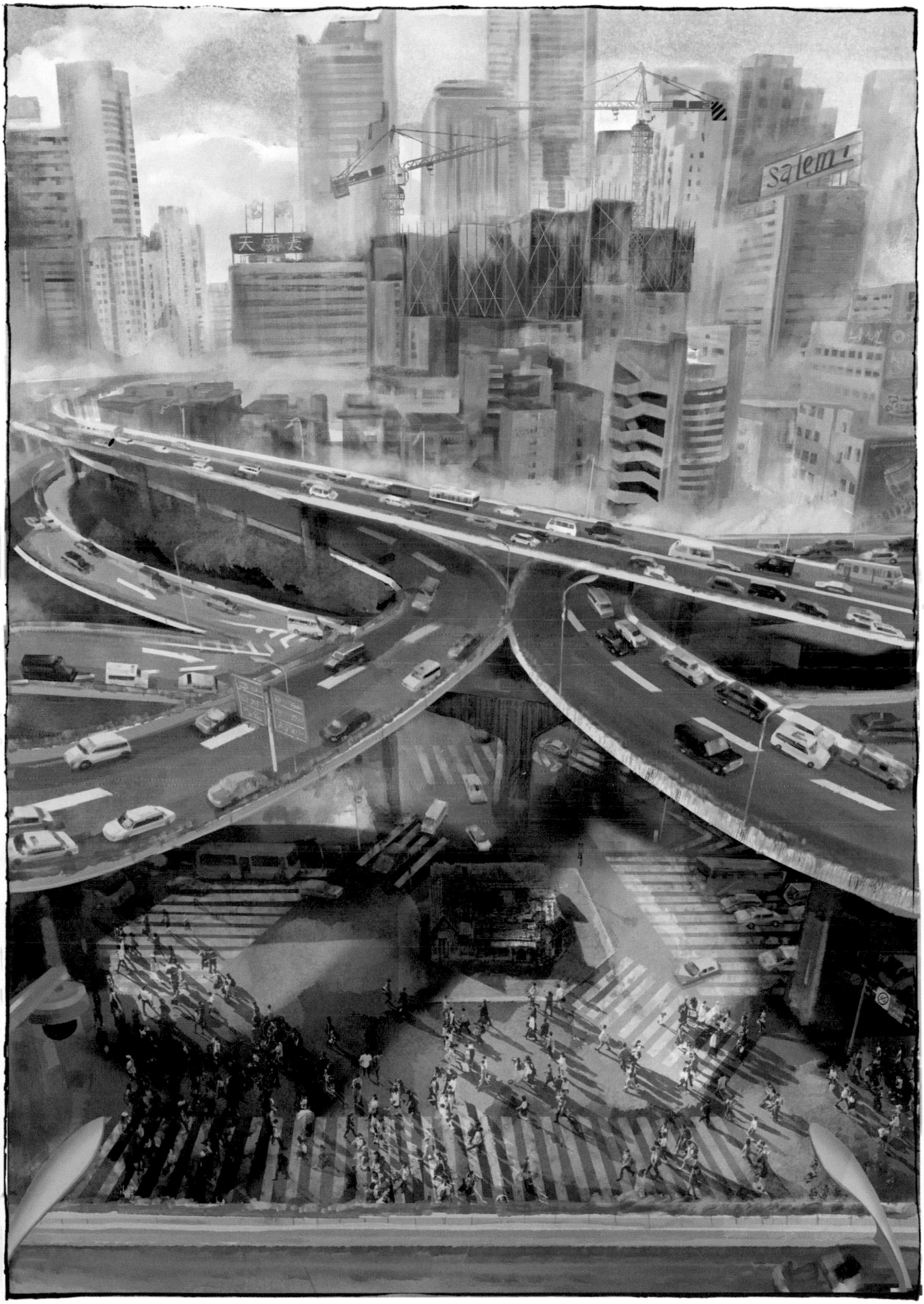
salem

MoMo's Story

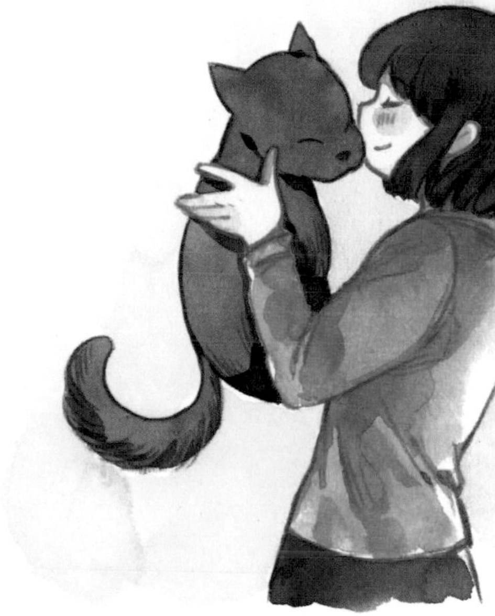

AUTHOR: WANG NING   ARTIST: WU YAO

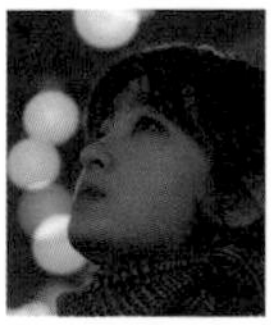

Wu Yao (artist)
Mia graduated from the Animation Department of the Xi'an Academy of Fine Arts. In 2007, she started to publish comic booklets. She was involved in the creation of many series of comic book collections. In 2019 she won the gold award in the "Second Sino-Japanese comic strip competition" jointly held by China and Japan.

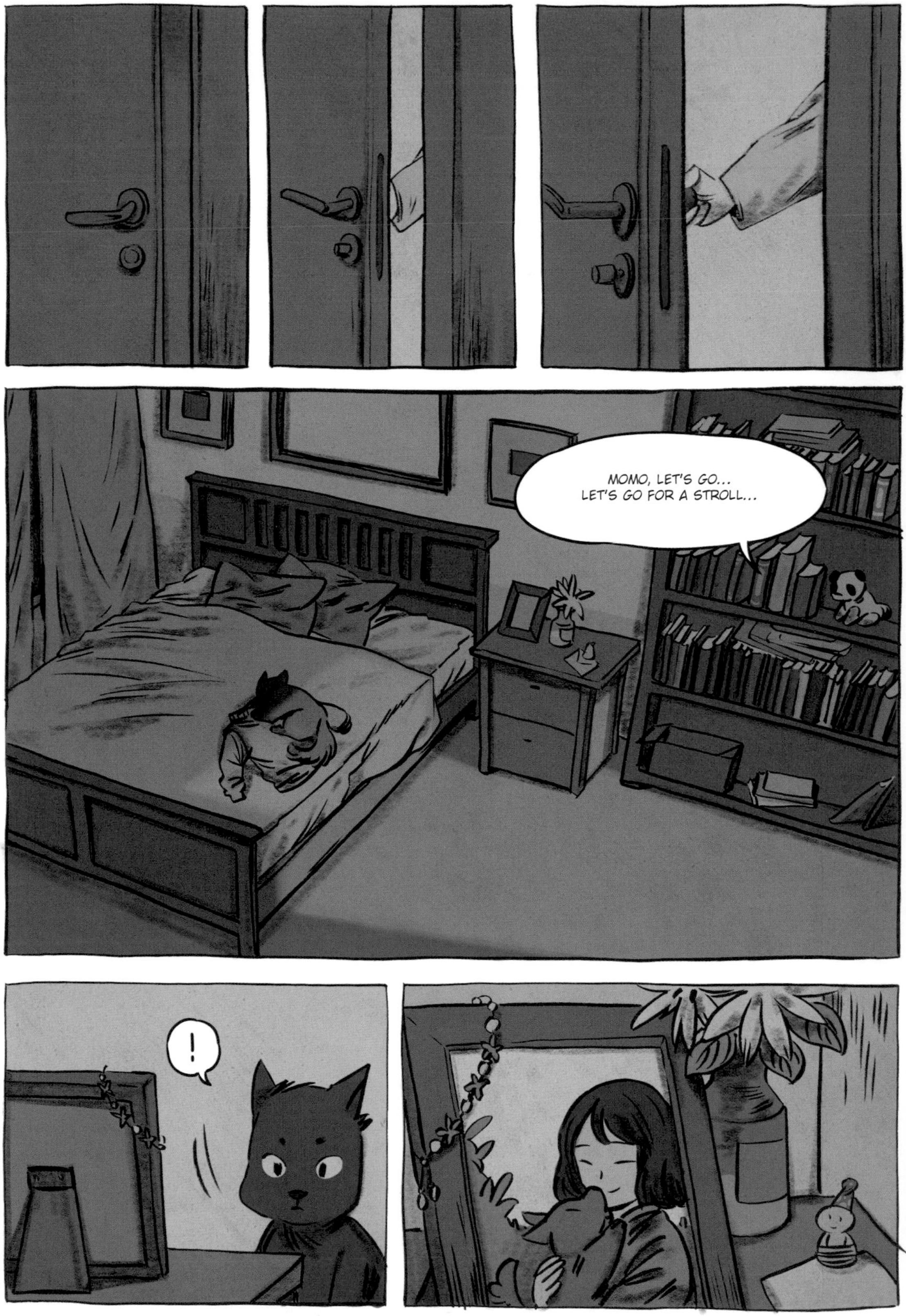
MOMO, LET'S GO...
LET'S GO FOR A STROLL...
!

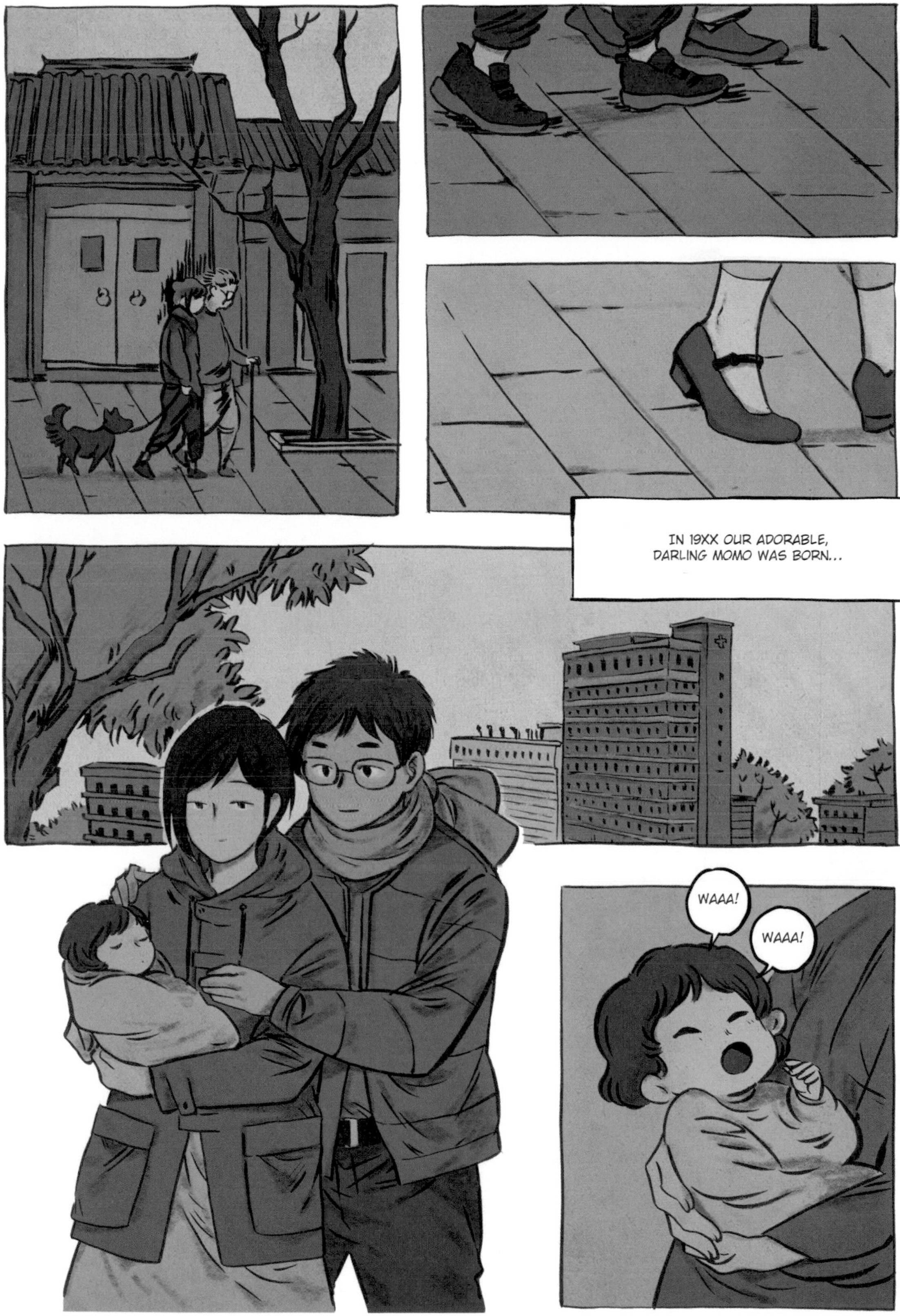
IN 19XX OUR ADORABLE,
DARLING MOMO WAS BORN...
WAAA!
WAAA!

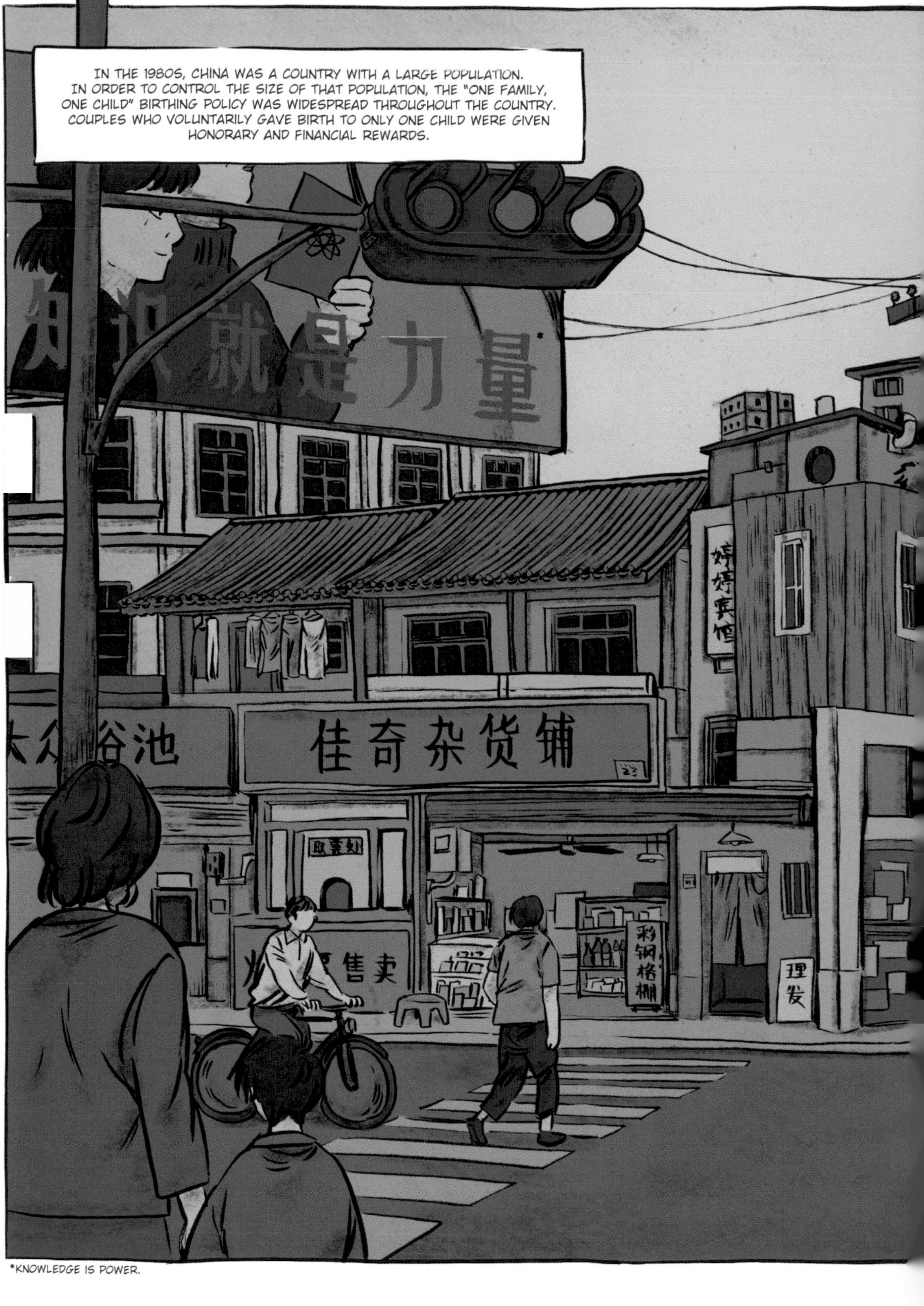
IN THE 1980S, CHINA WAS A COUNTRY WITH A LARGE POPULATION. IN ORDER TO CONTROL THE SIZE OF THAT POPULATION, THE "ONE FAMILY, ONE CHILD" BIRTHING POLICY WAS WIDESPREAD THROUGHOUT THE COUNTRY. COUPLES WHO VOLUNTARILY GAVE BIRTH TO ONLY ONE CHILD WERE GIVEN HONORARY AND FINANCIAL REWARDS.
知识就是力量*
佳奇杂货铺
理发

*KNOWLEDGE IS POWER.

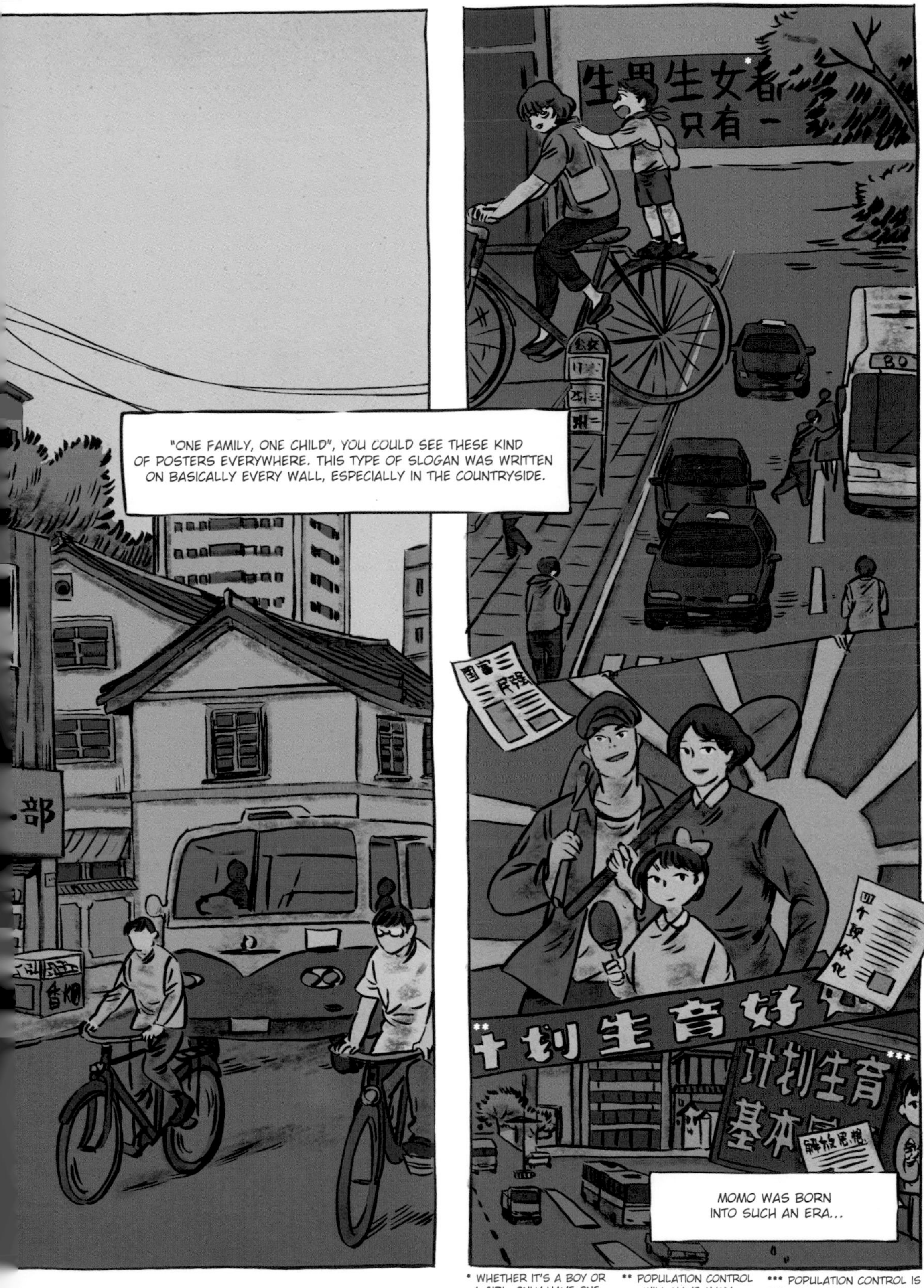
"ONE FAMILY, ONE CHILD", YOU COULD SEE THESE KIND OF POSTERS EVERYWHERE. THIS TYPE OF SLOGAN WAS WRITTEN ON BASICALLY EVERY WALL, ESPECIALLY IN THE COUNTRYSIDE.
部
香烟
只有一
BO
计划生育
MOMO WAS BORN INTO SUCH AN ERA...

* WHETHER IT'S A BOY OR A GIRL, ONLY HAVE ONE

** POPULATION CONTROL WILL HAVE MANY BENEFITS.

*** POPULATION CONTROL IS THE BASIC NATIONAL POLICY.

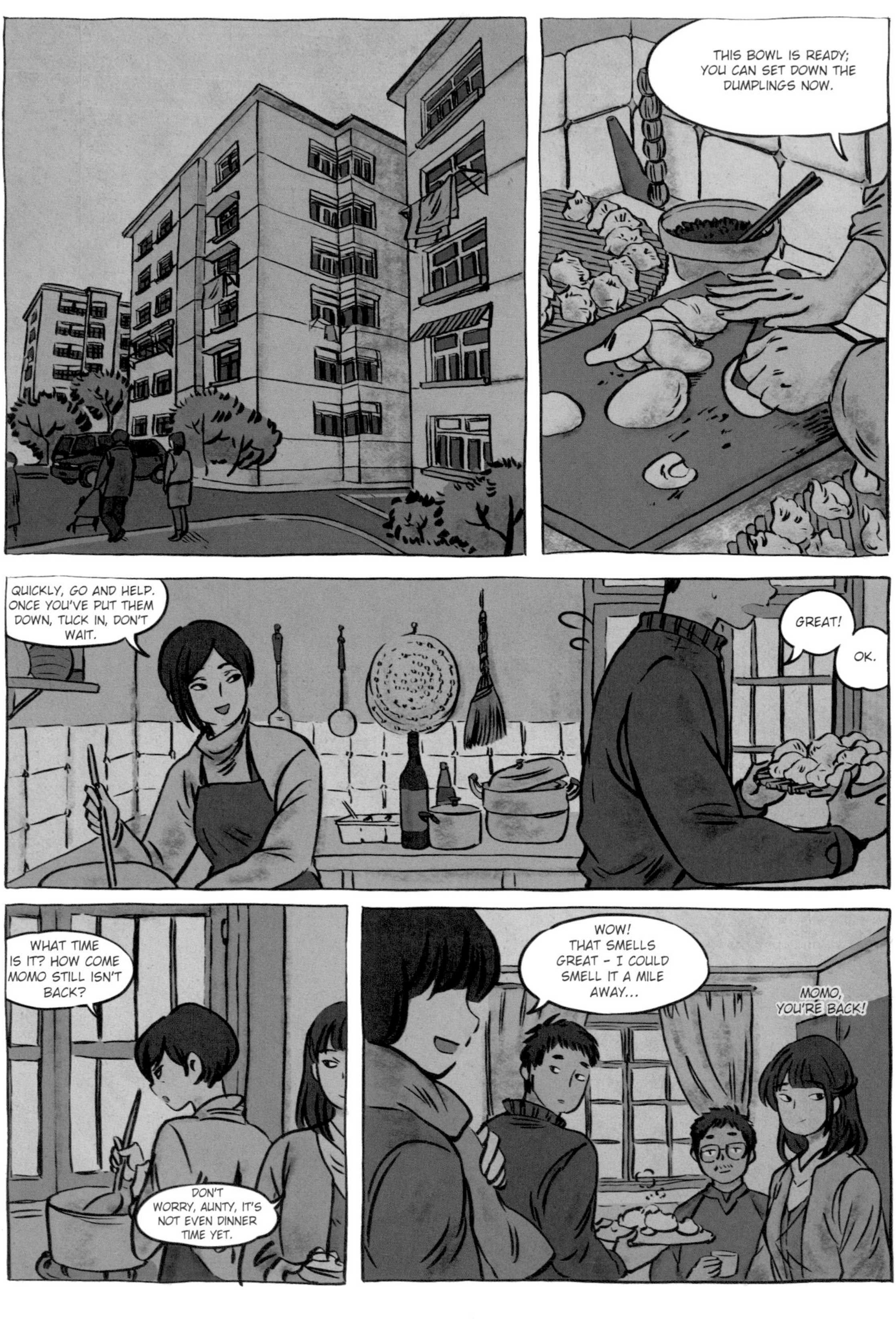

THIS BOWL IS READY; YOU CAN SET DOWN THE DUMPLINGS NOW.
QUICKLY, GO AND HELP. ONCE YOU'VE PUT THEM DOWN, TUCK IN, DON'T WAIT.
GREAT!
OK.
WHAT TIME IS IT? HOW COME MOMO STILL ISN'T BACK?
DON'T WORRY, AUNTY, IT'S NOT EVEN DINNER TIME YET.
WOW! THAT SMELLS GREAT - I COULD SMELL IT A MILE AWAY...
MOMO, YOU'RE BACK!

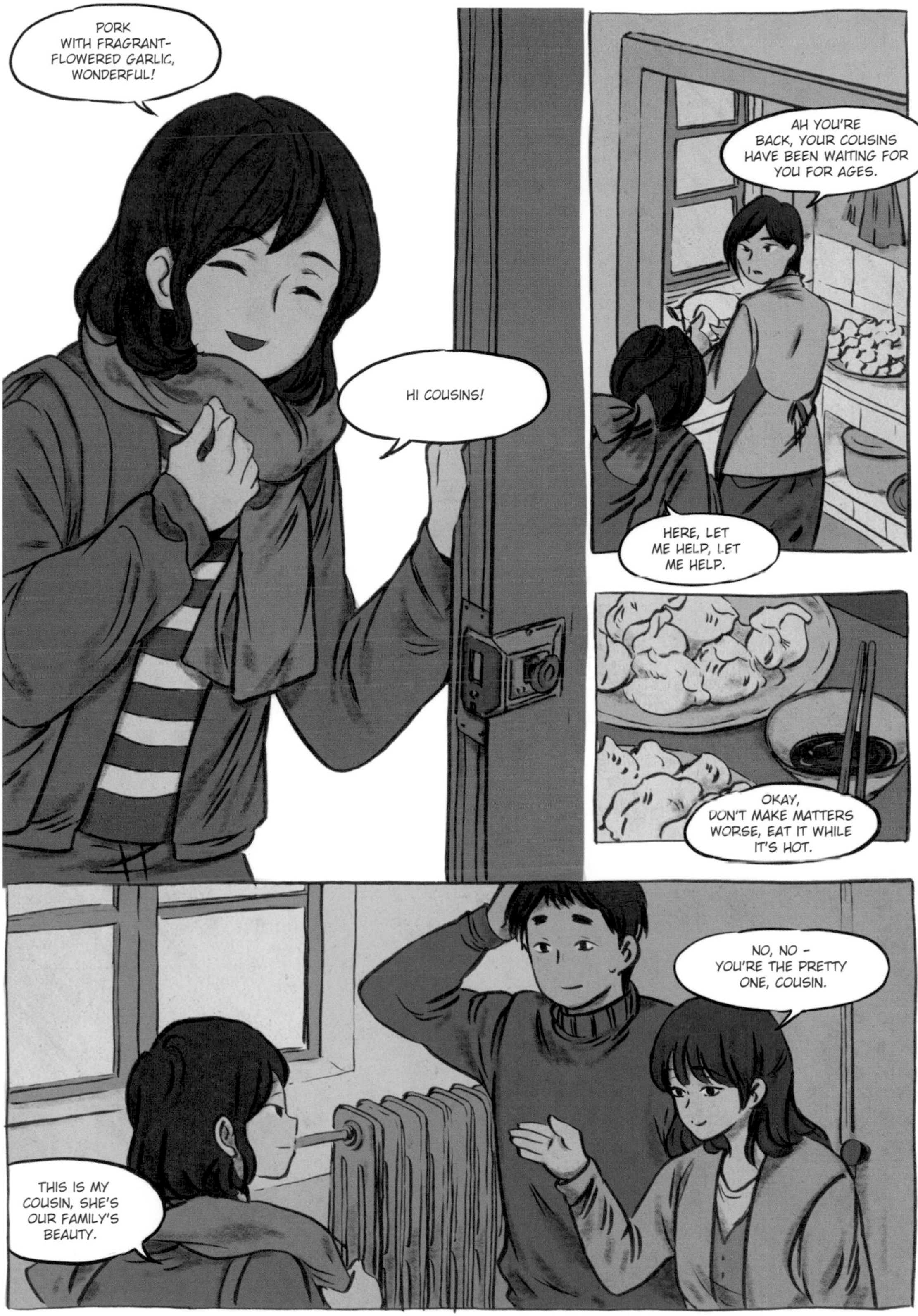
PORK WITH FRAGRANT-FLOWERED GARLIC, WONDERFUL!
HI COUSINS!
AH YOU'RE BACK, YOUR COUSINS HAVE BEEN WAITING FOR YOU FOR AGES.
HERE, LET ME HELP, LET ME HELP.
OKAY, DON'T MAKE MATTERS WORSE, EAT IT WHILE IT'S HOT.
THIS IS MY COUSIN, SHE'S OUR FAMILY'S BEAUTY.
NO, NO - YOU'RE THE PRETTY ONE, COUSIN.

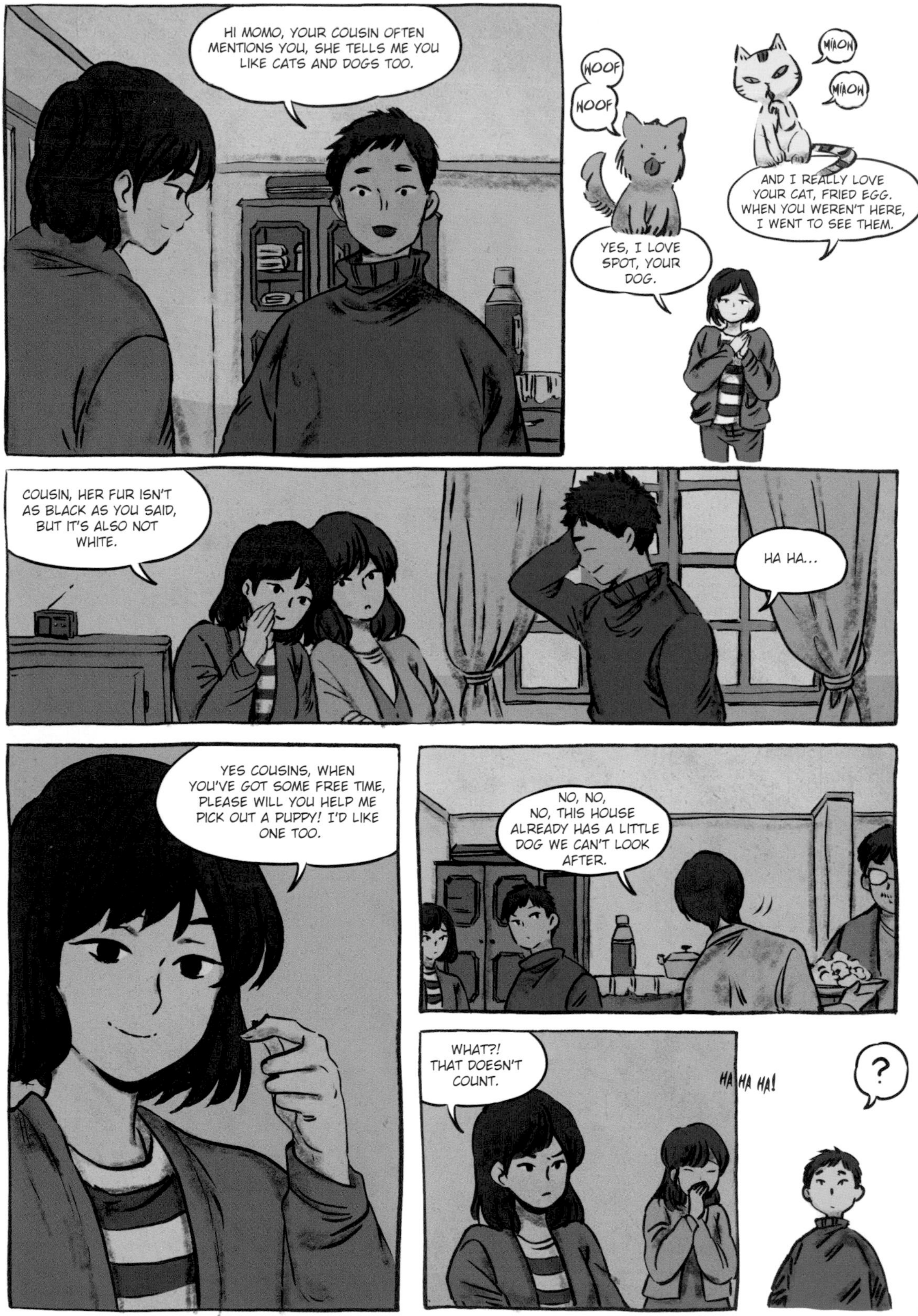
HI MOMO, YOUR COUSIN OFTEN MENTIONS YOU, SHE TELLS ME YOU LIKE CATS AND DOGS TOO.
WOOF
WOOF
MIAOW
MIAOW
YES, I LOVE SPOT, YOUR DOG.
AND I REALLY LOVE YOUR CAT, FRIED EGG. WHEN YOU WEREN'T HERE, I WENT TO SEE THEM.
COUSIN, HER FUR ISN'T AS BLACK AS YOU SAID, BUT IT'S ALSO NOT WHITE.
HA HA...
YES COUSINS, WHEN YOU'VE GOT SOME FREE TIME, PLEASE WILL YOU HELP ME PICK OUT A PUPPY! I'D LIKE ONE TOO.
NO, NO, NO, THIS HOUSE ALREADY HAS A LITTLE DOG WE CAN'T LOOK AFTER.
WHAT?! THAT DOESN'T COUNT.
HA HA HA!
?

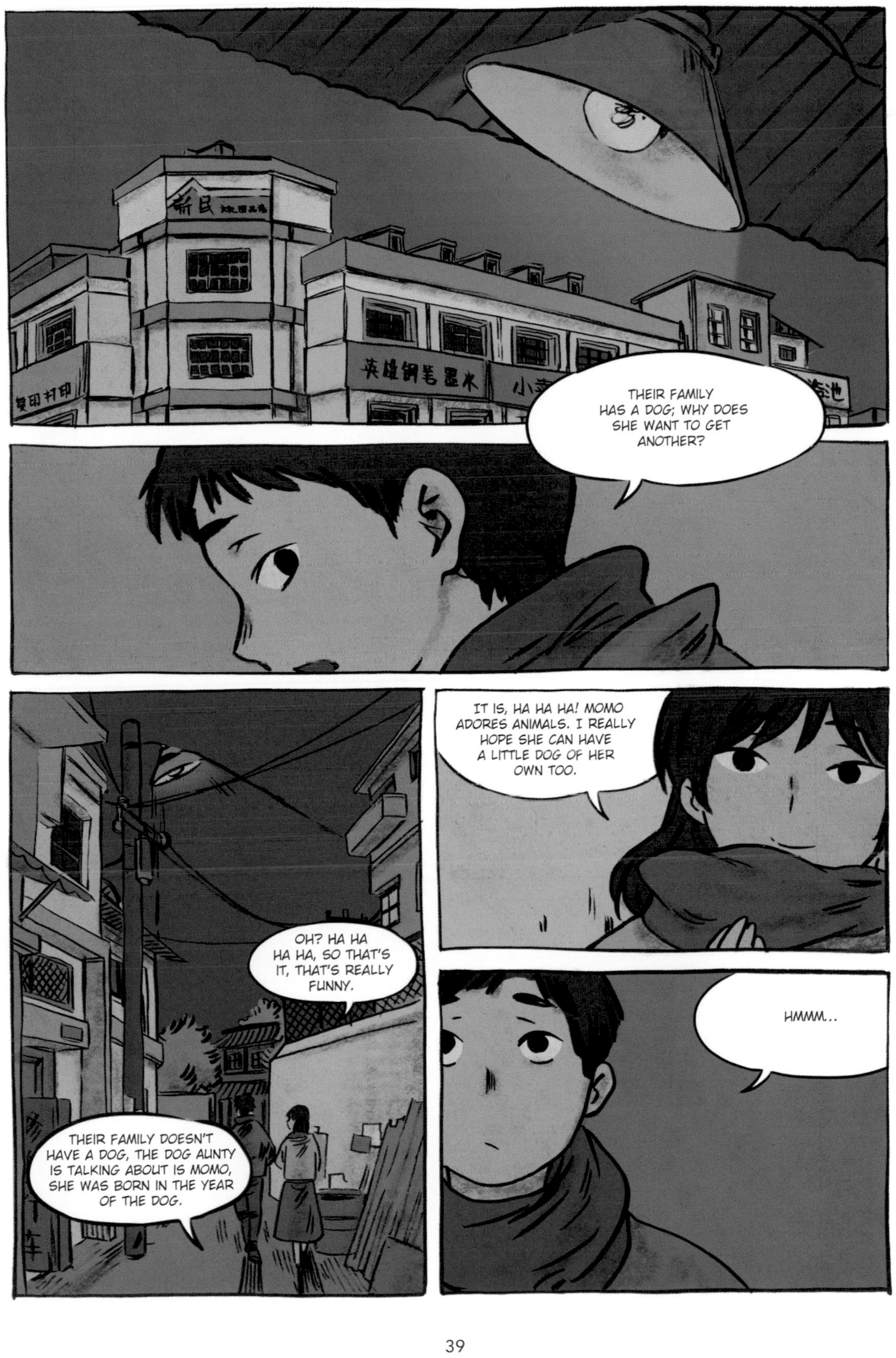
新民
英雄钢笔墨水
复印打印
THEIR FAMILY HAS A DOG; WHY DOES SHE WANT TO GET ANOTHER?
OH? HA HA HA HA, SO THAT'S IT, THAT'S REALLY FUNNY.
THEIR FAMILY DOESN'T HAVE A DOG, THE DOG AUNTY IS TALKING ABOUT IS MOMO, SHE WAS BORN IN THE YEAR OF THE DOG.
IT IS, HA HA HA! MOMO ADORES ANIMALS. I REALLY HOPE SHE CAN HAVE A LITTLE DOG OF HER OWN TOO.
HMMM...

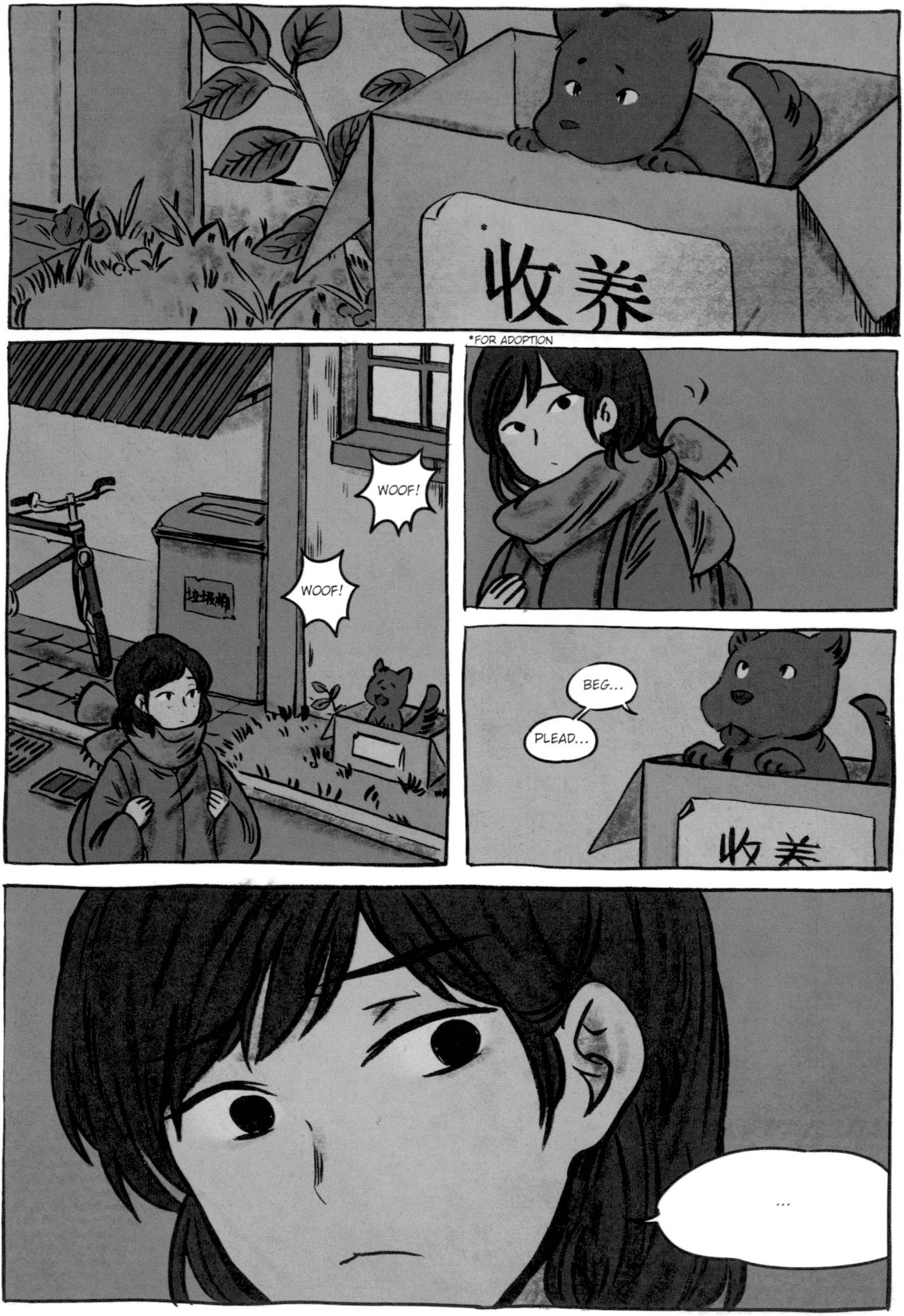
*收养
*FOR ADOPTION
WOOF!
WOOF!
BEG...
PLEAD...
收养
...

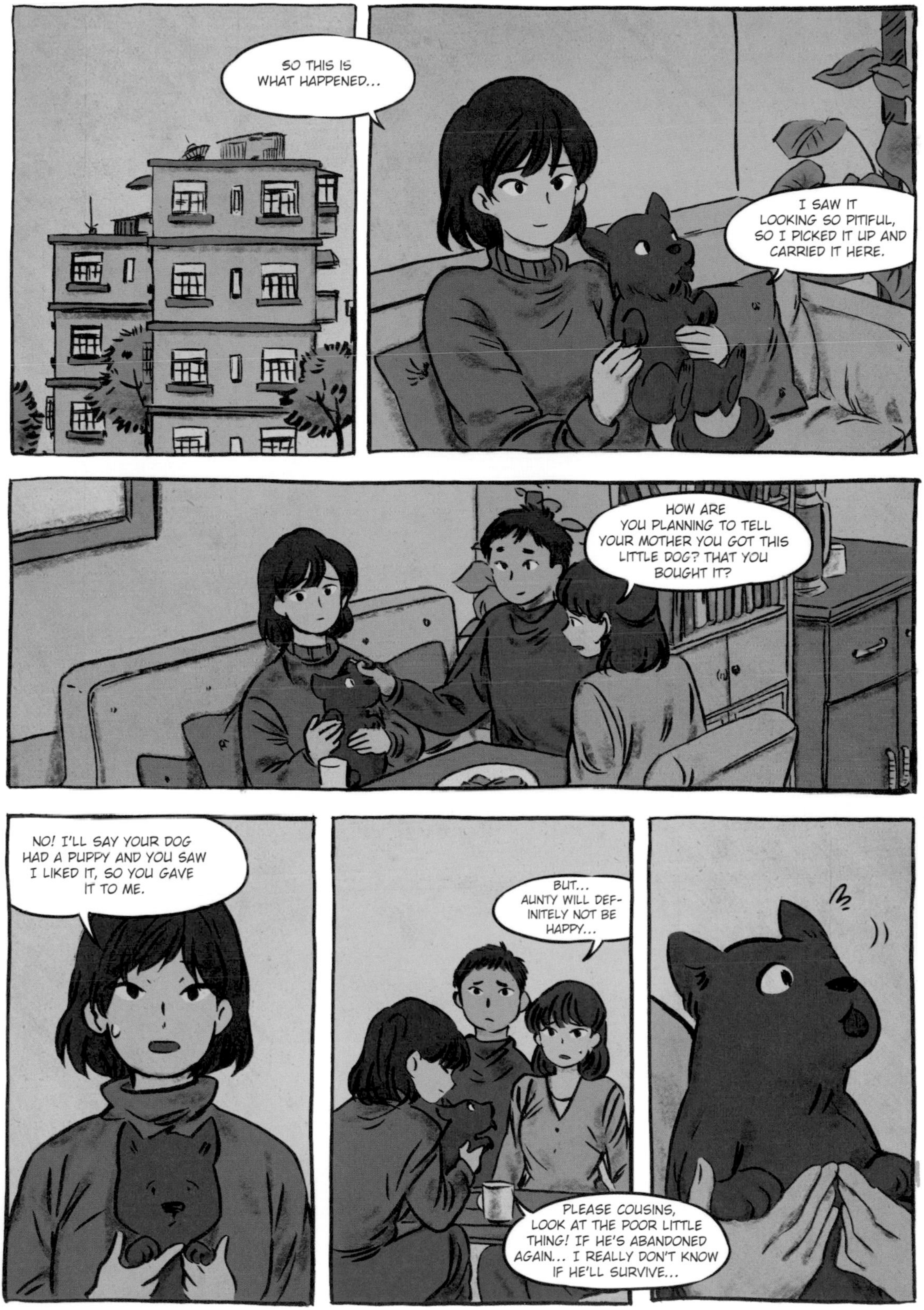
SO THIS IS WHAT HAPPENED...
I SAW IT LOOKING SO PITIFUL, SO I PICKED IT UP AND CARRIED IT HERE.
HOW ARE YOU PLANNING TO TELL YOUR MOTHER YOU GOT THIS LITTLE DOG? THAT YOU BOUGHT IT?
NO! I'LL SAY YOUR DOG HAD A PUPPY AND YOU SAW I LIKED IT, SO YOU GAVE IT TO ME.
BUT... AUNTY WILL DEF-INITELY NOT BE HAPPY...
PLEASE COUSINS, LOOK AT THE POOR LITTLE THING! IF HE'S ABANDONED AGAIN... I REALLY DON'T KNOW IF HE'LL SURVIVE...

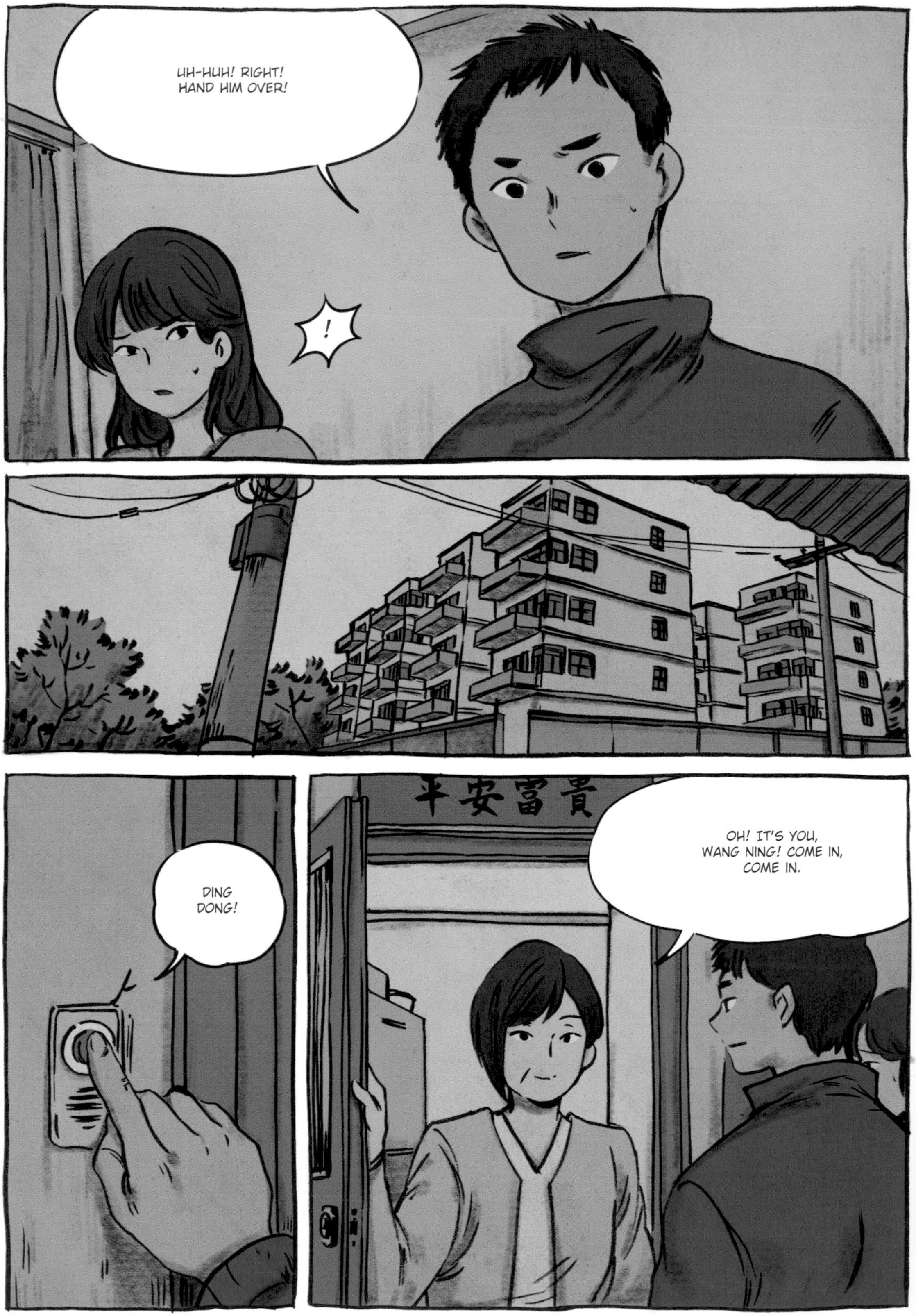
UH-HUH! RIGHT! HAND HIM OVER!
!
DING DONG!
平安富貴
OH! IT'S YOU, WANG NING! COME IN, COME IN.

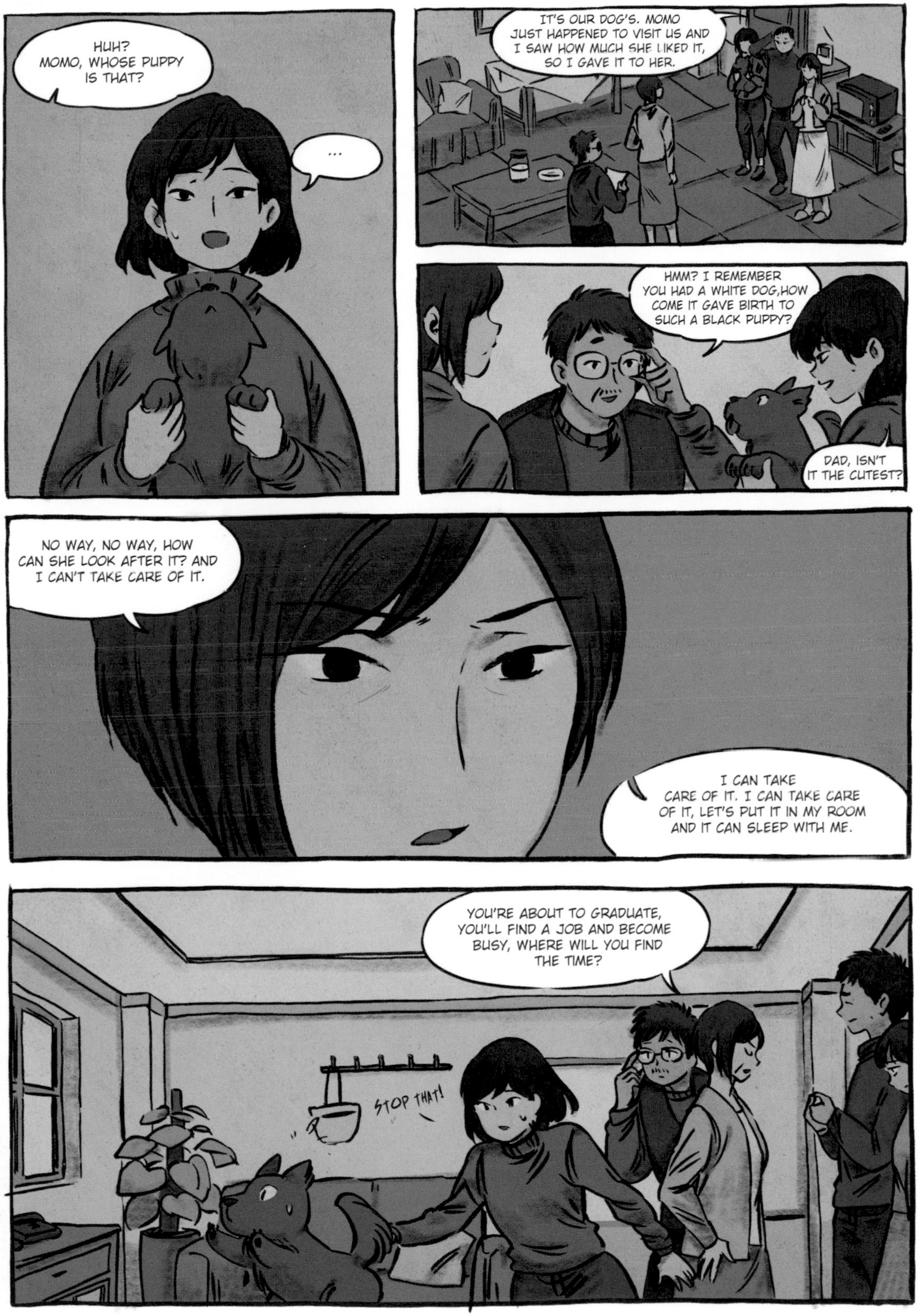
HUH?
MOMO, WHOSE PUPPY IS THAT?
...
IT'S OUR DOG'S. MOMO JUST HAPPENED TO VISIT US AND I SAW HOW MUCH SHE LIKED IT, SO I GAVE IT TO HER.
HMM? I REMEMBER YOU HAD A WHITE DOG,HOW COME IT GAVE BIRTH TO SUCH A BLACK PUPPY?
DAD, ISN'T IT THE CUTEST?
NO WAY, NO WAY, HOW CAN SHE LOOK AFTER IT? AND I CAN'T TAKE CARE OF IT.
I CAN TAKE CARE OF IT. I CAN TAKE CARE OF IT, LET'S PUT IT IN MY ROOM AND IT CAN SLEEP WITH ME.
YOU'RE ABOUT TO GRADUATE, YOU'LL FIND A JOB AND BECOME BUSY, WHERE WILL YOU FIND THE TIME?
STOP THAT!

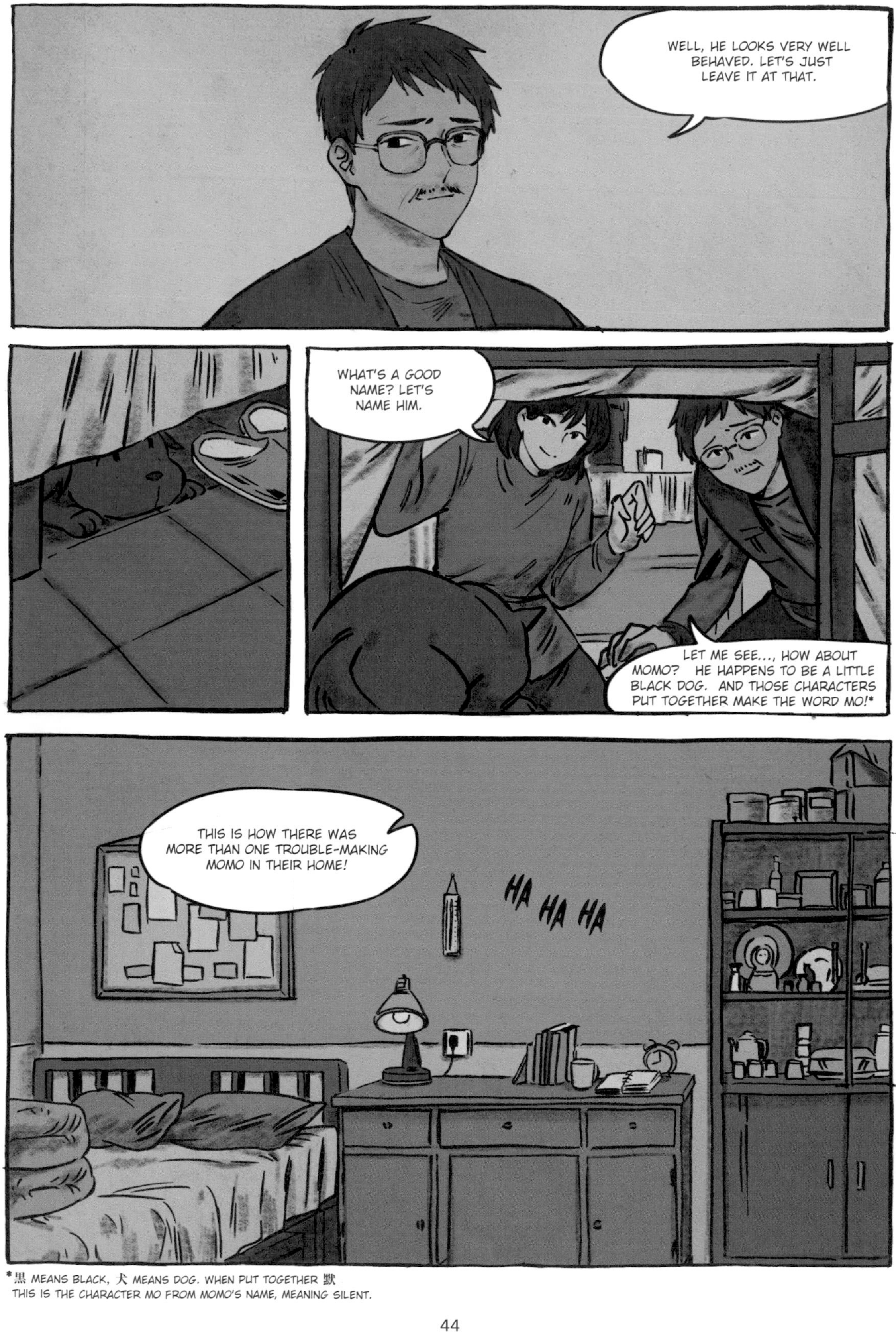
WELL, HE LOOKS VERY WELL BEHAVED. LET'S JUST LEAVE IT AT THAT.
WHAT'S A GOOD NAME? LET'S NAME HIM.
LET ME SEE..., HOW ABOUT MOMO? HE HAPPENS TO BE A LITTLE BLACK DOG. AND THOSE CHARACTERS PUT TOGETHER MAKE THE WORD MO!*
THIS IS HOW THERE WAS MORE THAN ONE TROUBLE-MAKING MOMO IN THEIR HOME!
HA HA HA

*黑 MEANS BLACK, 犬 MEANS DOG. WHEN PUT TOGETHER 默 THIS IS THE CHARACTER MO FROM MOMO'S NAME, MEANING SILENT.

THIS IS HOW THERE WAS MORE THAN
ONE MOMO IN OUR HOUSE ...MY
BELOVED LITTLE MOMO...

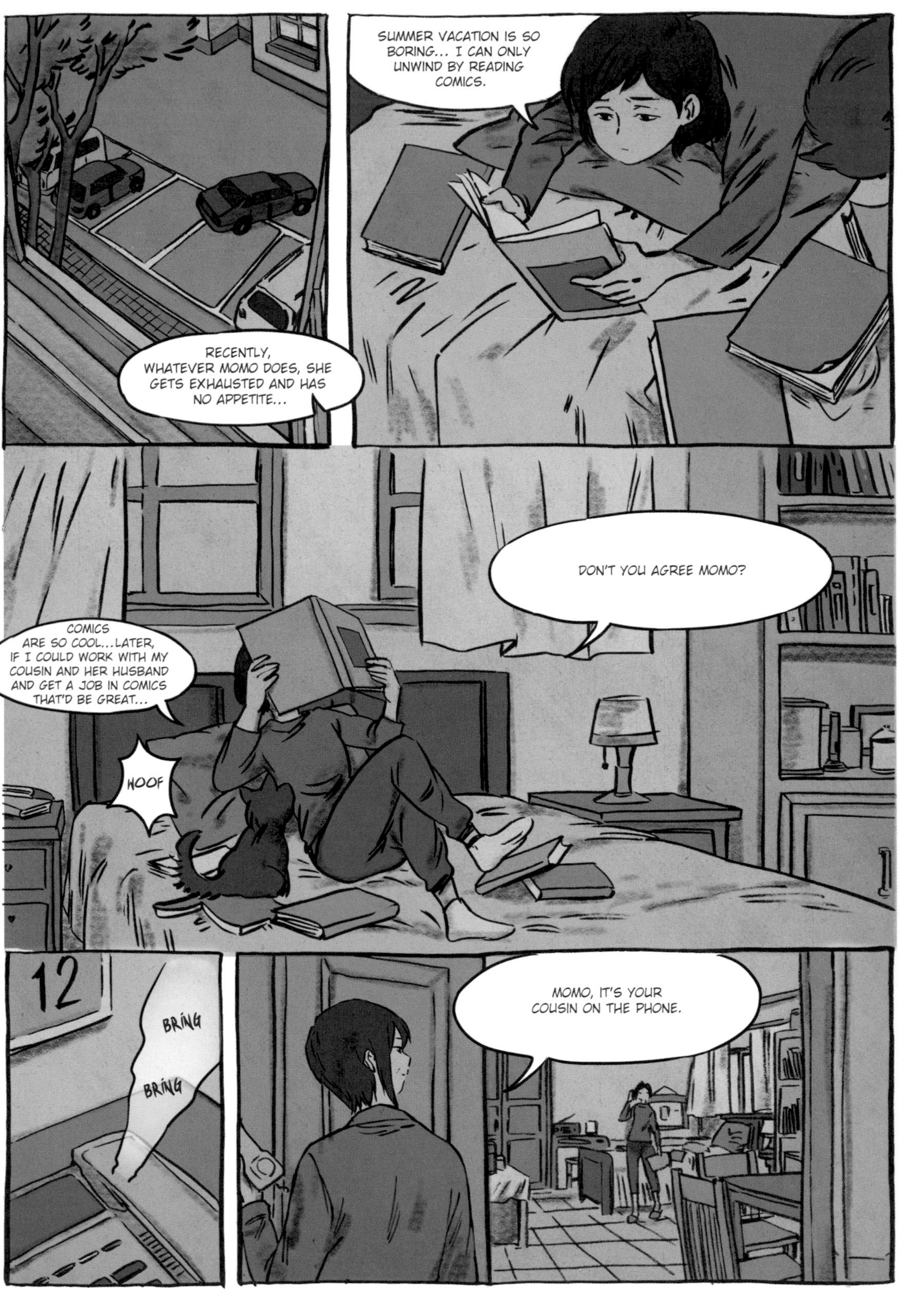
RECENTLY, WHATEVER MOMO DOES, SHE GETS EXHAUSTED AND HAS NO APPETITE...
SUMMER VACATION IS SO BORING... I CAN ONLY UNWIND BY READING COMICS.
COMICS ARE SO COOL...LATER, IF I COULD WORK WITH MY COUSIN AND HER HUSBAND AND GET A JOB IN COMICS THAT'D BE GREAT...
WOOF
DON'T YOU AGREE MOMO?
12
BRING
BRING
MOMO, IT'S YOUR COUSIN ON THE PHONE.

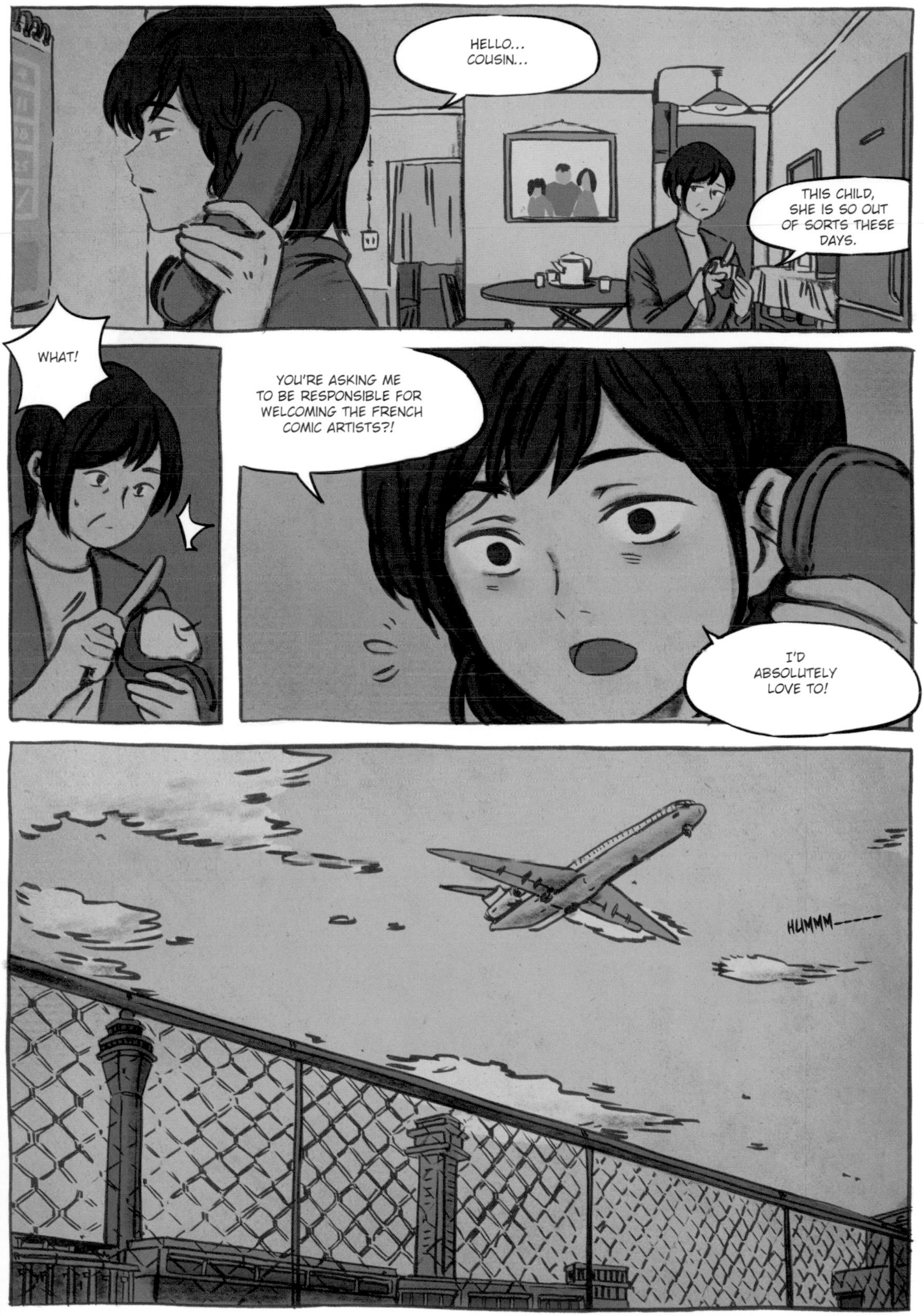
HELLO... COUSIN...
THIS CHILD, SHE IS SO OUT OF SORTS THESE DAYS.
WHAT!
YOU'RE ASKING ME TO BE RESPONSIBLE FOR WELCOMING THE FRENCH COMIC ARTISTS?!
I'D ABSOLUTELY LOVE TO!
HUMMM------

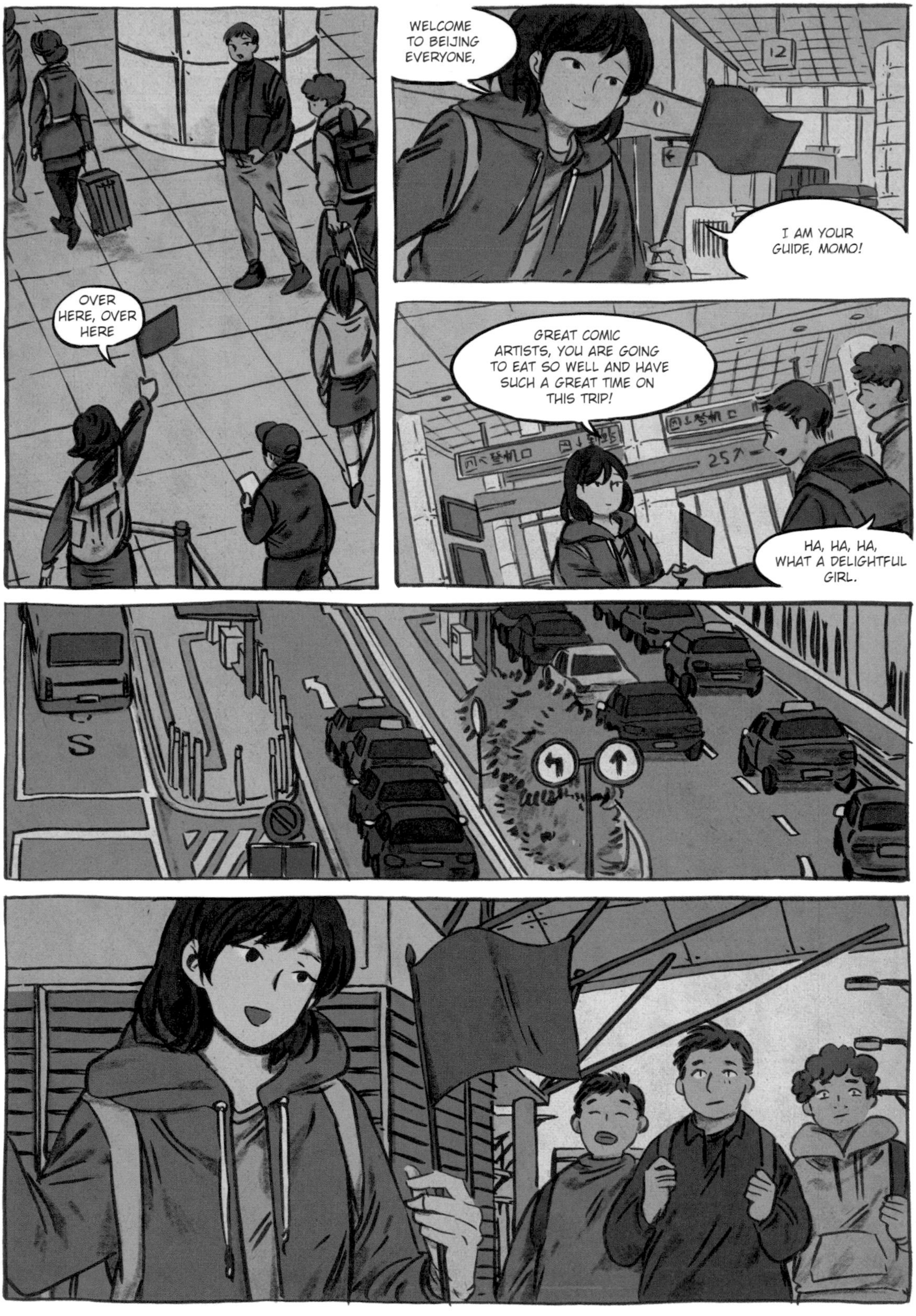
OVER HERE, OVER HERE
WELCOME TO BEIJING EVERYONE,
I AM YOUR GUIDE, MOMO!
GREAT COMIC ARTISTS, YOU ARE GOING TO EAT SO WELL AND HAVE SUCH A GREAT TIME ON THIS TRIP!
HA, HA, HA, WHAT A DELIGHTFUL GIRL.

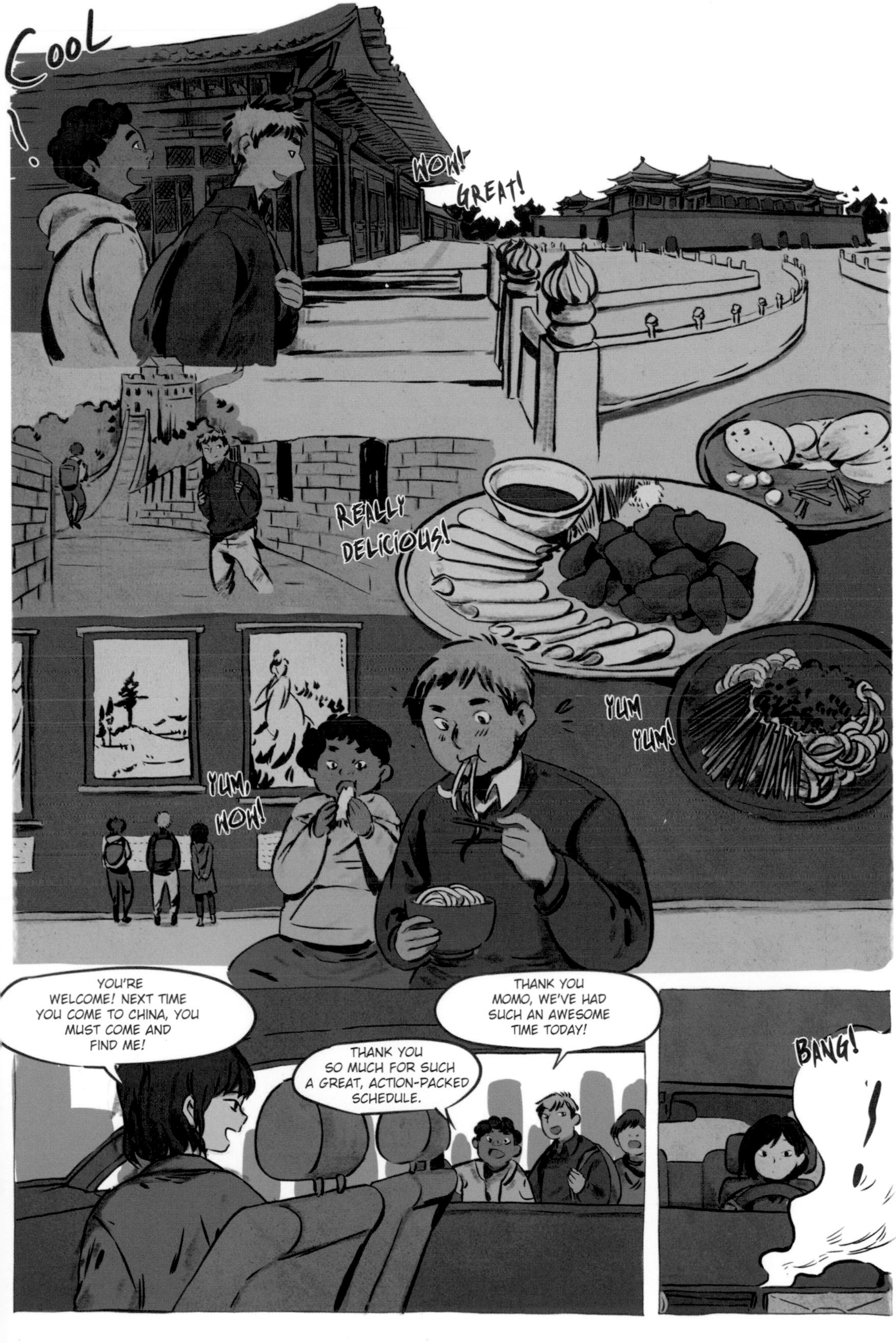
COOL!
WOW!
GREAT!
REALLY DELICIOUS!
YUM, WOW!
YUM YUM!
YOU'RE WELCOME! NEXT TIME YOU COME TO CHINA, YOU MUST COME AND FIND ME!
THANK YOU SO MUCH FOR SUCH A GREAT, ACTION-PACKED SCHEDULE.
THANK YOU MOMO, WE'VE HAD SUCH AN AWESOME TIME TODAY!
BANG!

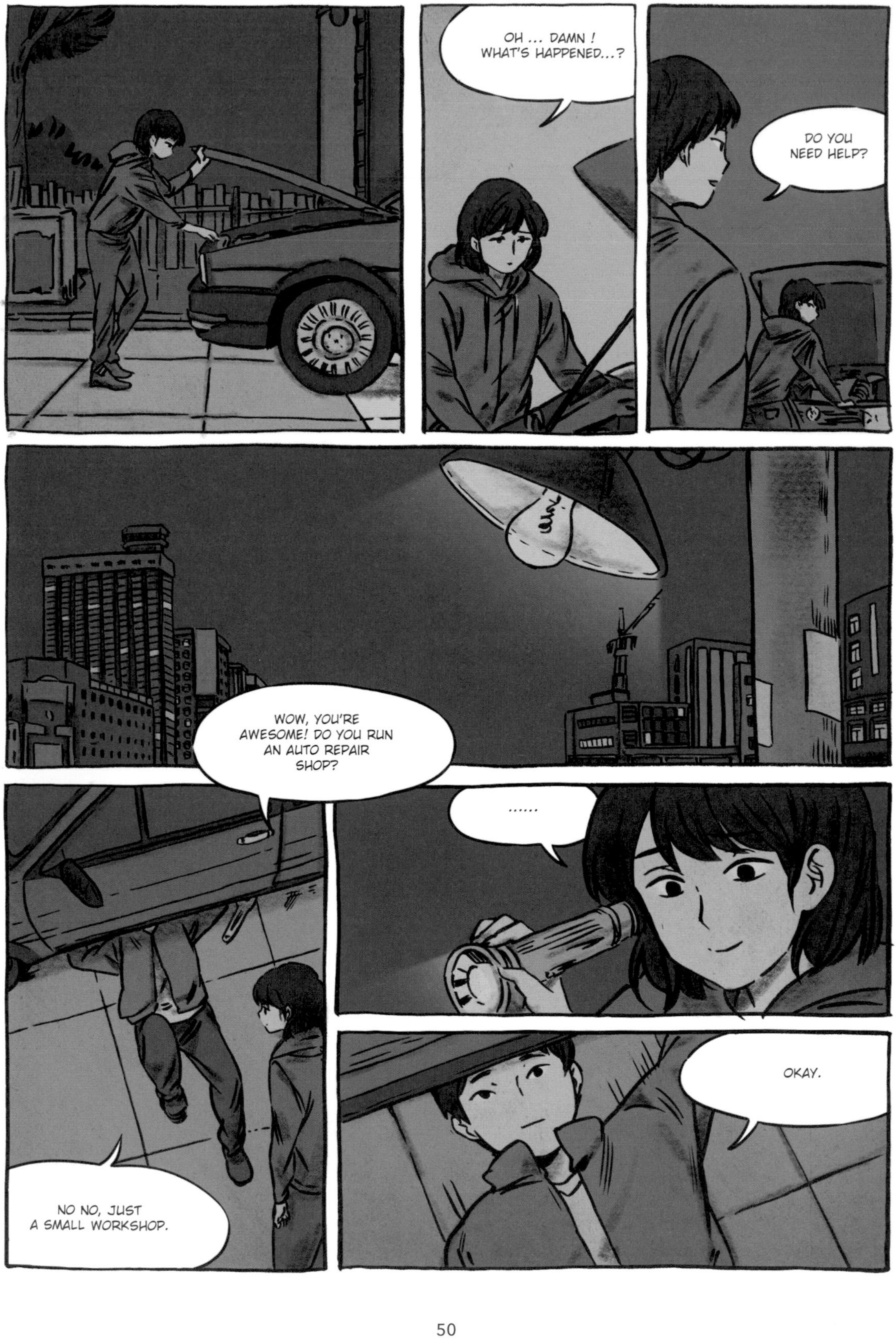
OH ... DAMN ! WHAT'S HAPPENED...?
DO YOU NEED HELP?
WOW, YOU'RE AWESOME! DO YOU RUN AN AUTO REPAIR SHOP?
NO NO, JUST A SMALL WORKSHOP.
......
OKAY.

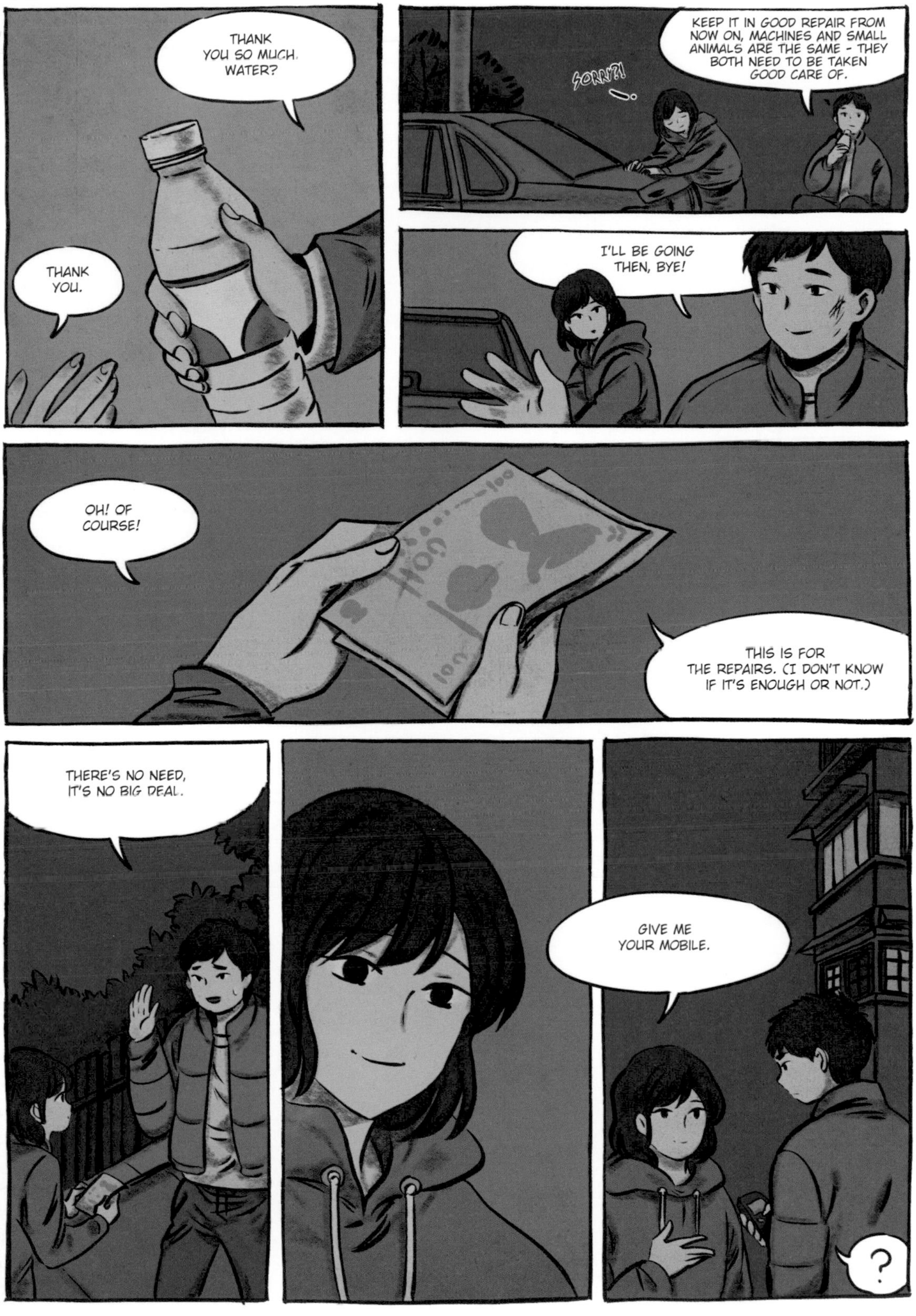
THANK YOU SO MUCH. WATER?
THANK YOU.
SORRY?!
KEEP IT IN GOOD REPAIR FROM NOW ON, MACHINES AND SMALL ANIMALS ARE THE SAME - THEY BOTH NEED TO BE TAKEN GOOD CARE OF.
I'LL BE GOING THEN, BYE!
OH! OF COURSE!
THIS IS FOR THE REPAIRS. (I DON'T KNOW IF IT'S ENOUGH OR NOT.)
THERE'S NO NEED, IT'S NO BIG DEAL.
GIVE ME YOUR MOBILE.
?

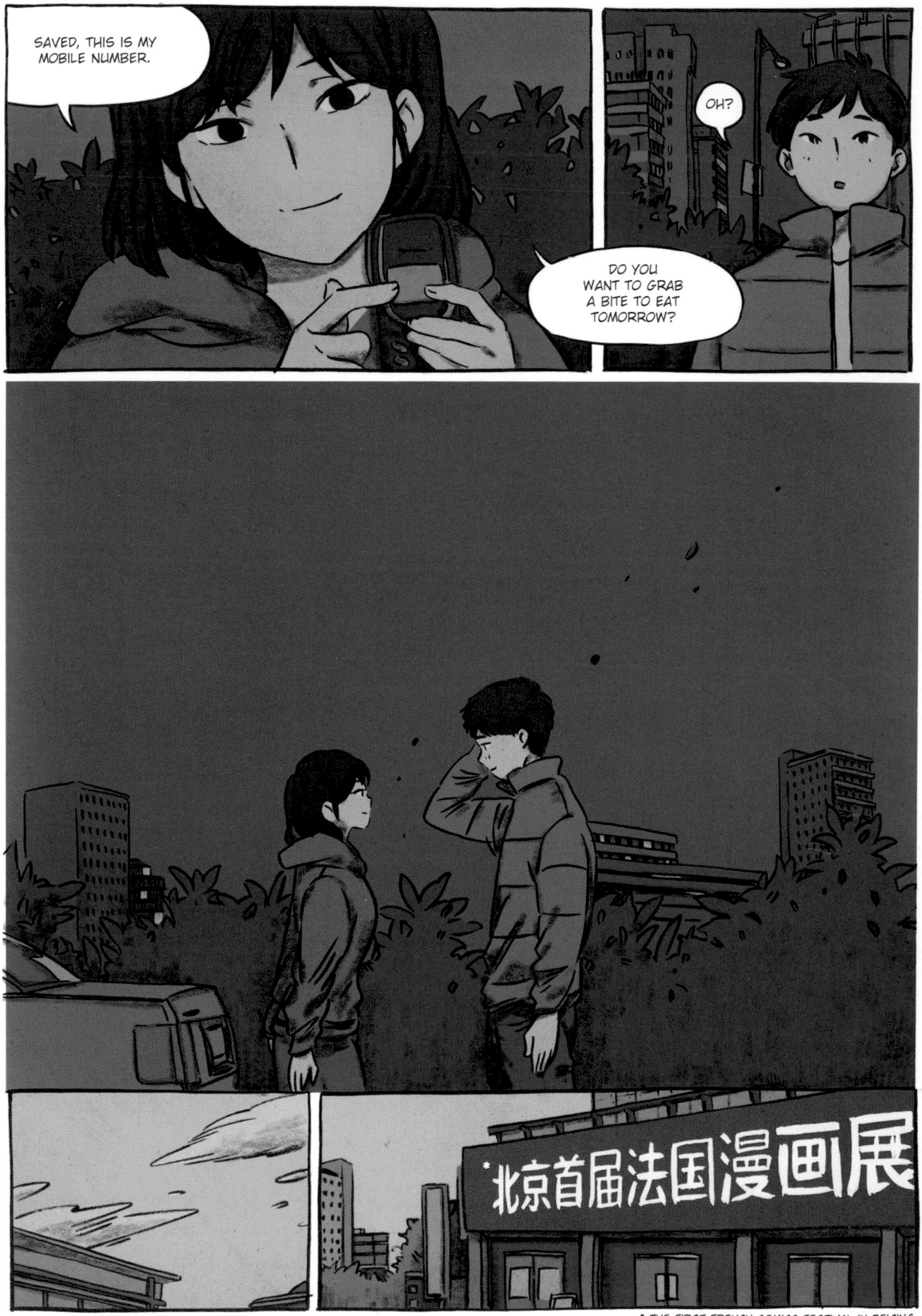
SAVED, THIS IS MY MOBILE NUMBER.
OH?
DO YOU WANT TO GRAB A BITE TO EAT TOMORROW?
*北京首届法国漫画展

* THE FIRST FRENCH COMICS FESTIVAL IN BEIJING

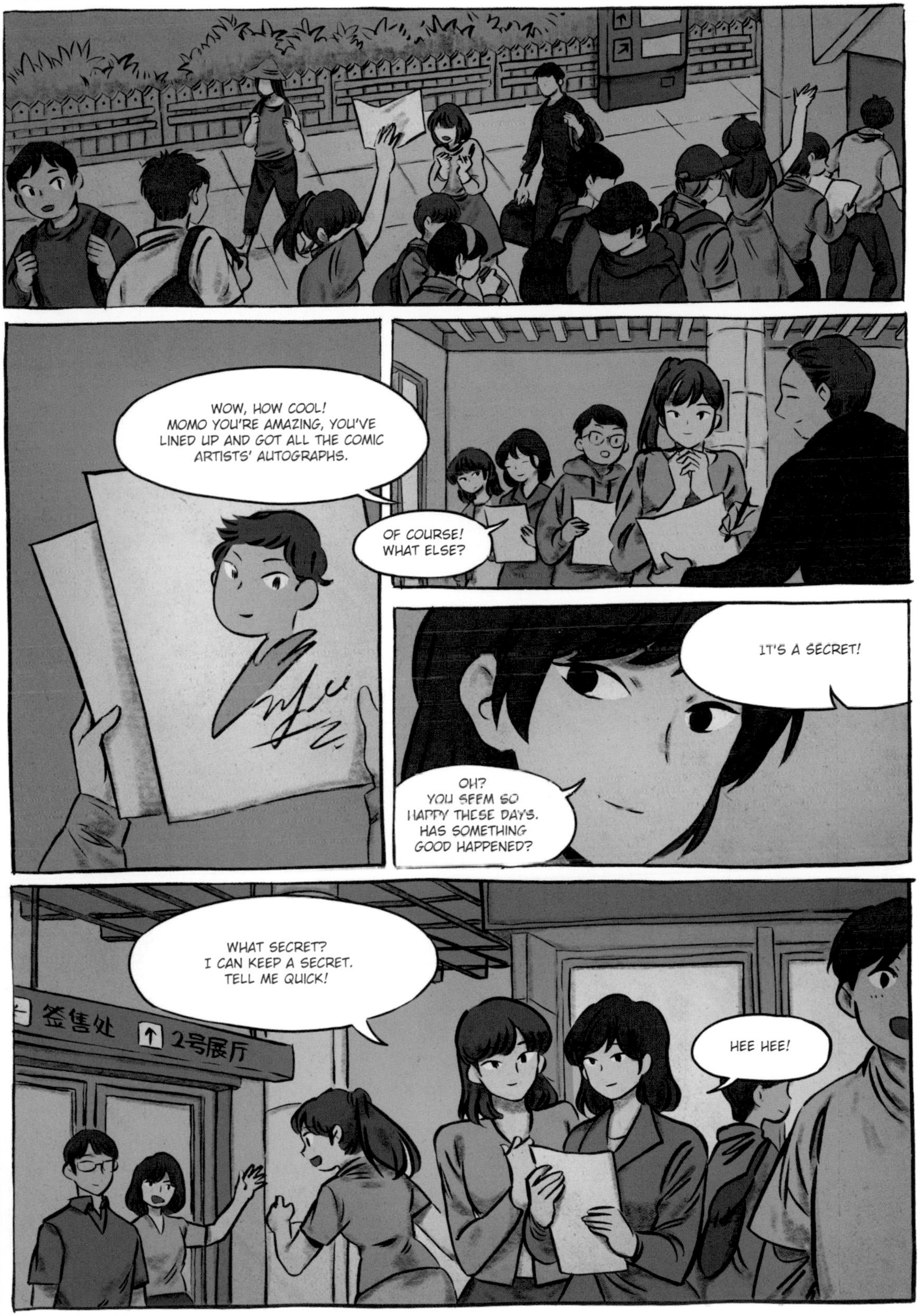
WOW, HOW COOL! MOMO YOU'RE AMAZING, YOU'VE LINED UP AND GOT ALL THE COMIC ARTISTS' AUTOGRAPHS.
OF COURSE! WHAT ELSE?
OH? YOU SEEM SO HAPPY THESE DAYS. HAS SOMETHING GOOD HAPPENED?
IT'S A SECRET!
WHAT SECRET? I CAN KEEP A SECRET. TELL ME QUICK!
签售处
2号展厅
HEE HEE!

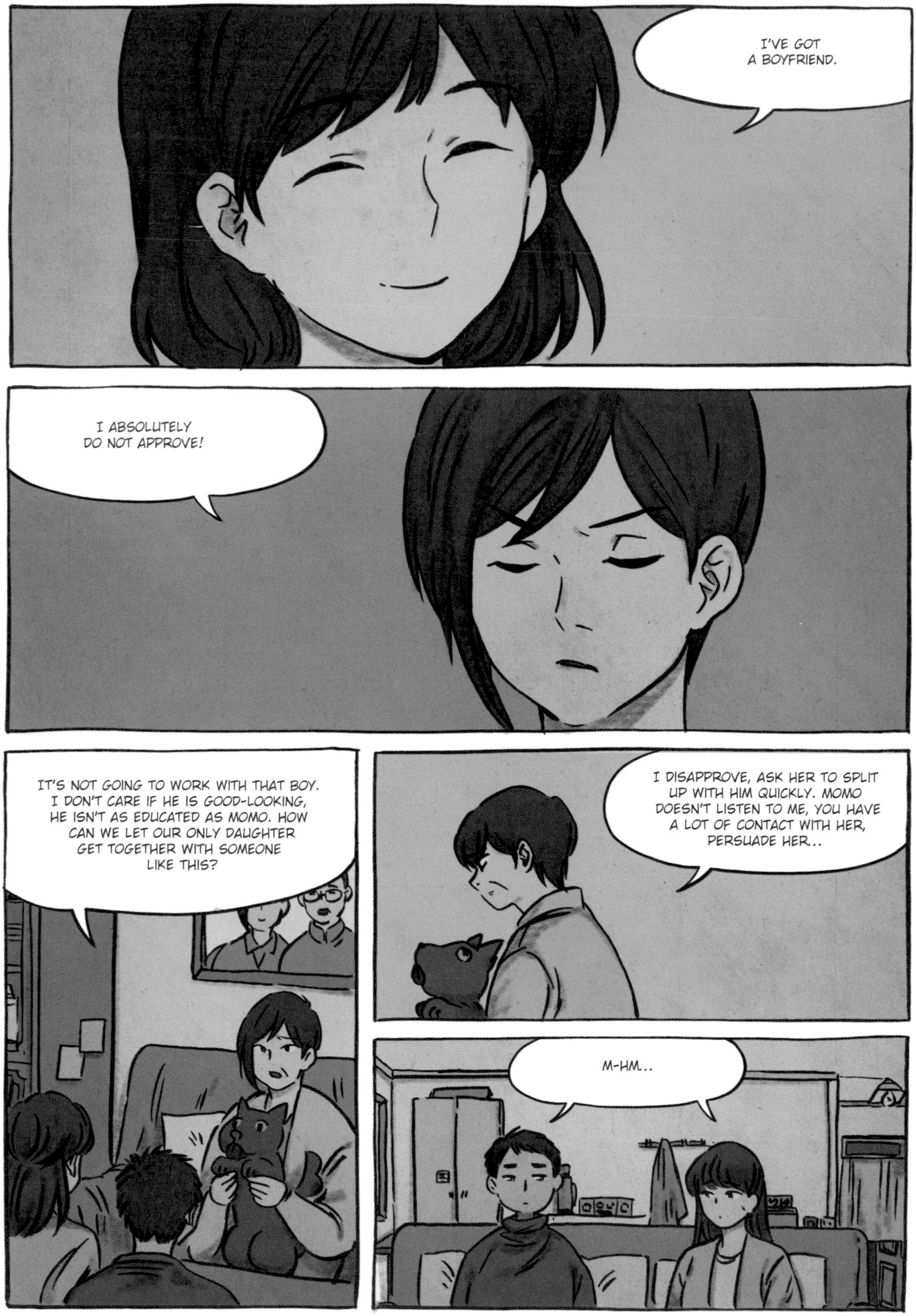
I'VE GOT A BOYFRIEND.
I ABSOLUTELY DO NOT APPROVE!
IT'S NOT GOING TO WORK WITH THAT BOY. I DON'T CARE IF HE IS GOOD-LOOKING, HE ISN'T AS EDUCATED AS MOMO. HOW CAN WE LET OUR ONLY DAUGHTER GET TOGETHER WITH SOMEONE LIKE THIS?
I DISAPPROVE, ASK HER TO SPLIT UP WITH HIM QUICKLY. MOMO DOESN'T LISTEN TO ME, YOU HAVE A LOT OF CONTACT WITH HER, PERSUADE HER..
M-HM..

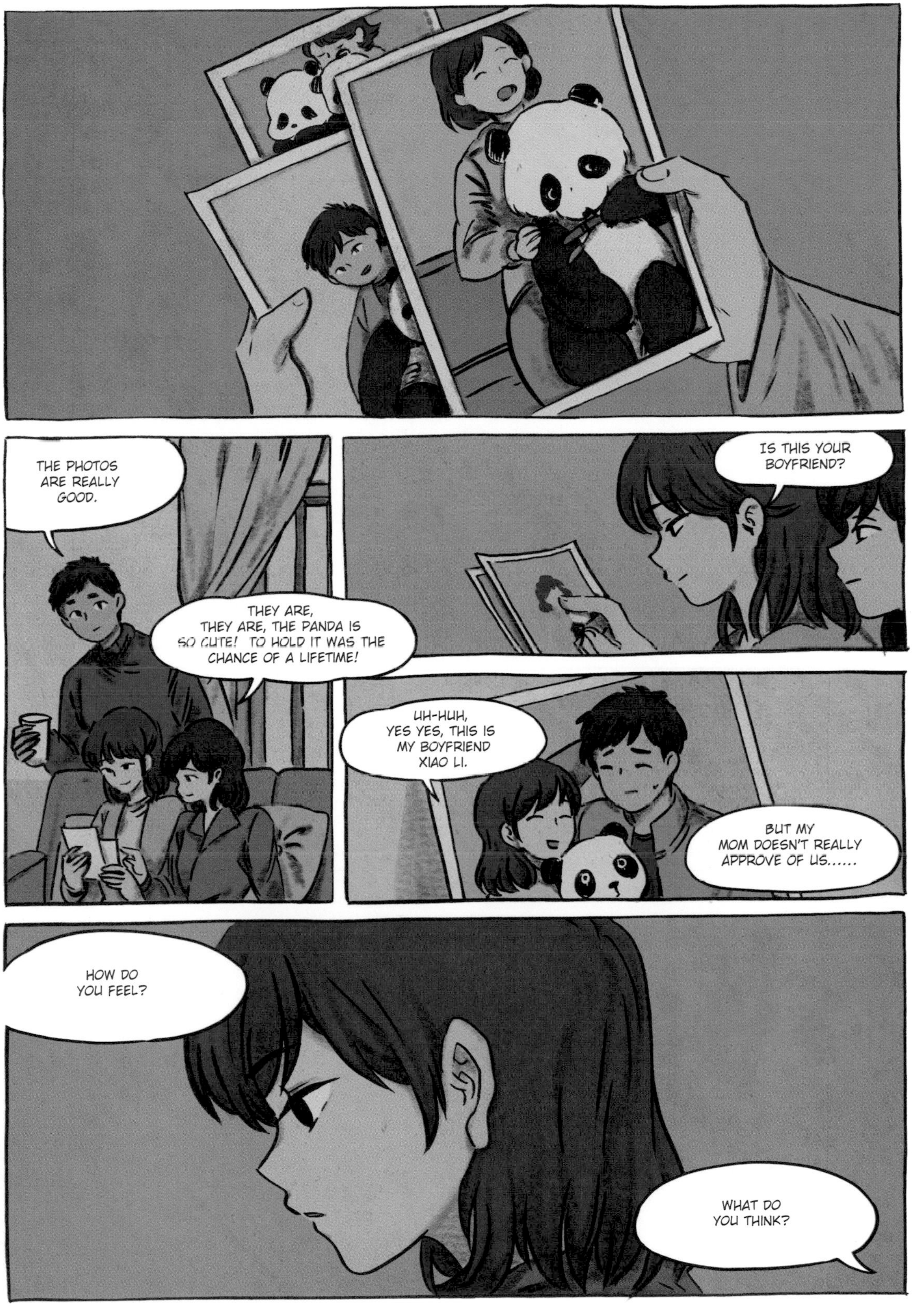
THE PHOTOS ARE REALLY GOOD.
THEY ARE, THEY ARE, THE PANDA IS SO CUTE! TO HOLD IT WAS THE CHANCE OF A LIFETIME!
IS THIS YOUR BOYFRIEND?
UH-HUH, YES YES, THIS IS MY BOYFRIEND XIAO LI.
BUT MY MOM DOESN'T REALLY APPROVE OF US……
HOW DO YOU FEEL?
WHAT DO YOU THINK?

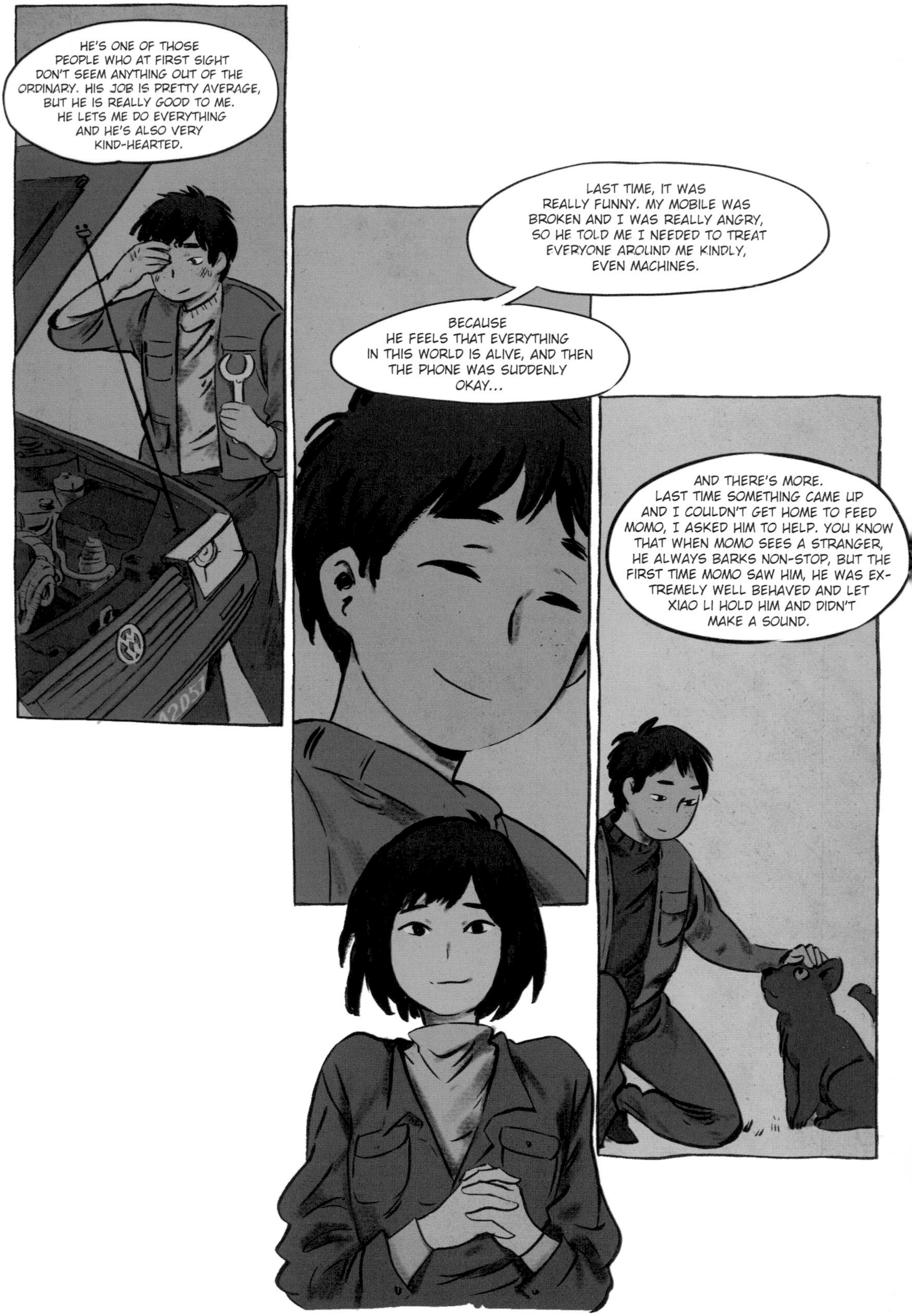
HE'S ONE OF THOSE PEOPLE WHO AT FIRST SIGHT DON'T SEEM ANYTHING OUT OF THE ORDINARY. HIS JOB IS PRETTY AVERAGE, BUT HE IS REALLY GOOD TO ME. HE LETS ME DO EVERYTHING AND HE'S ALSO VERY KIND-HEARTED.
LAST TIME, IT WAS REALLY FUNNY. MY MOBILE WAS BROKEN AND I WAS REALLY ANGRY, SO HE TOLD ME I NEEDED TO TREAT EVERYONE AROUND ME KINDLY, EVEN MACHINES.
BECAUSE HE FEELS THAT EVERYTHING IN THIS WORLD IS ALIVE, AND THEN THE PHONE WAS SUDDENLY OKAY...
AND THERE'S MORE. LAST TIME SOMETHING CAME UP AND I COULDN'T GET HOME TO FEED MOMO, I ASKED HIM TO HELP. YOU KNOW THAT WHEN MOMO SEES A STRANGER, HE ALWAYS BARKS NON-STOP, BUT THE FIRST TIME MOMO SAW HIM, HE WAS EXTREMELY WELL BEHAVED AND LET XIAO LI HOLD HIM AND DIDN'T MAKE A SOUND.

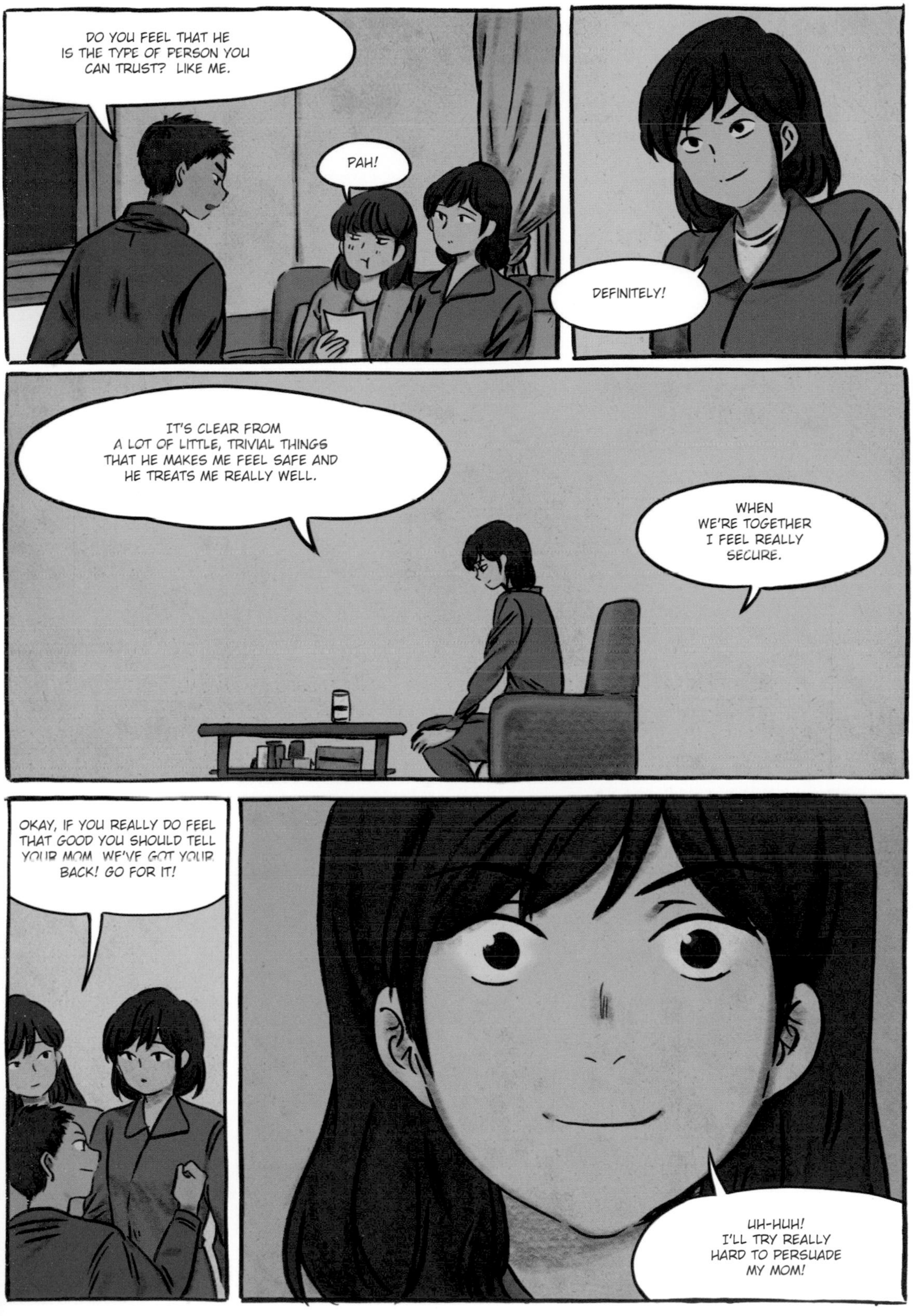
DO YOU FEEL THAT HE IS THE TYPE OF PERSON YOU CAN TRUST? LIKE ME.
PAH!
DEFINITELY!
IT'S CLEAR FROM A LOT OF LITTLE, TRIVIAL THINGS THAT HE MAKES ME FEEL SAFE AND HE TREATS ME REALLY WELL.
WHEN WE'RE TOGETHER I FEEL REALLY SECURE.
OKAY, IF YOU REALLY DO FEEL THAT GOOD YOU SHOULD TELL YOUR MOM. WE'VE GOT YOUR BACK! GO FOR IT!
UH-HUH! I'LL TRY REALLY HARD TO PERSUADE MY MOM!

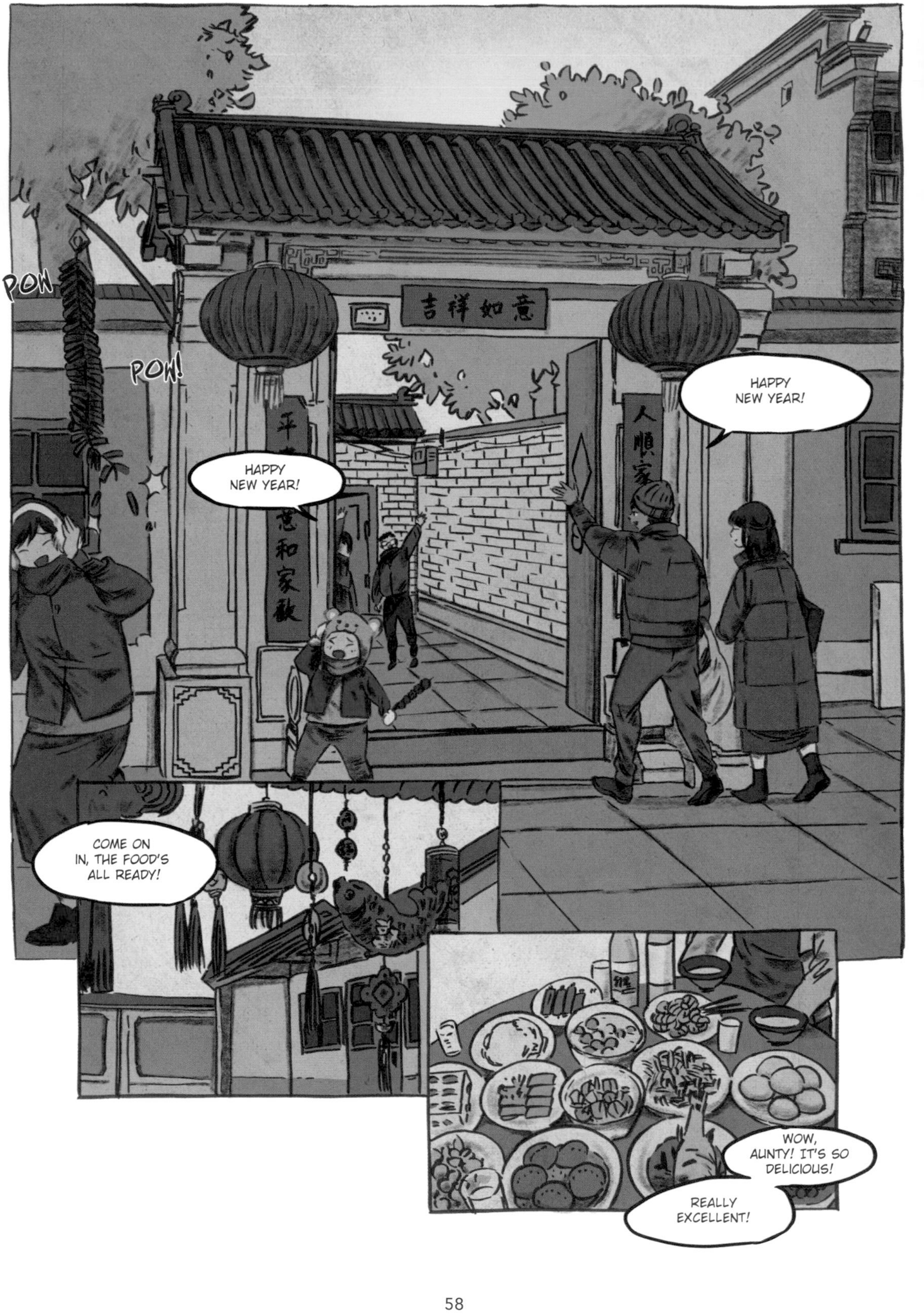
POW
POW!
吉祥如意
HAPPY NEW YEAR!
HAPPY NEW YEAR!
COME ON IN, THE FOOD'S ALL READY!
WOW, AUNTY! IT'S SO DELICIOUS!
REALLY EXCELLENT!

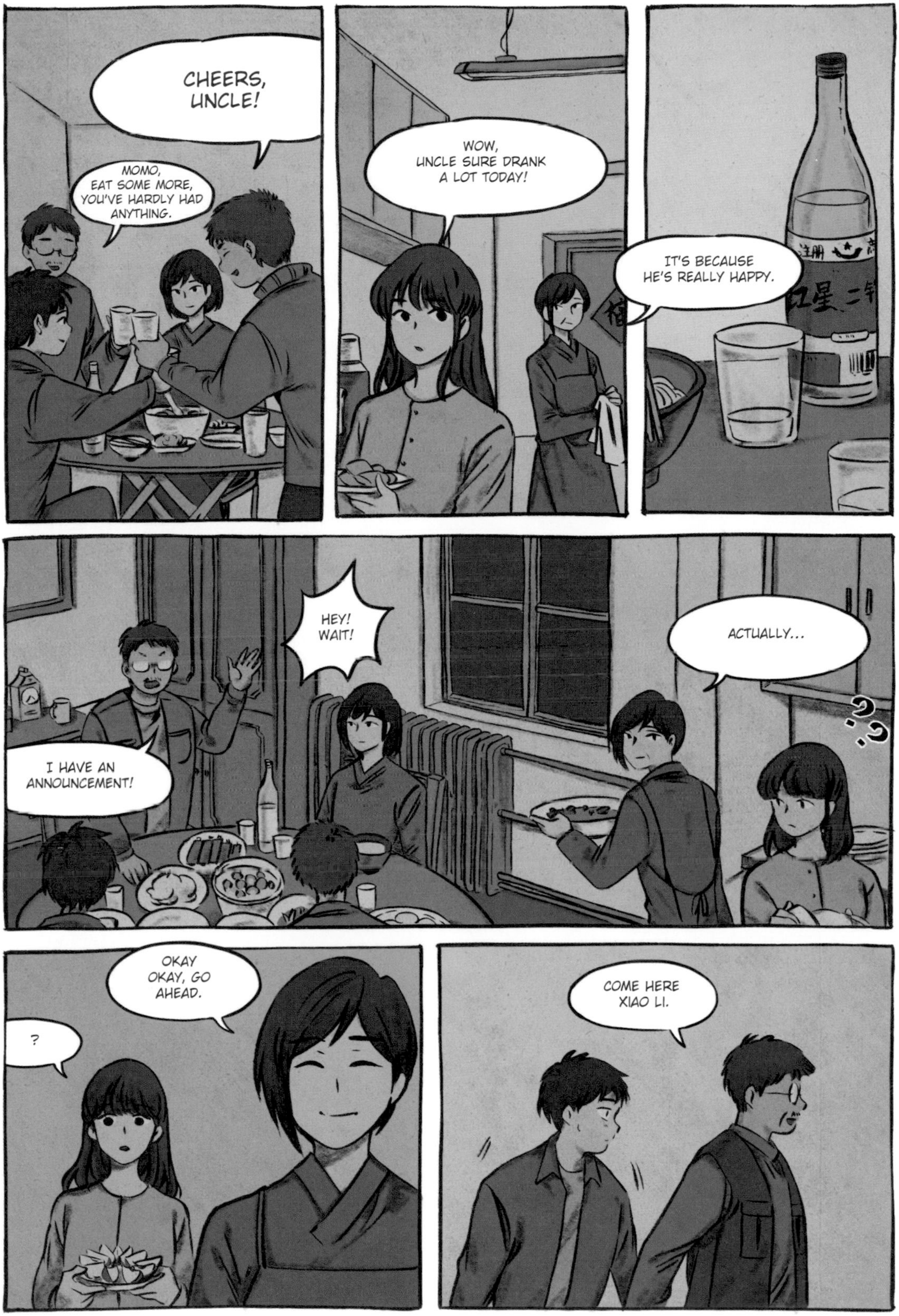
CHEERS, UNCLE!
MOMO, EAT SOME MORE, YOU'VE HARDLY HAD ANYTHING.
WOW, UNCLE SURE DRANK A LOT TODAY!
IT'S BECAUSE HE'S REALLY HAPPY.
HEY! WAIT!
I HAVE AN ANNOUNCEMENT!
ACTUALLY...
OKAY OKAY, GO AHEAD.
?
COME HERE XIAO LI.

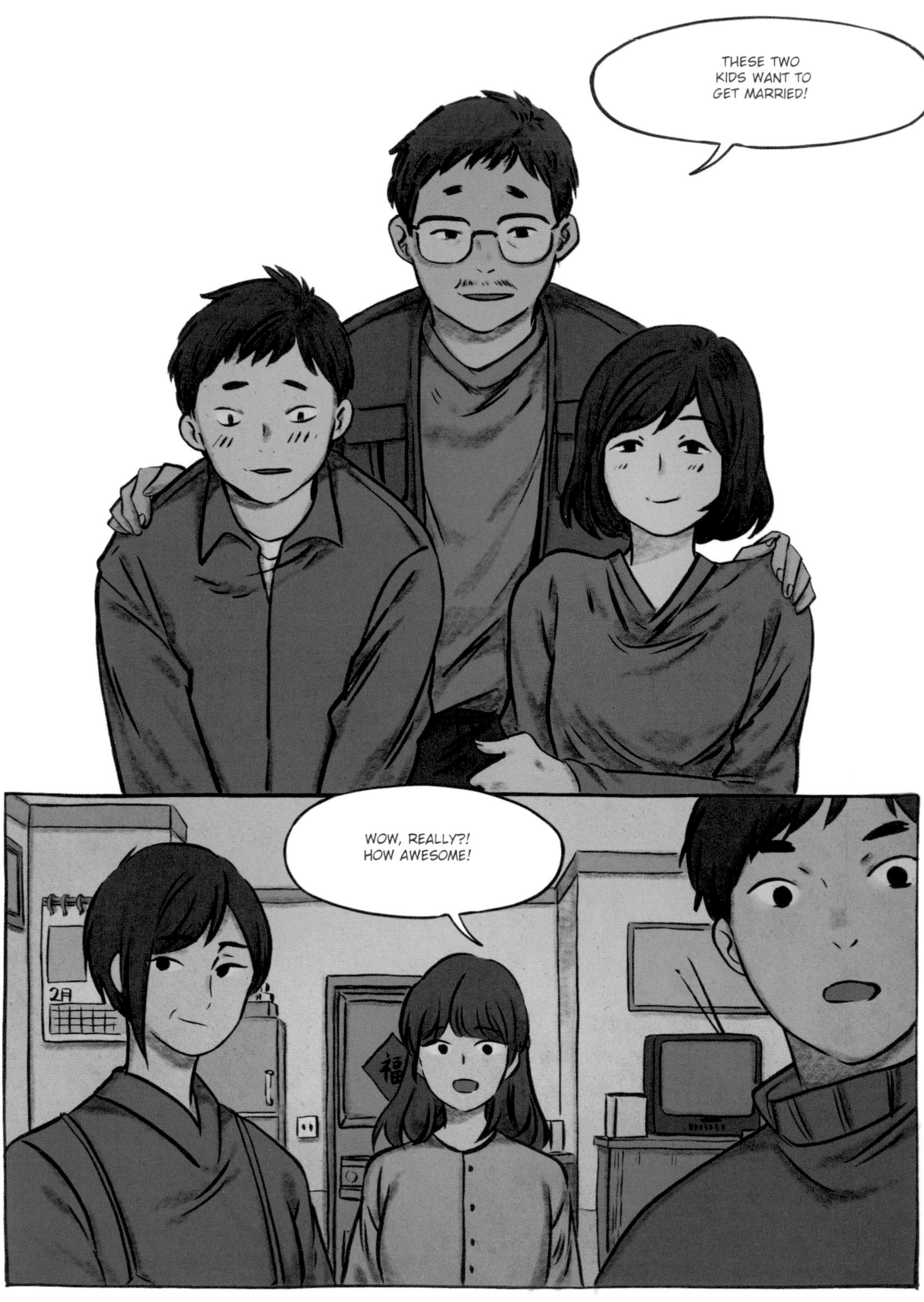
THESE TWO KIDS WANT TO GET MARRIED!
WOW, REALLY?! HOW AWESOME!

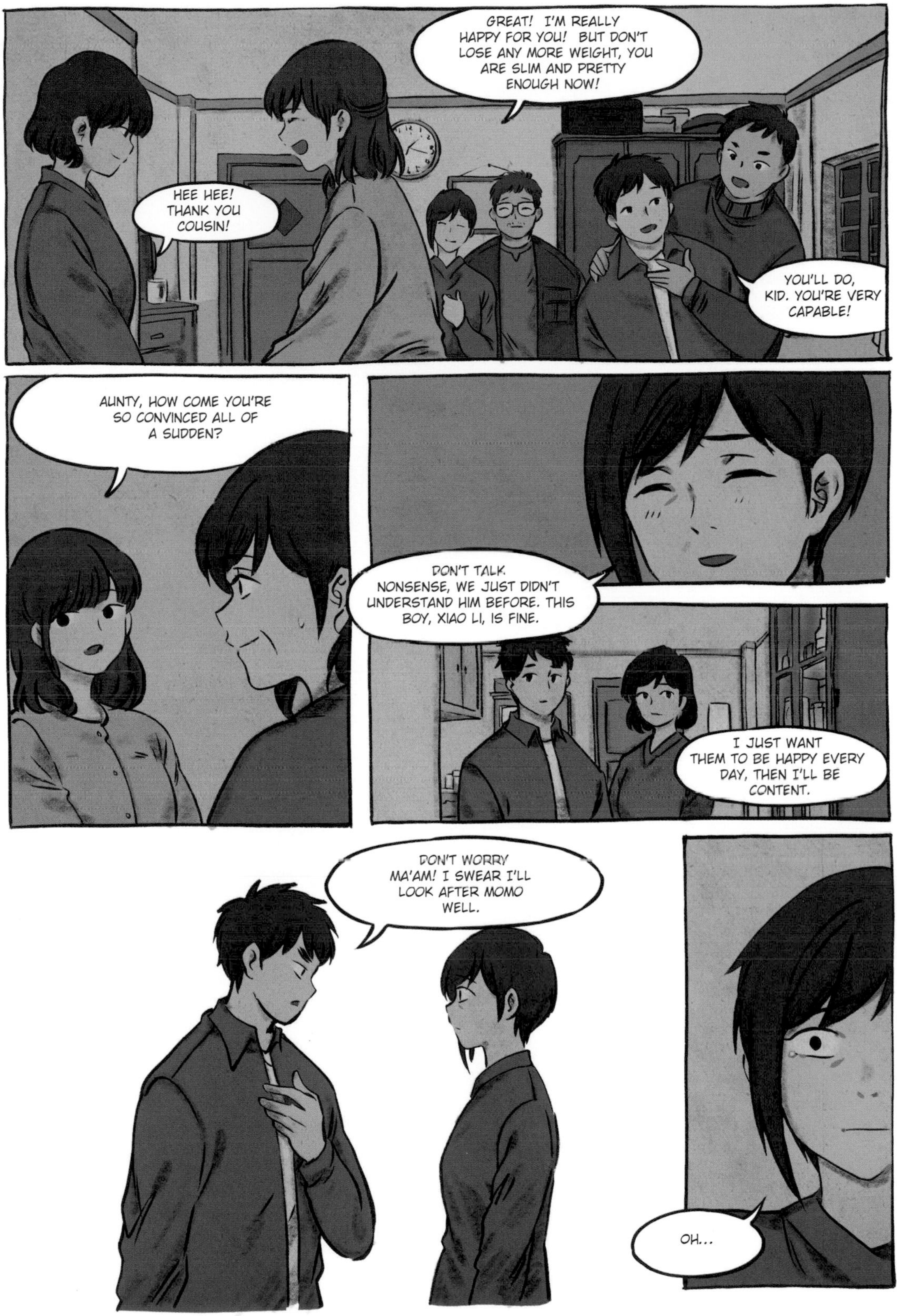
GREAT! I'M REALLY HAPPY FOR YOU! BUT DON'T LOSE ANY MORE WEIGHT, YOU ARE SLIM AND PRETTY ENOUGH NOW!
HEE HEE! THANK YOU COUSIN!
YOU'LL DO, KID. YOU'RE VERY CAPABLE!
AUNTY, HOW COME YOU'RE SO CONVINCED ALL OF A SUDDEN?
DON'T TALK NONSENSE, WE JUST DIDN'T UNDERSTAND HIM BEFORE. THIS BOY, XIAO LI, IS FINE.
I JUST WANT THEM TO BE HAPPY EVERY DAY, THEN I'LL BE CONTENT.
DON'T WORRY MA'AM! I SWEAR I'LL LOOK AFTER MOMO WELL.
OH...

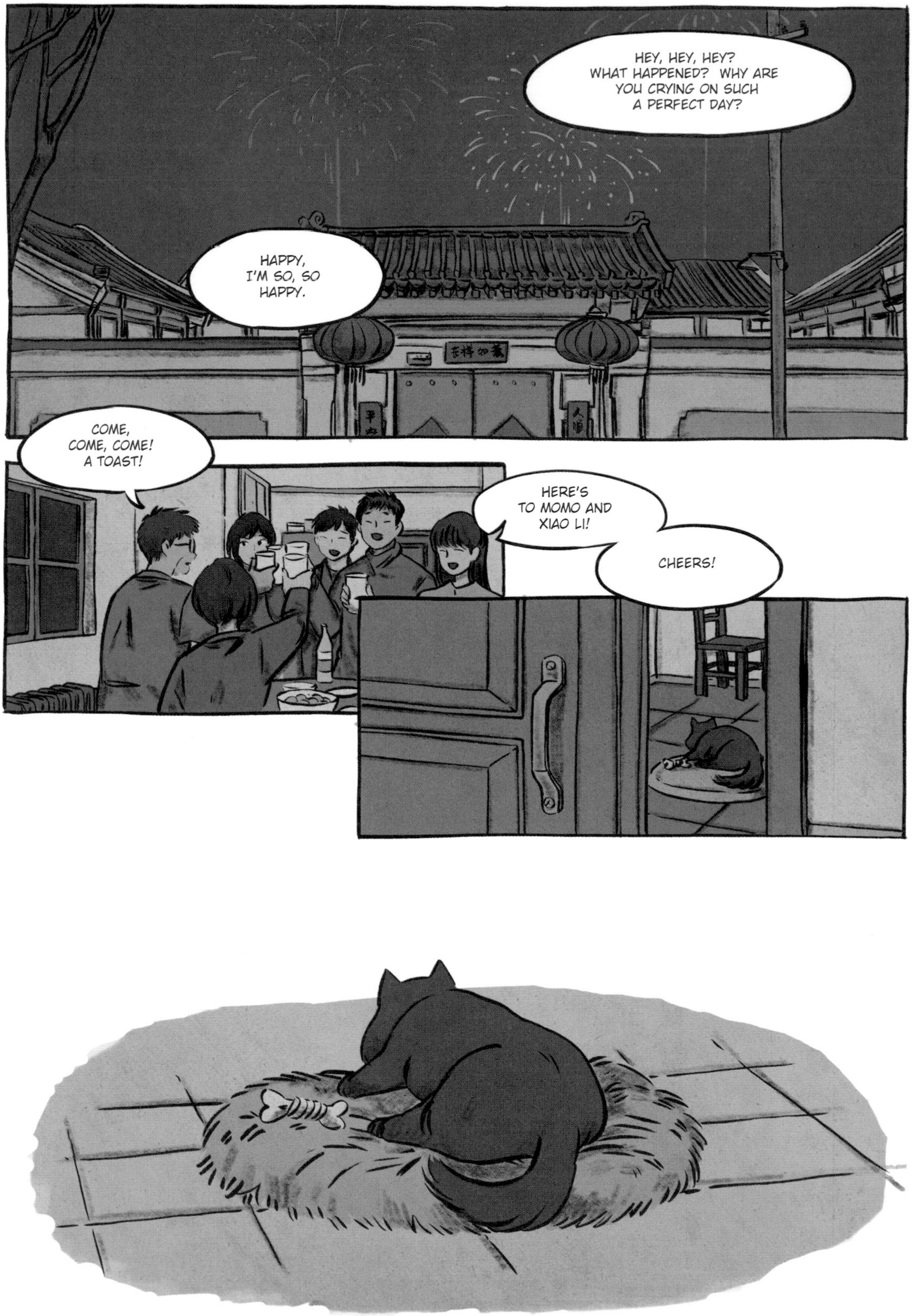
HEY, HEY, HEY? WHAT HAPPENED? WHY ARE YOU CRYING ON SUCH A PERFECT DAY?
HAPPY, I'M SO, SO HAPPY.
COME, COME, COME! A TOAST!
HERE'S TO MOMO AND XIAO LI!
CHEERS!

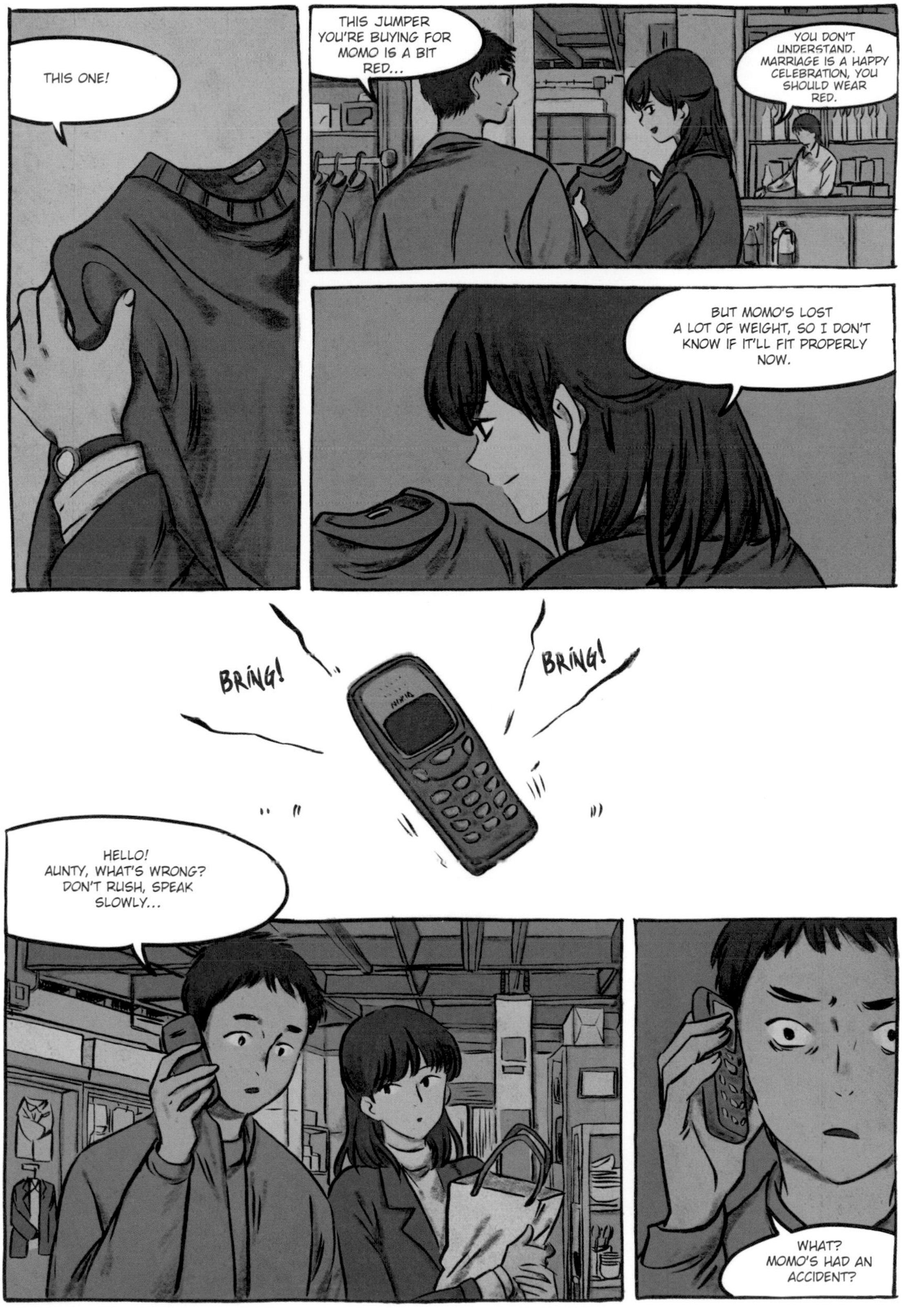

THIS ONE!
THIS JUMPER YOU'RE BUYING FOR MOMO IS A BIT RED...
YOU DON'T UNDERSTAND. A MARRIAGE IS A HAPPY CELEBRATION, YOU SHOULD WEAR RED.
BUT MOMO'S LOST A LOT OF WEIGHT, SO I DON'T KNOW IF IT'LL FIT PROPERLY NOW.
BRING!
BRING!
HELLO! AUNTY, WHAT'S WRONG? DON'T RUSH, SPEAK SLOWLY...
WHAT? MOMO'S HAD AN ACCIDENT?

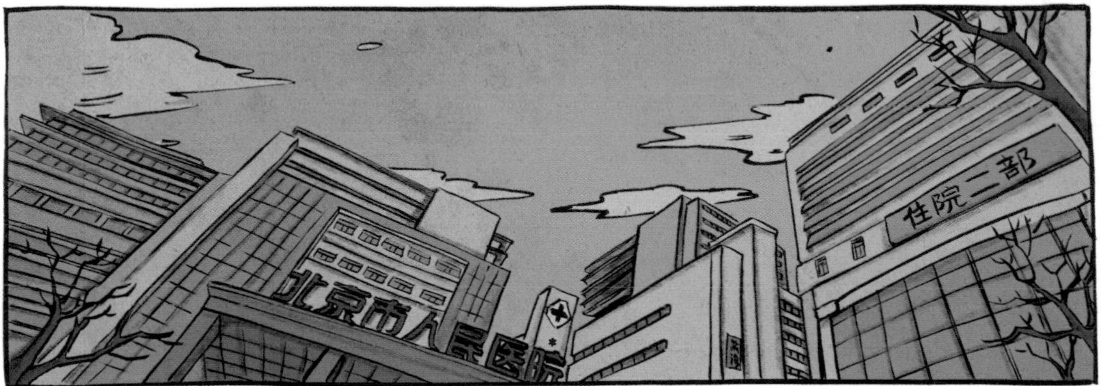
住院二部
北京市人民医院*

*BEIJING PEOPLE'S HOSPITAL

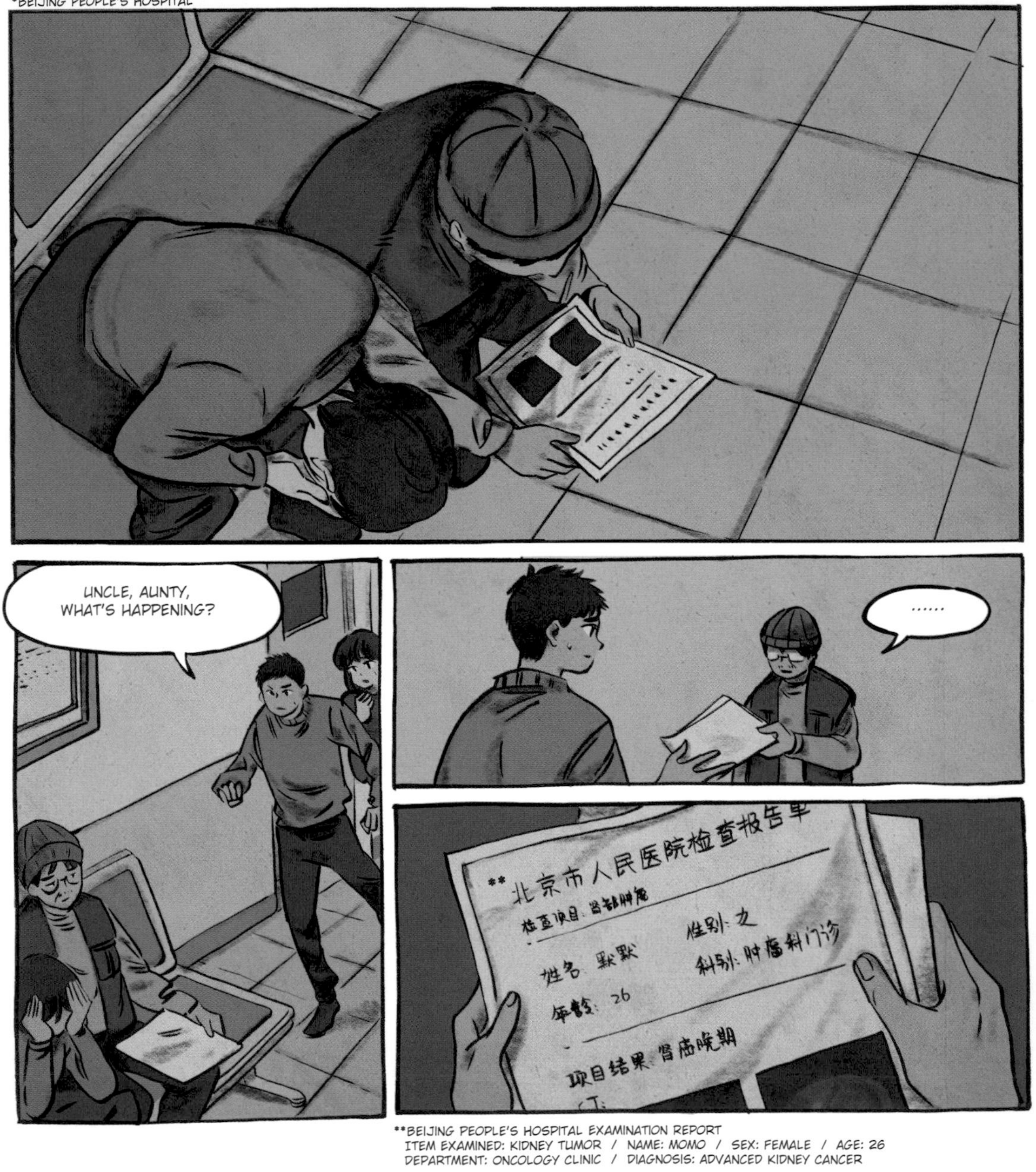
UNCLE, AUNTY,
WHAT'S HAPPENING?
......
**北京市人民医院检查报告单
检查项目: 肾部肿瘤
性别: 女
姓名: 默默
科别: 肿瘤科门诊
年龄: 26
项目结果: 肾癌晚期

**BEIJING PEOPLE'S HOSPITAL EXAMINATION REPORT
ITEM EXAMINED: KIDNEY TUMOR / NAME: MOMO / SEX: FEMALE / AGE: 26
DEPARTMENT: ONCOLOGY CLINIC / DIAGNOSIS: ADVANCED KIDNEY CANCER

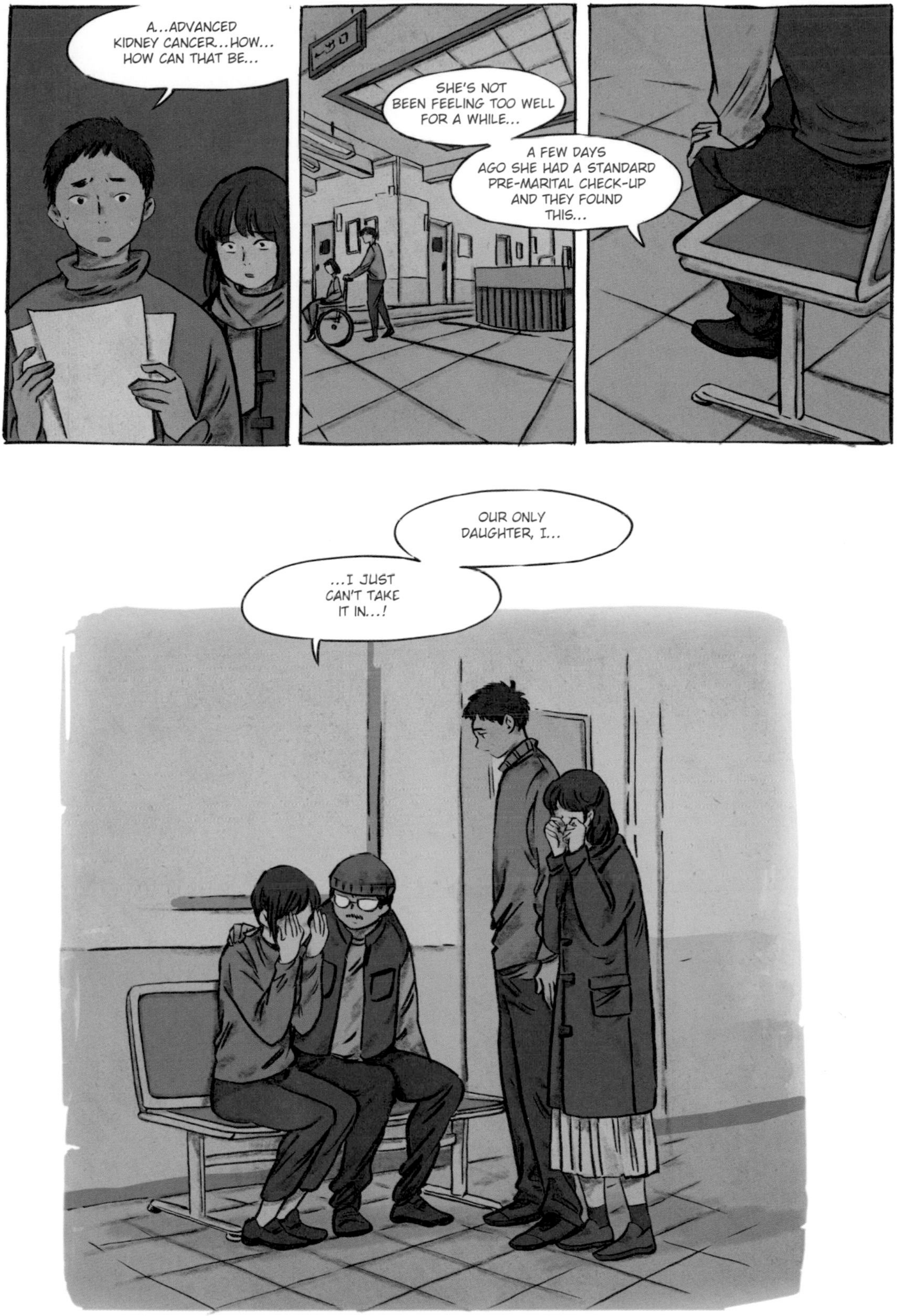
A...ADVANCED KIDNEY CANCER...HOW... HOW CAN THAT BE...
SHE'S NOT BEEN FEELING TOO WELL FOR A WHILE...
A FEW DAYS AGO SHE HAD A STANDARD PRE-MARITAL CHECK-UP AND THEY FOUND THIS...
OUR ONLY DAUGHTER, I...
...I JUST CAN'T TAKE IT IN...!

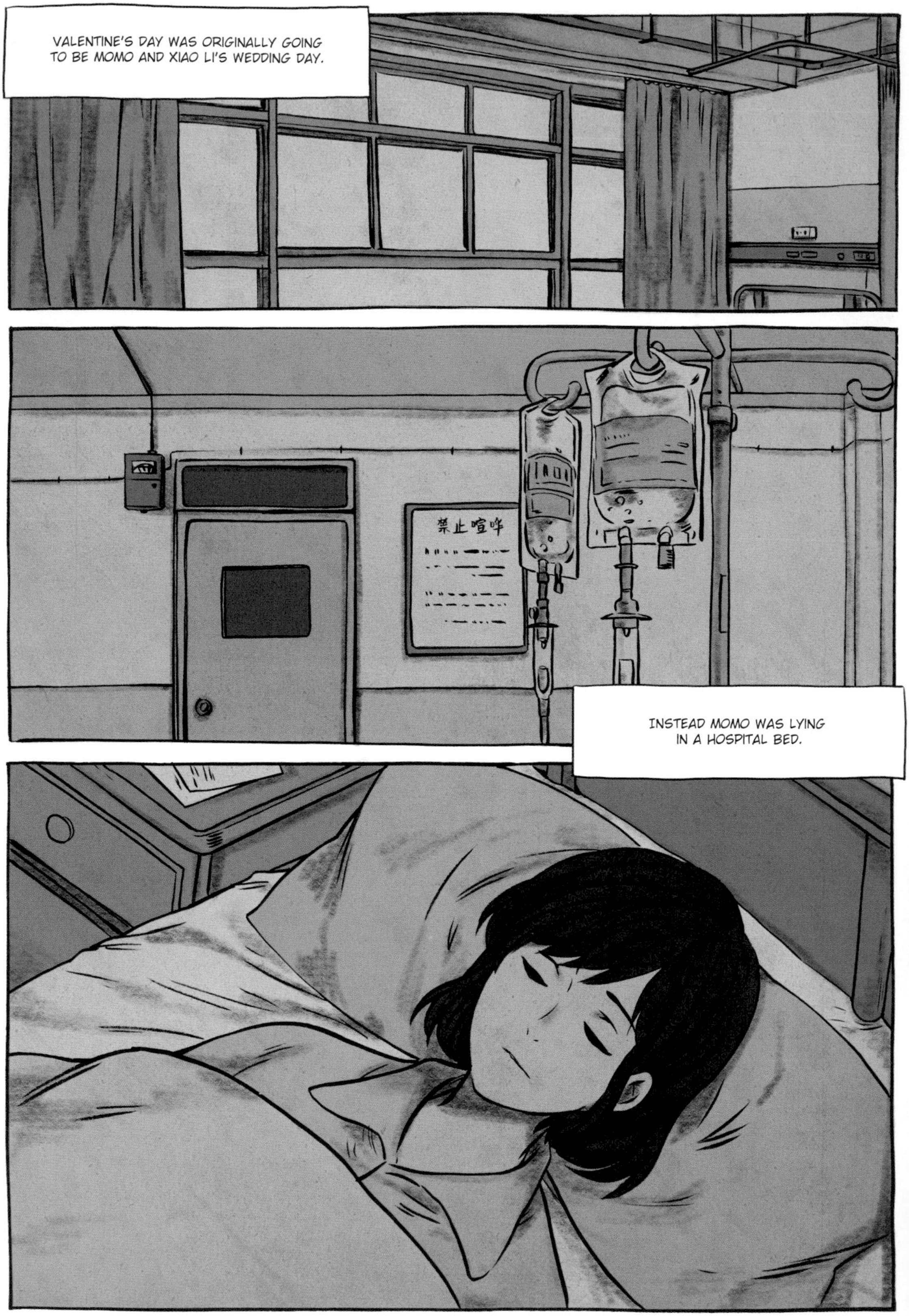
VALENTINE'S DAY WAS ORIGINALLY GOING TO BE MOMO AND XIAO LI'S WEDDING DAY.
禁止喧哗
INSTEAD MOMO WAS LYING IN A HOSPITAL BED.

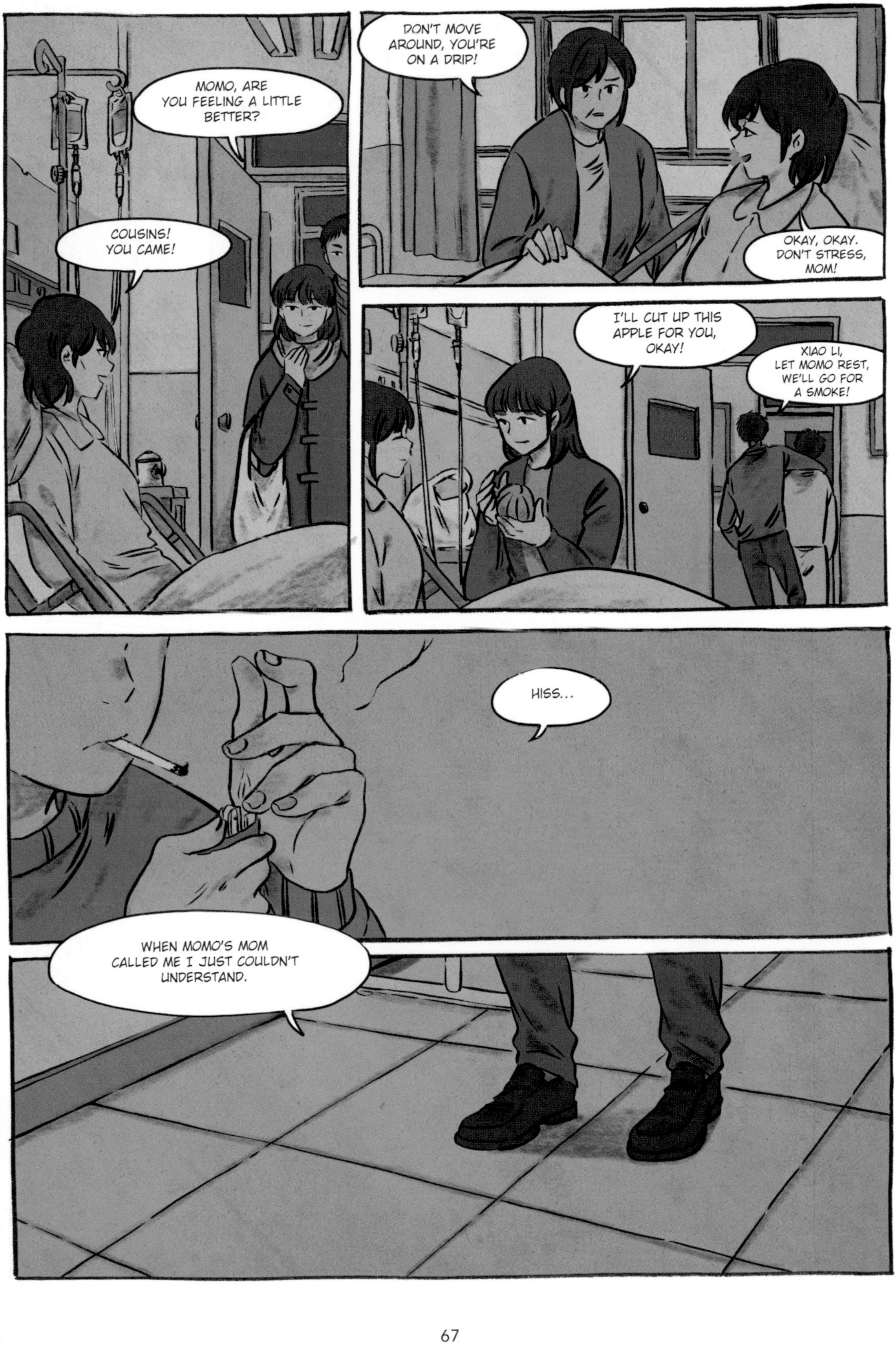
MOMO, ARE YOU FEELING A LITTLE BETTER?
COUSINS! YOU CAME!
DON'T MOVE AROUND, YOU'RE ON A DRIP!
OKAY, OKAY. DON'T STRESS, MOM!
I'LL CUT UP THIS APPLE FOR YOU, OKAY!
XIAO LI, LET MOMO REST, WE'LL GO FOR A SMOKE!
HISS...
WHEN MOMO'S MOM CALLED ME I JUST COULDN'T UNDERSTAND.

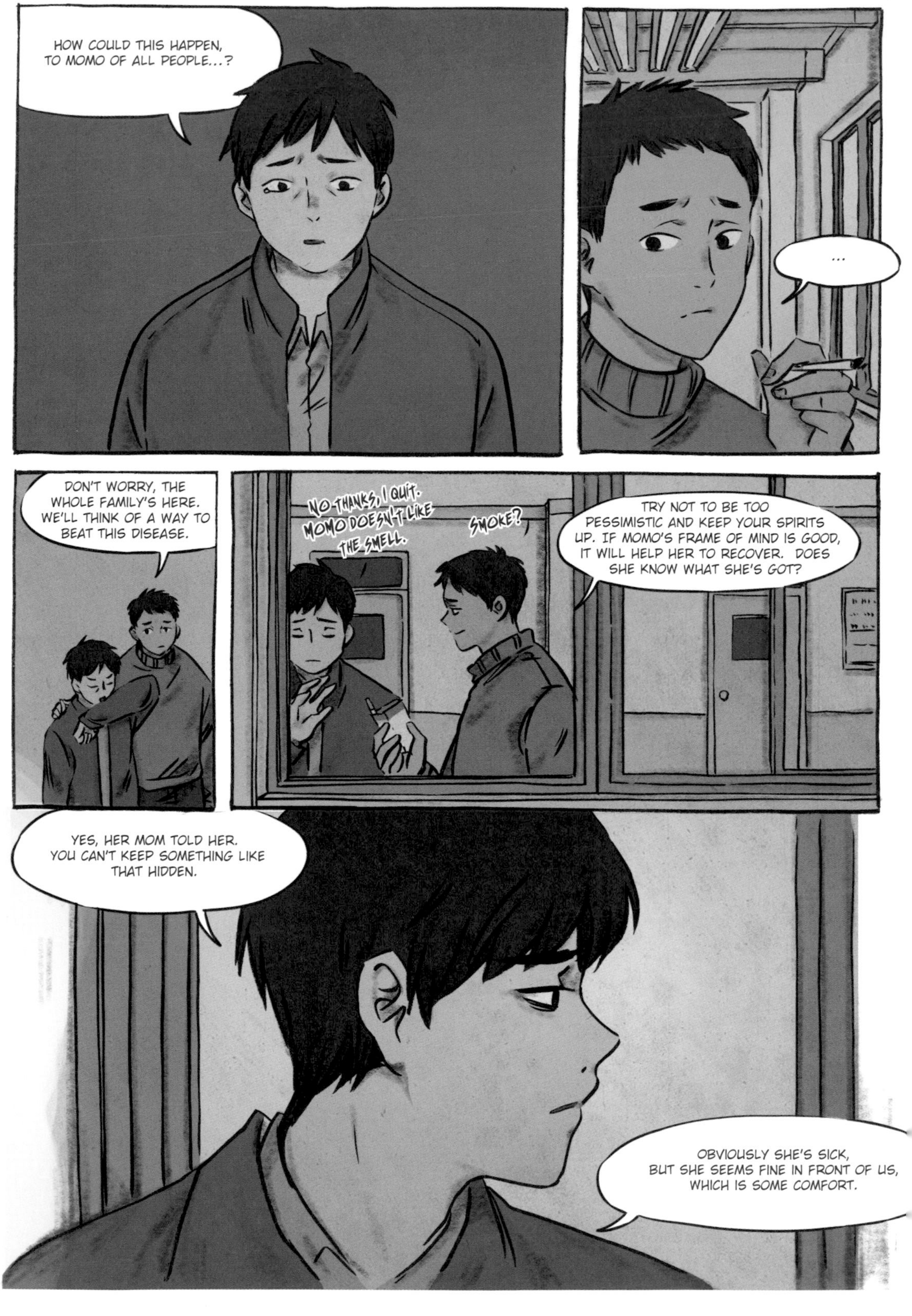
HOW COULD THIS HAPPEN, TO MOMO OF ALL PEOPLE...?
...
DON'T WORRY, THE WHOLE FAMILY'S HERE. WE'LL THINK OF A WAY TO BEAT THIS DISEASE.
SMOKE?
NO THANKS, I QUIT. MOMO DOESN'T LIKE THE SMELL.
TRY NOT TO BE TOO PESSIMISTIC AND KEEP YOUR SPIRITS UP. IF MOMO'S FRAME OF MIND IS GOOD, IT WILL HELP HER TO RECOVER. DOES SHE KNOW WHAT SHE'S GOT?
YES, HER MOM TOLD HER. YOU CAN'T KEEP SOMETHING LIKE THAT HIDDEN.
OBVIOUSLY SHE'S SICK, BUT SHE SEEMS FINE IN FRONT OF US, WHICH IS SOME COMFORT.

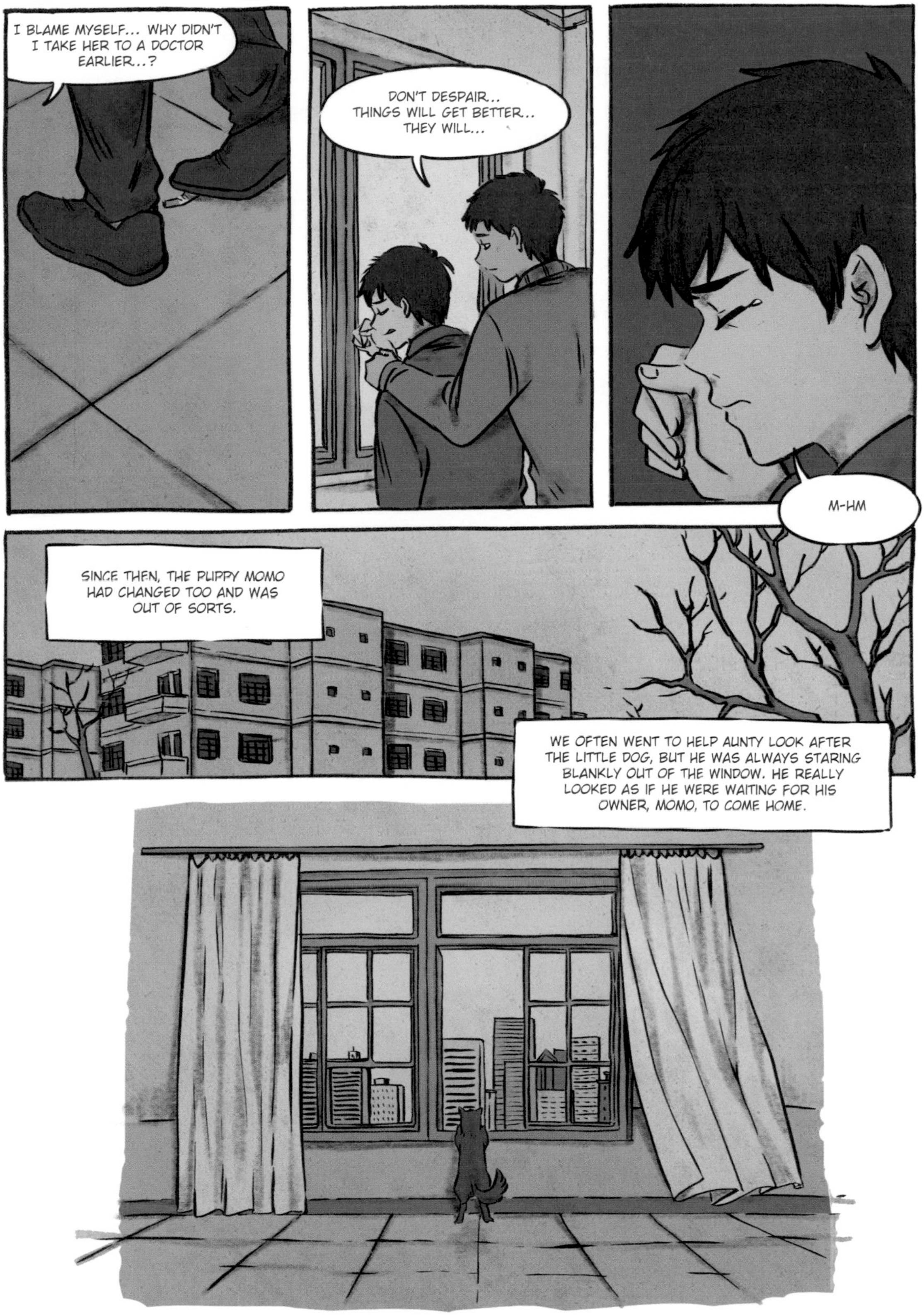
I BLAME MYSELF... WHY DIDN'T I TAKE HER TO A DOCTOR EARLIER..?
DON'T DESPAIR.. THINGS WILL GET BETTER.. THEY WILL...
M-HM
SINCE THEN, THE PUPPY MOMO HAD CHANGED TOO AND WAS OUT OF SORTS.
WE OFTEN WENT TO HELP AUNTY LOOK AFTER THE LITTLE DOG, BUT HE WAS ALWAYS STARING BLANKLY OUT OF THE WINDOW. HE REALLY LOOKED AS IF HE WERE WAITING FOR HIS OWNER, MOMO, TO COME HOME.

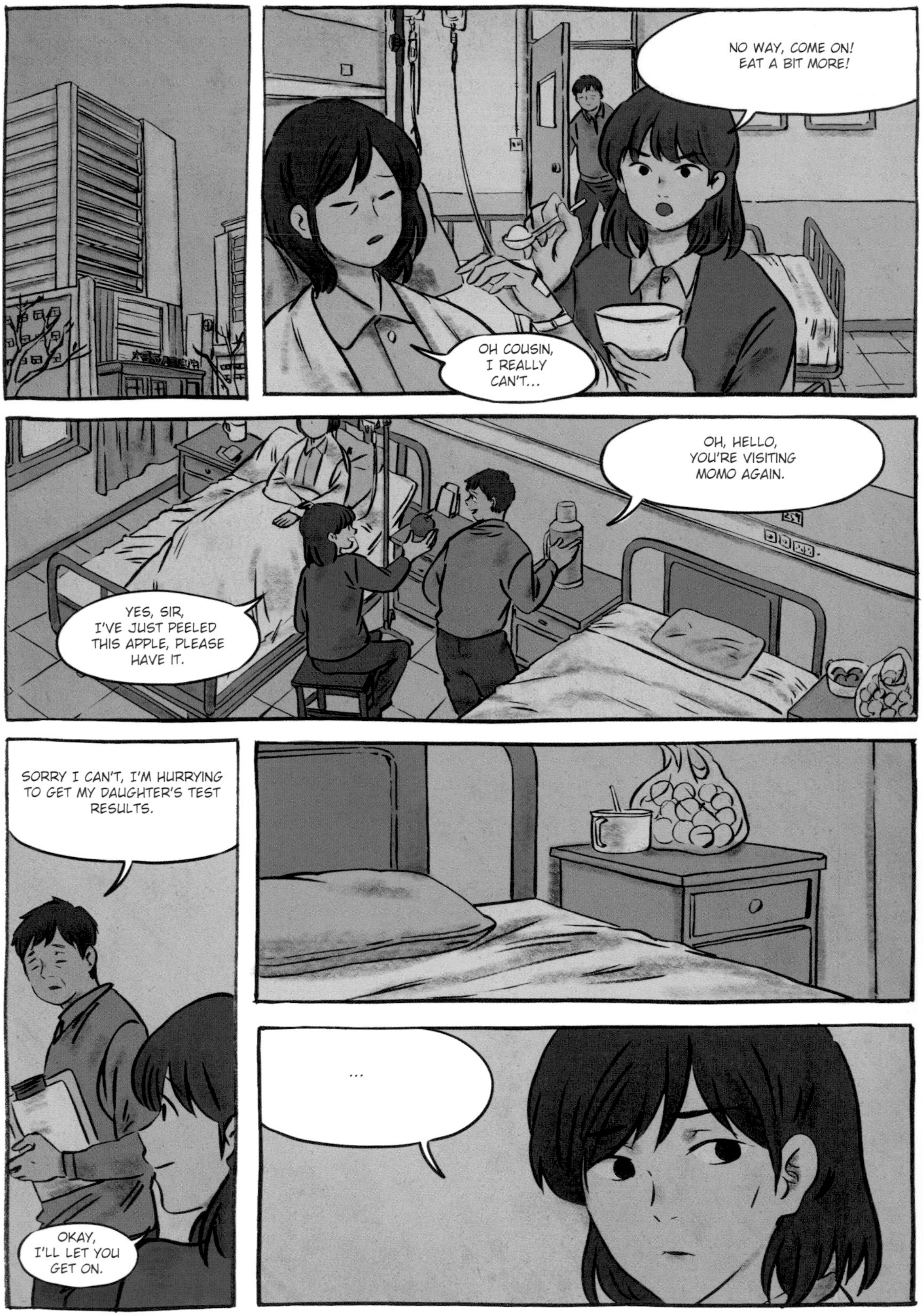
NO WAY, COME ON! EAT A BIT MORE!
OH COUSIN, I REALLY CAN'T...
OH, HELLO, YOU'RE VISITING MOMO AGAIN.
YES, SIR, I'VE JUST PEELED THIS APPLE, PLEASE HAVE IT.
SORRY I CAN'T, I'M HURRYING TO GET MY DAUGHTER'S TEST RESULTS.
OKAY, I'LL LET YOU GET ON.
...

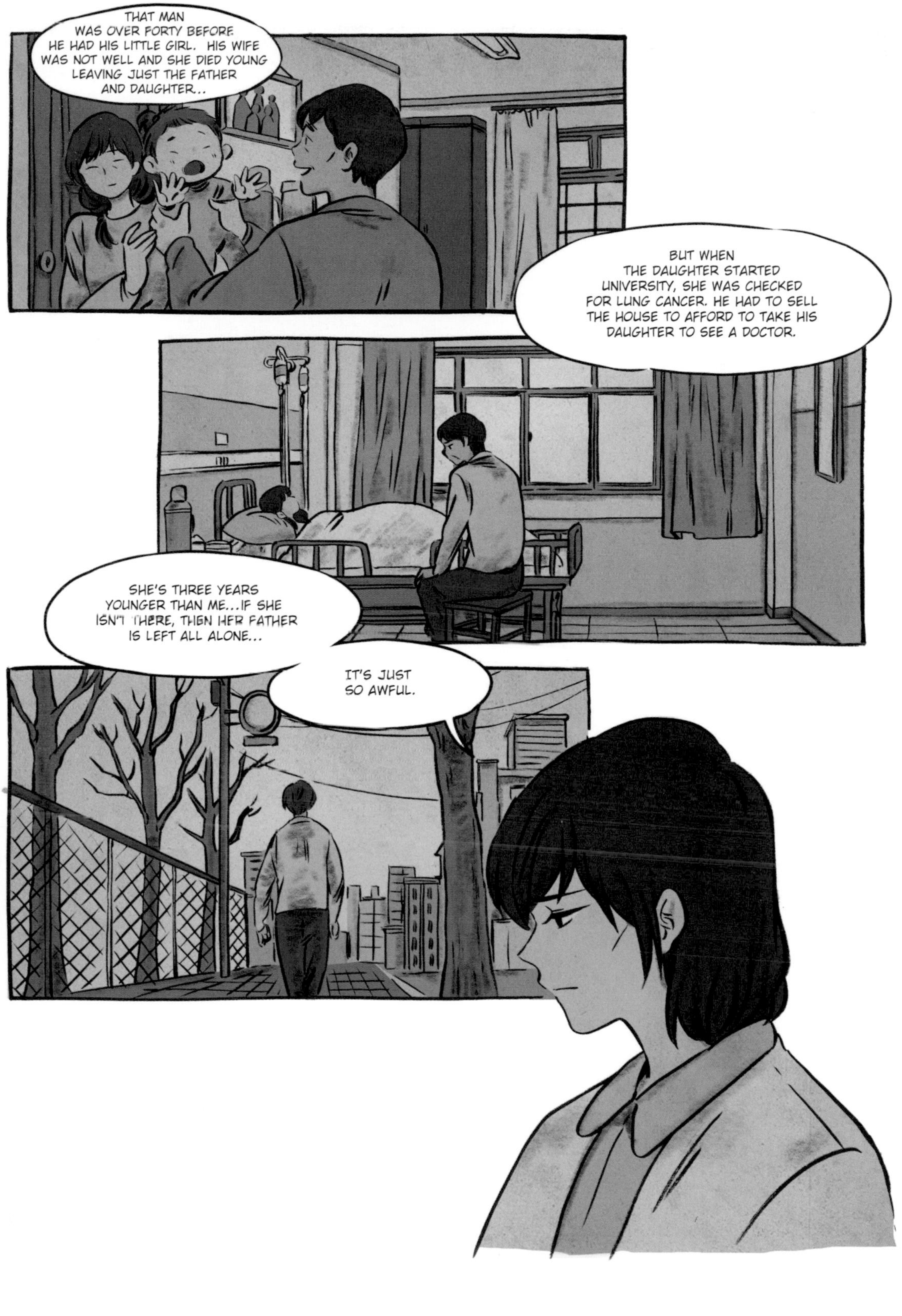
THAT MAN WAS OVER FORTY BEFORE HE HAD HIS LITTLE GIRL. HIS WIFE WAS NOT WELL AND SHE DIED YOUNG LEAVING JUST THE FATHER AND DAUGHTER...
BUT WHEN THE DAUGHTER STARTED UNIVERSITY, SHE WAS CHECKED FOR LUNG CANCER. HE HAD TO SELL THE HOUSE TO AFFORD TO TAKE HIS DAUGHTER TO SEE A DOCTOR.
SHE'S THREE YEARS YOUNGER THAN ME...IF SHE ISN'T THERE, THEN HER FATHER IS LEFT ALL ALONE...
IT'S JUST SO AWFUL.

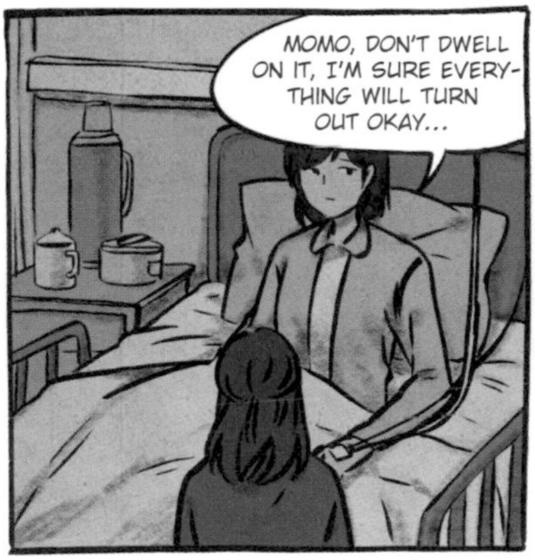
MOMO, DON'T DWELL ON IT, I'M SURE EVERY-THING WILL TURN OUT OKAY...

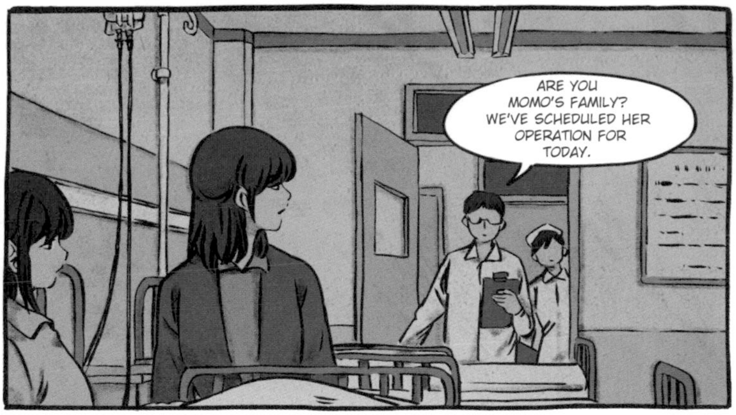
ARE YOU MOMO'S FAMILY? WE'VE SCHEDULED HER OPERATION FOR TODAY.

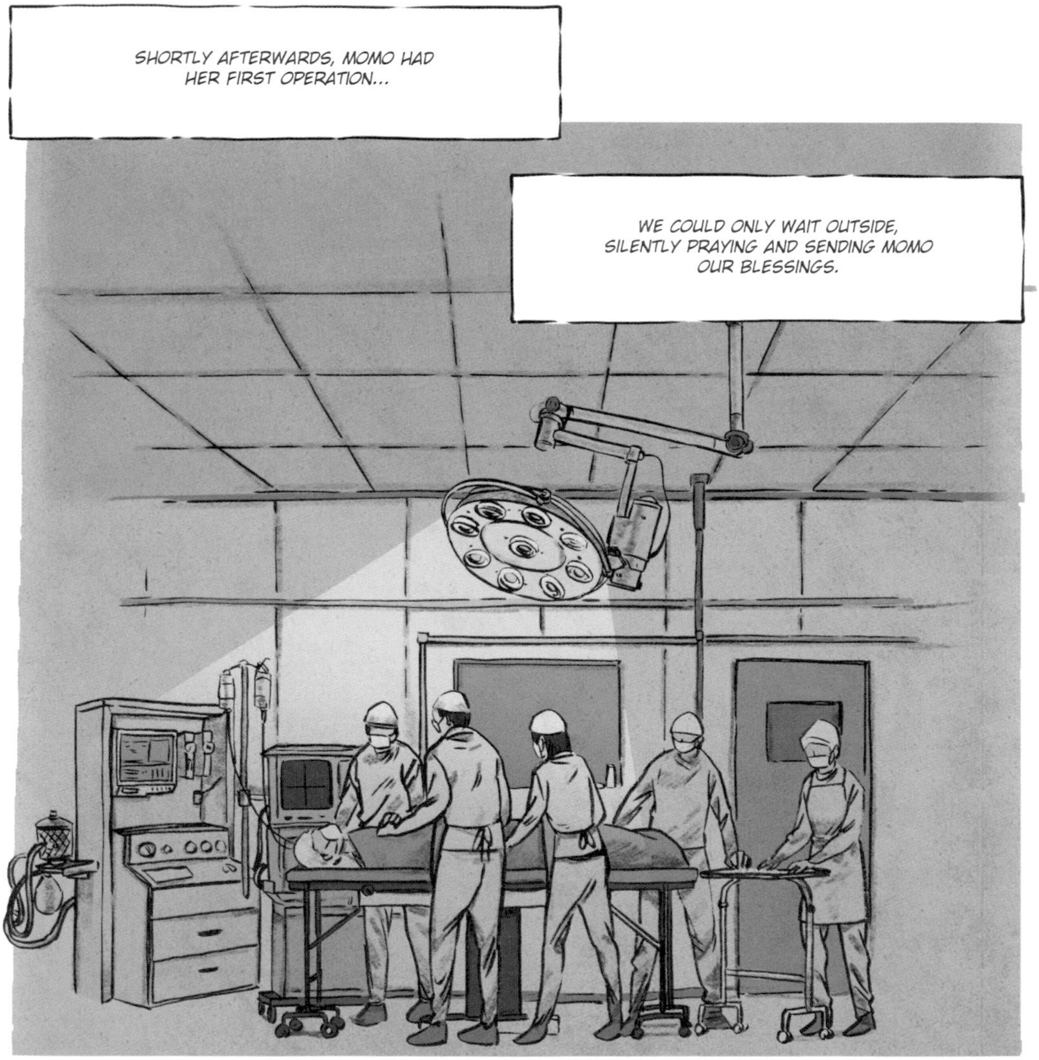
SHORTLY AFTERWARDS, MOMO HAD HER FIRST OPERATION...
WE COULD ONLY WAIT OUTSIDE, SILENTLY PRAYING AND SENDING MOMO OUR BLESSINGS.

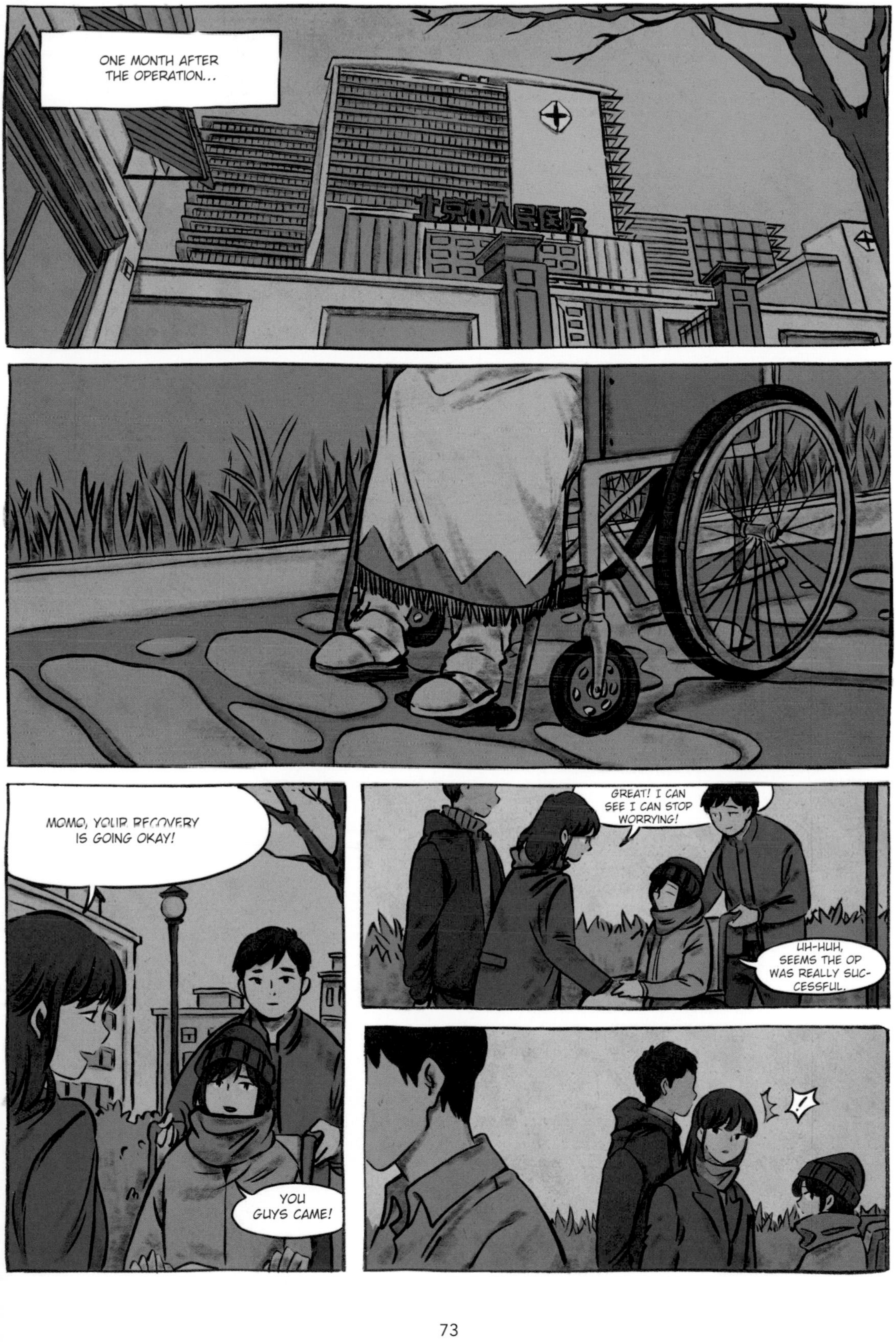
ONE MONTH AFTER THE OPERATION...
北京市人民医院
MOMO, YOUR RECOVERY IS GOING OKAY!
YOU GUYS CAME!
GREAT! I CAN SEE I CAN STOP WORRYING!
UH-HUH, SEEMS THE OP WAS REALLY SUC-CESSFUL.
!

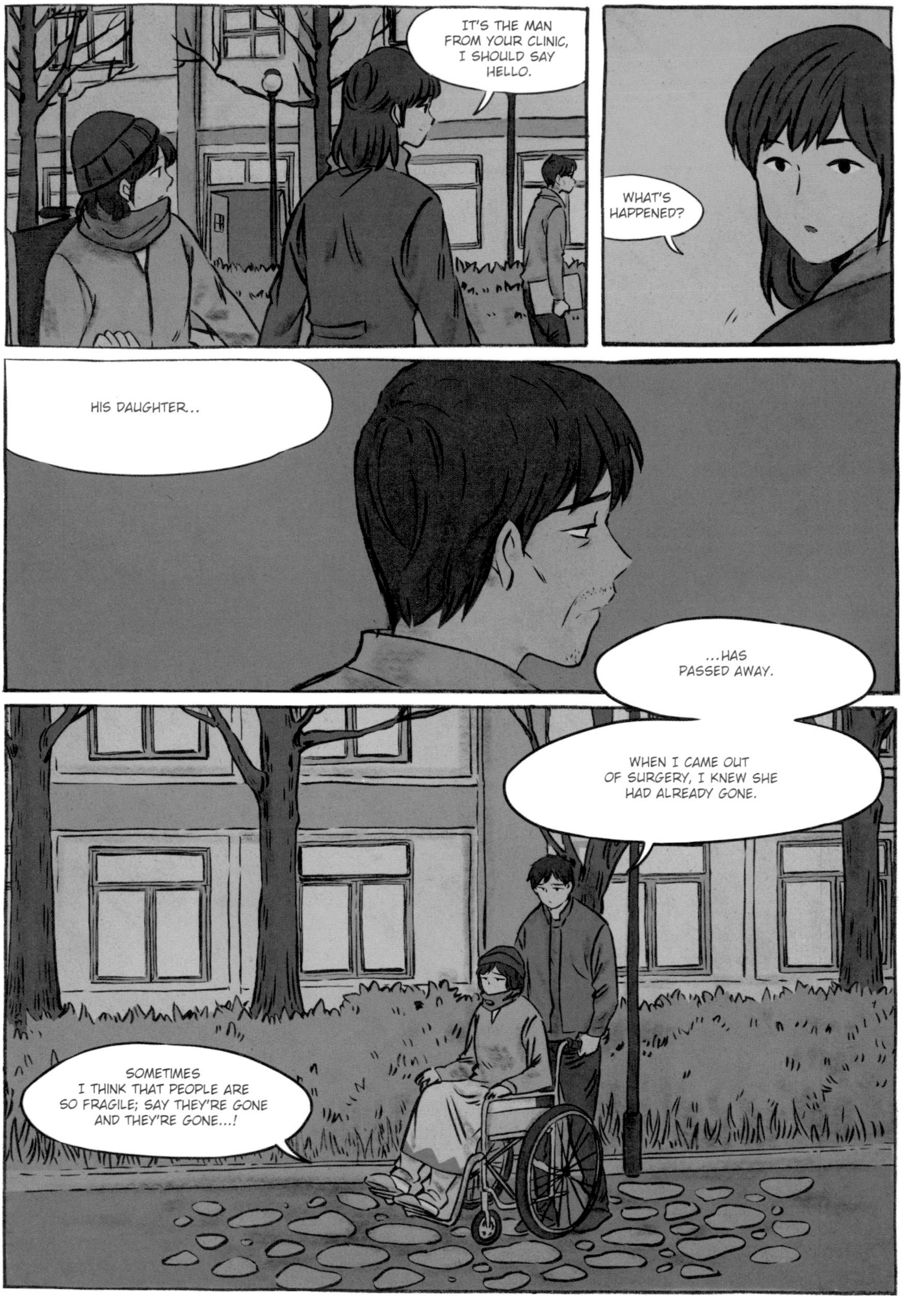
IT'S THE MAN FROM YOUR CLINIC, I SHOULD SAY HELLO.
WHAT'S HAPPENED?
HIS DAUGHTER..
...HAS PASSED AWAY.
WHEN I CAME OUT OF SURGERY, I KNEW SHE HAD ALREADY GONE.
SOMETIMES I THINK THAT PEOPLE ARE SO FRAGILE; SAY THEY'RE GONE AND THEY'RE GONE...!

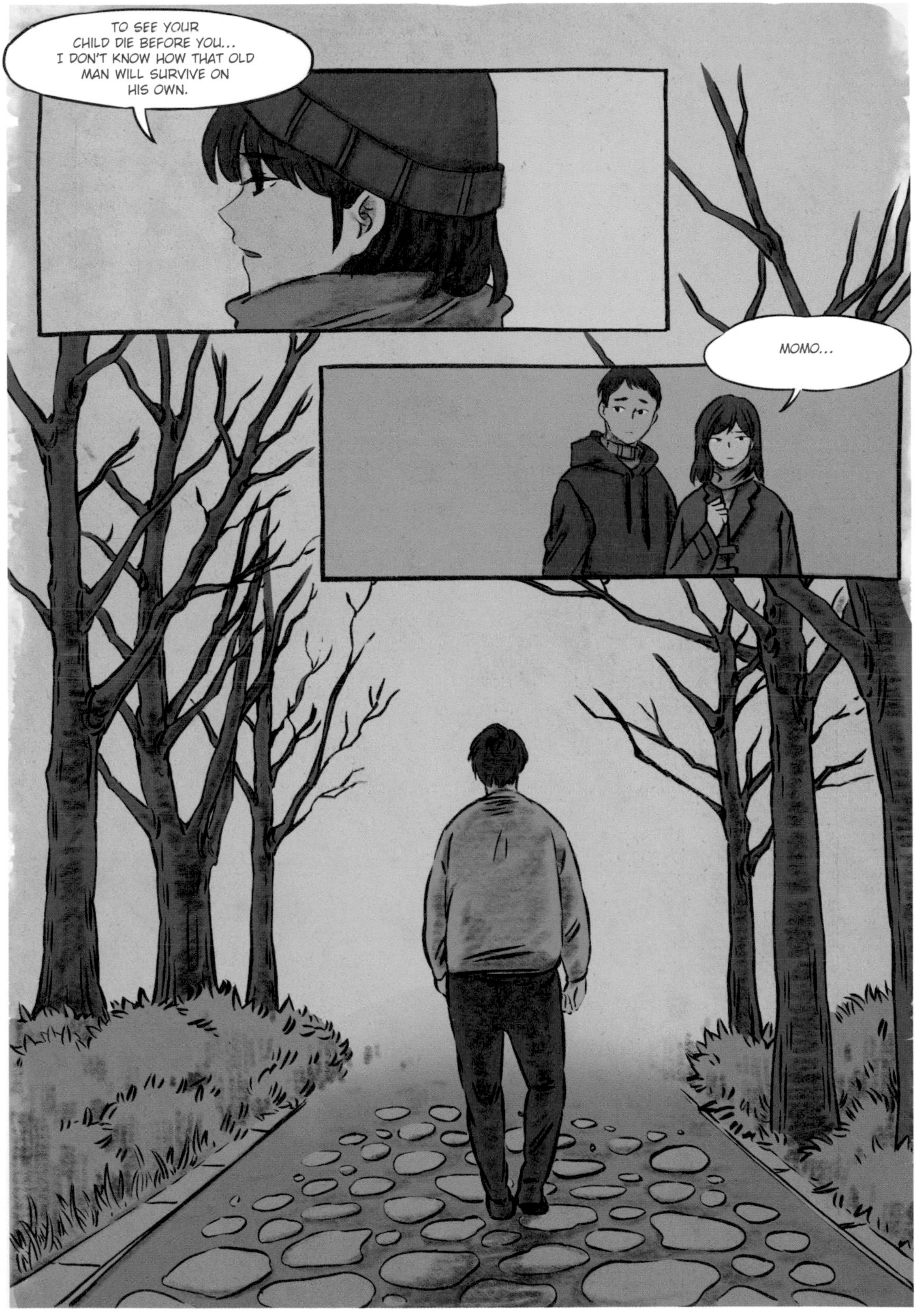
TO SEE YOUR CHILD DIE BEFORE YOU... I DON'T KNOW HOW THAT OLD MAN WILL SURVIVE ON HIS OWN.
MOMO...

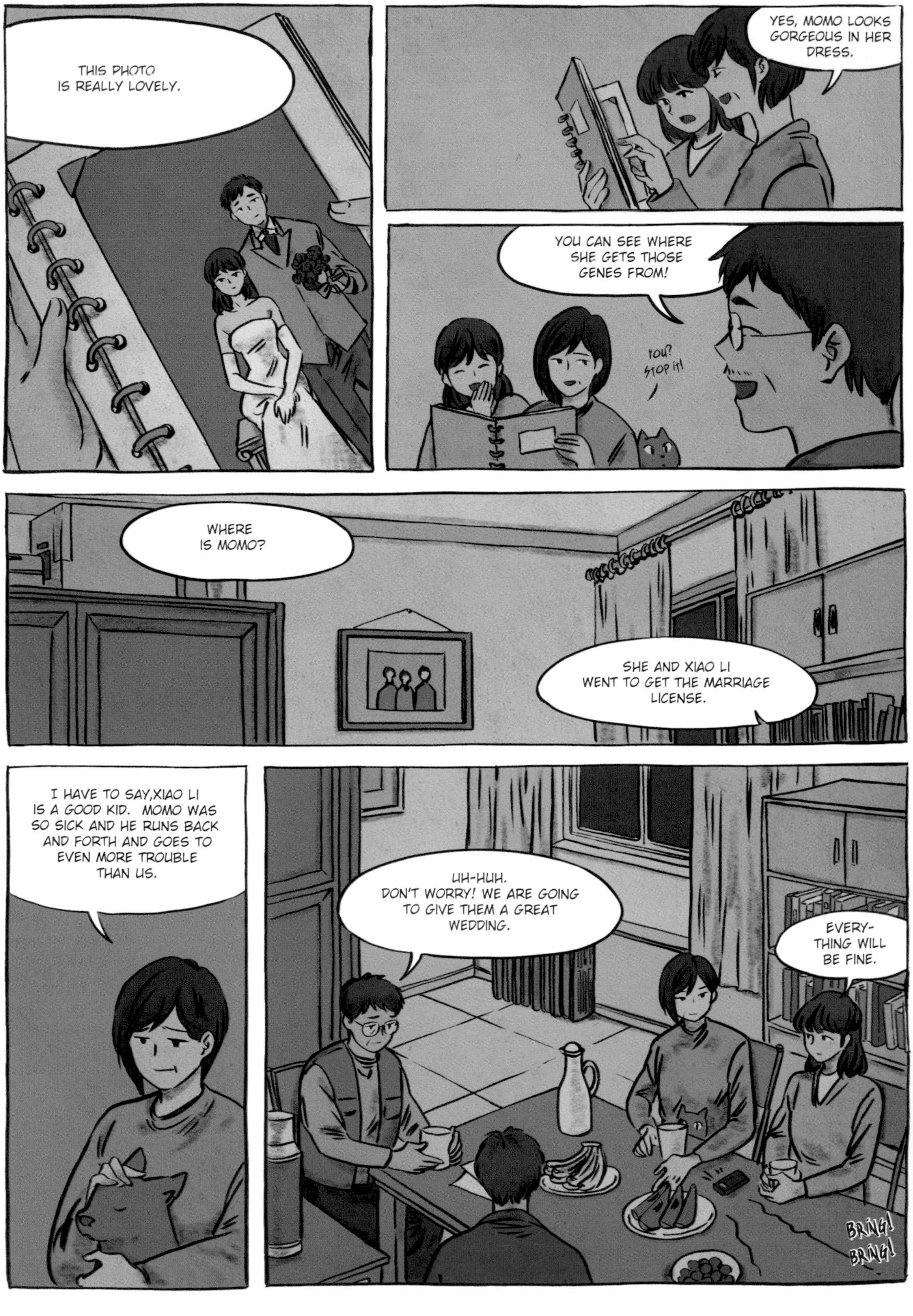
THIS PHOTO IS REALLY LOVELY.
YES, MOMO LOOKS GORGEOUS IN HER DRESS.
YOU CAN SEE WHERE SHE GETS THOSE GENES FROM!
YOU? STOP IT!
WHERE IS MOMO?
SHE AND XIAO LI WENT TO GET THE MARRIAGE LICENSE.
I HAVE TO SAY,XIAO LI IS A GOOD KID. MOMO WAS SO SICK AND HE RUNS BACK AND FORTH AND GOES TO EVEN MORE TROUBLE THAN US.
UH-HUH. DON'T WORRY! WE ARE GOING TO GIVE THEM A GREAT WEDDING.
EVERY-THING WILL BE FINE.
BRING! BRING!

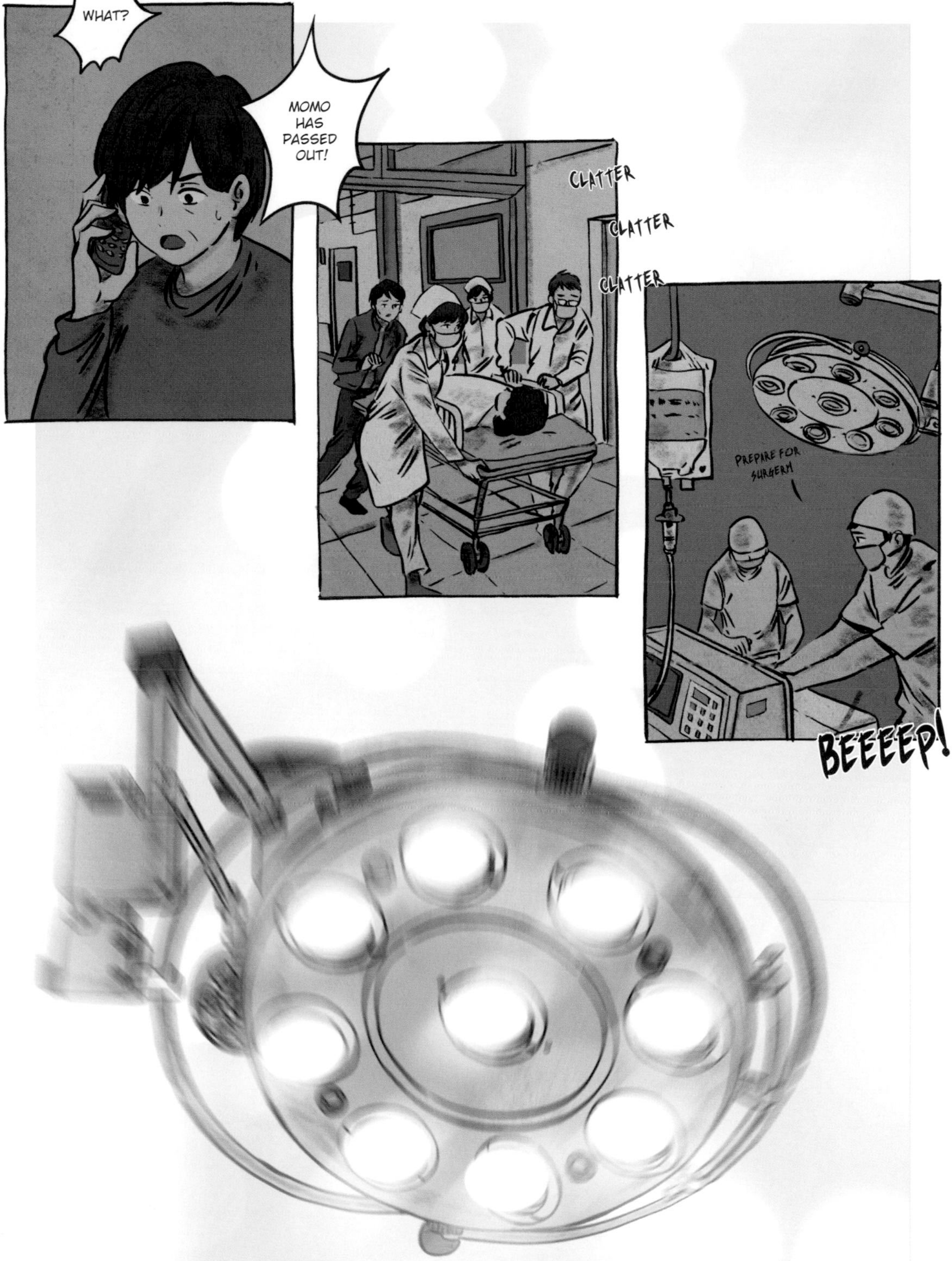
WHAT?
MOMO HAS PASSED OUT!
CLATTER
CLATTER
CLATTER
PREPARE FOR SURGERY!
BEEEEP!

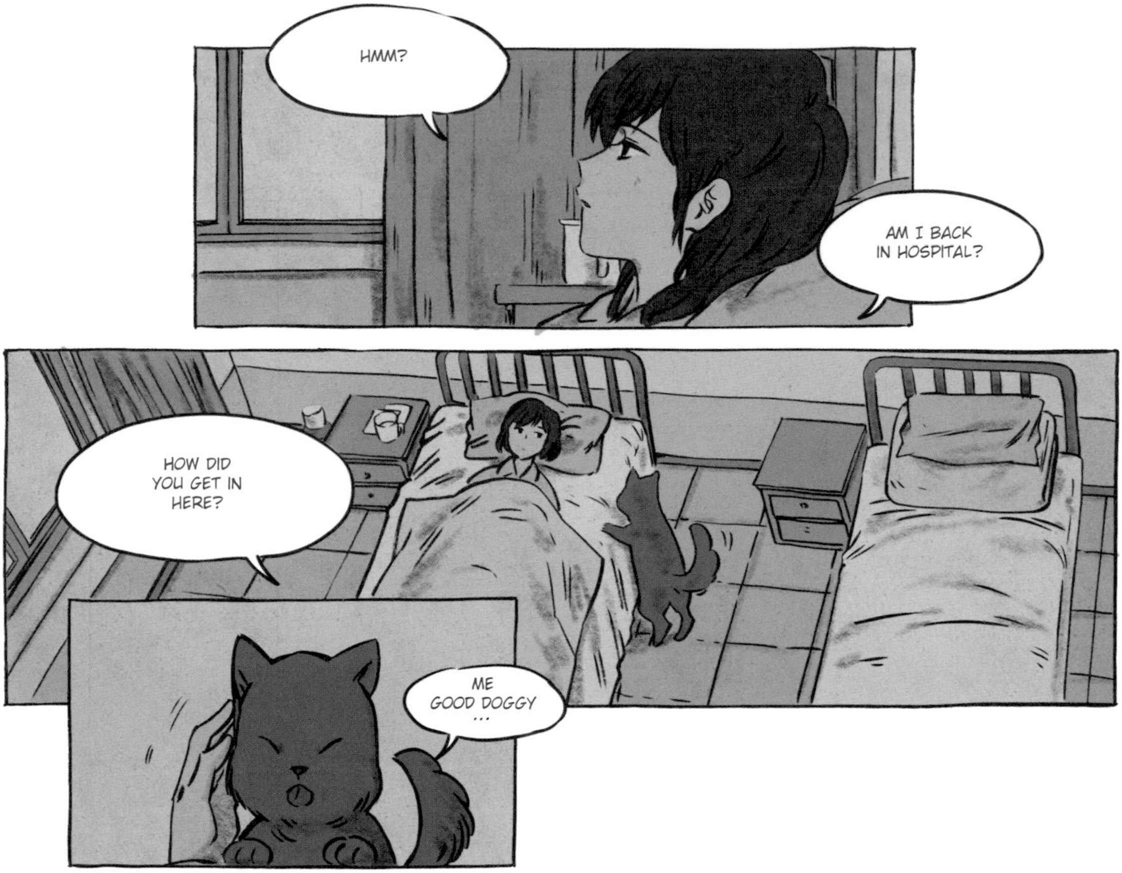
HMM?
AM I BACK IN HOSPITAL?
HOW DID YOU GET IN HERE?
ME GOOD DOGGY ...

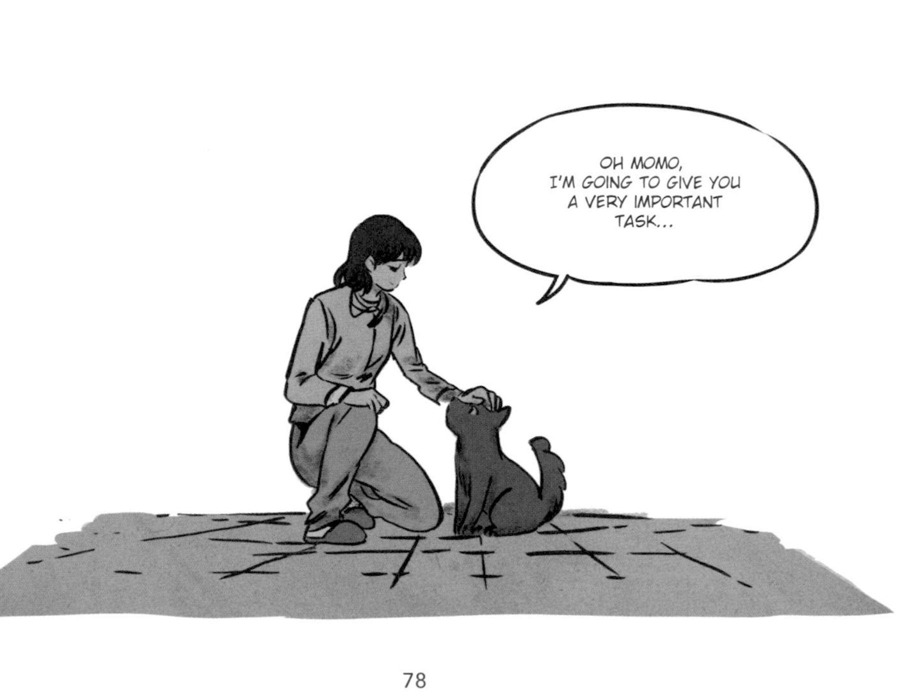
OH MOMO, I'M GOING TO GIVE YOU A VERY IMPORTANT TASK...

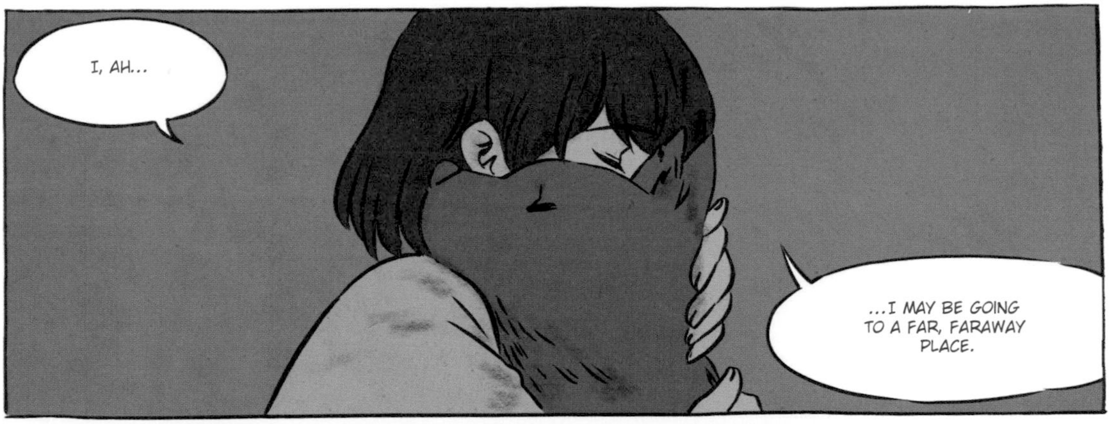
I, AH...
...I MAY BE GOING TO A FAR, FARAWAY PLACE.

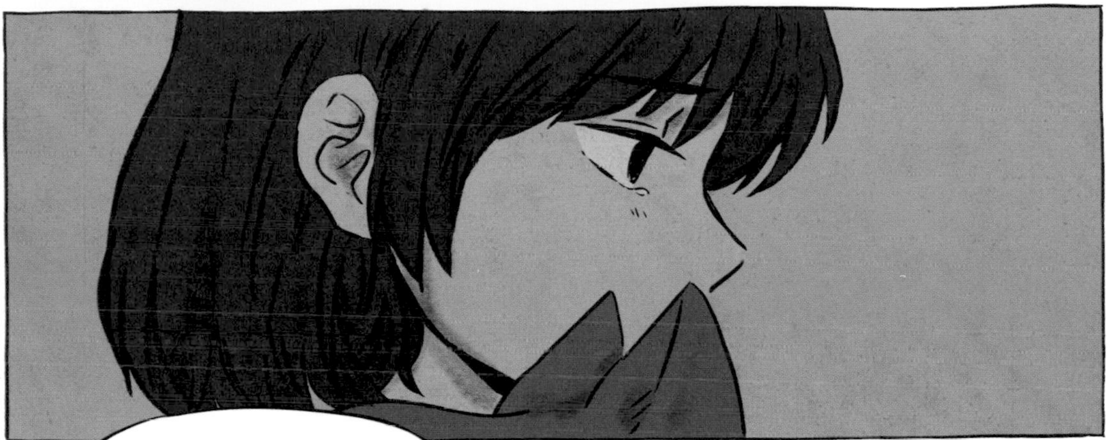
MOMO, CAN I ASK YOU TO LOOK AFTER MY FAMILY?

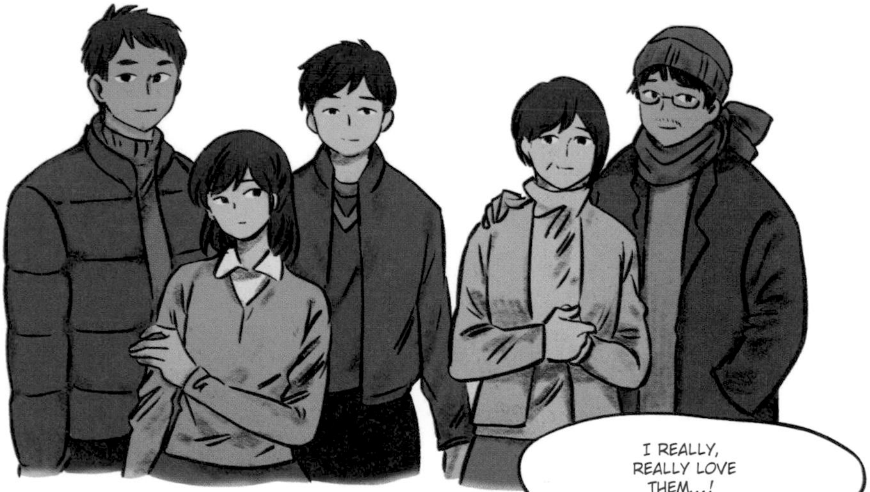
I REALLY, REALLY LOVE THEM...!

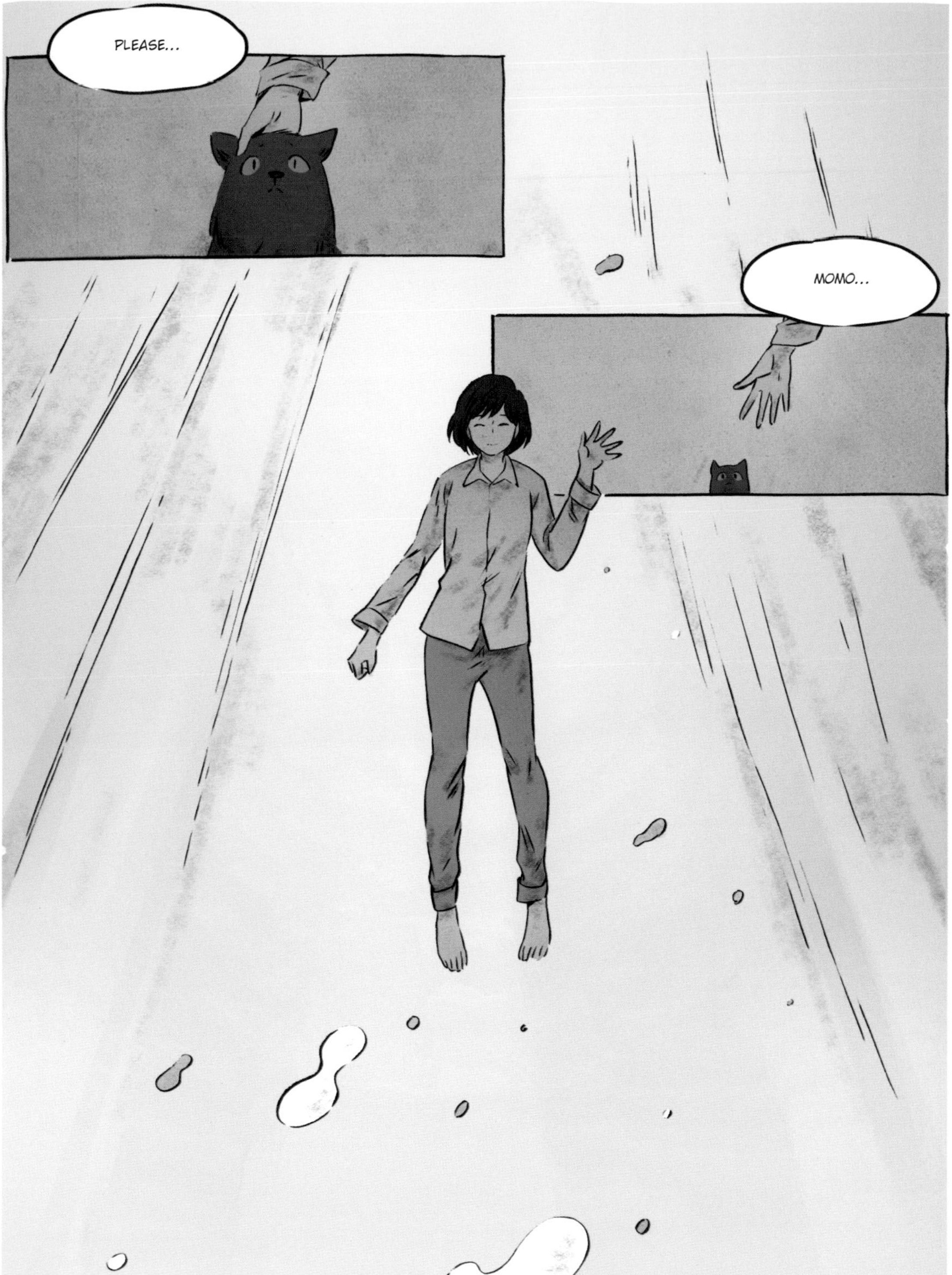
PLEASE...
MOMO...

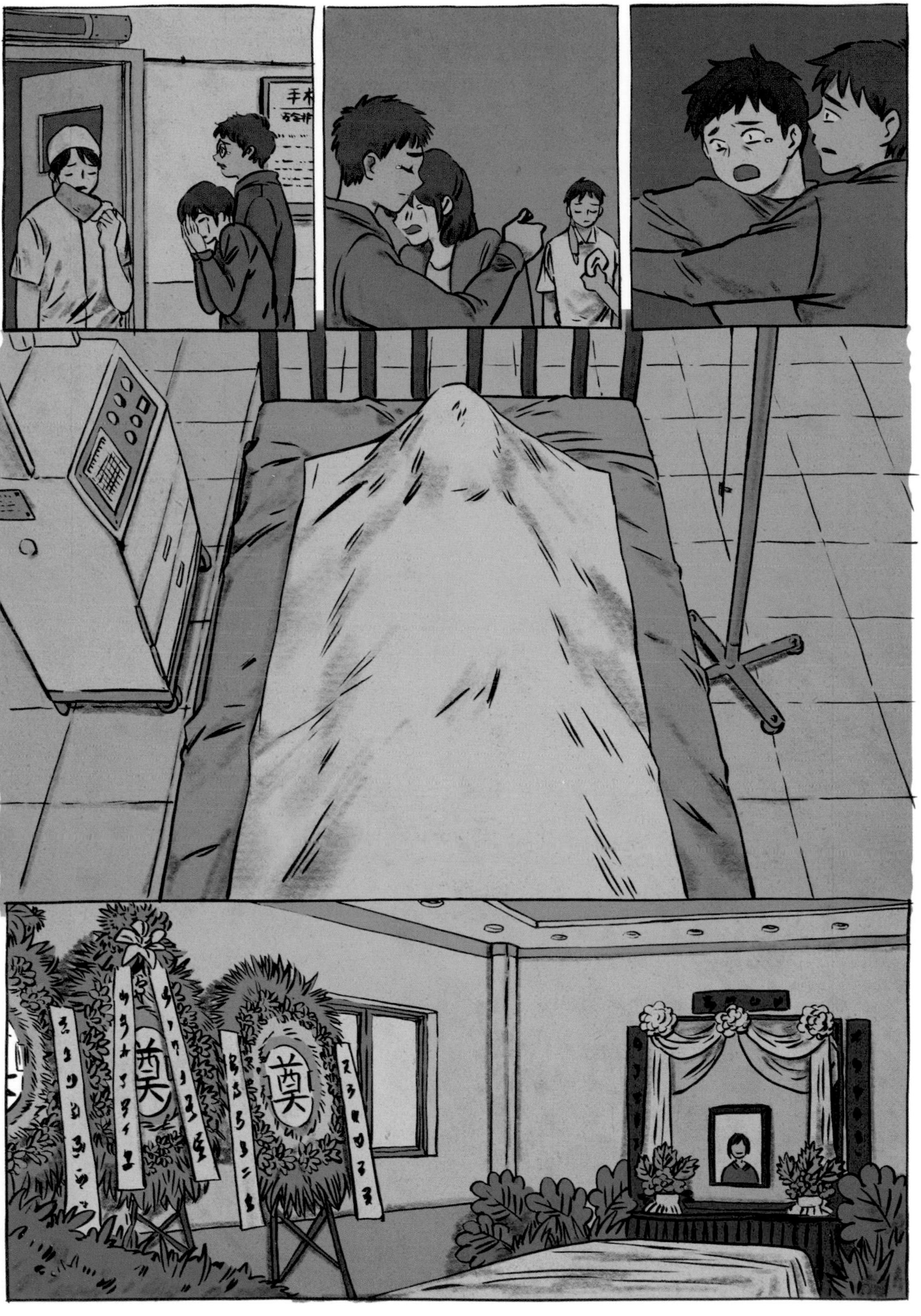
奠
奠

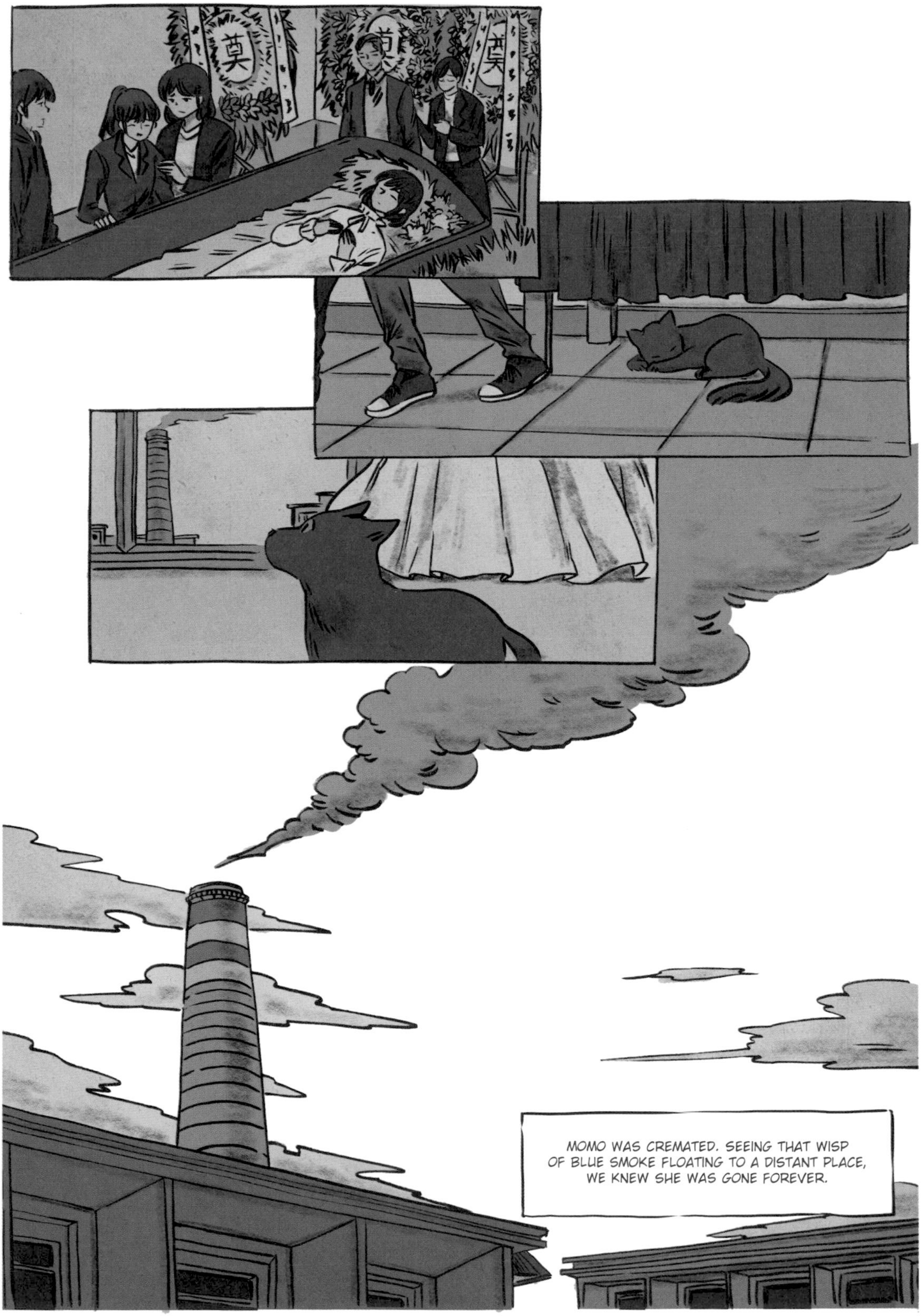
奠
奠
奠
MOMO WAS CREMATED. SEEING THAT WISP OF BLUE SMOKE FLOATING TO A DISTANT PLACE, WE KNEW SHE WAS GONE FOREVER.

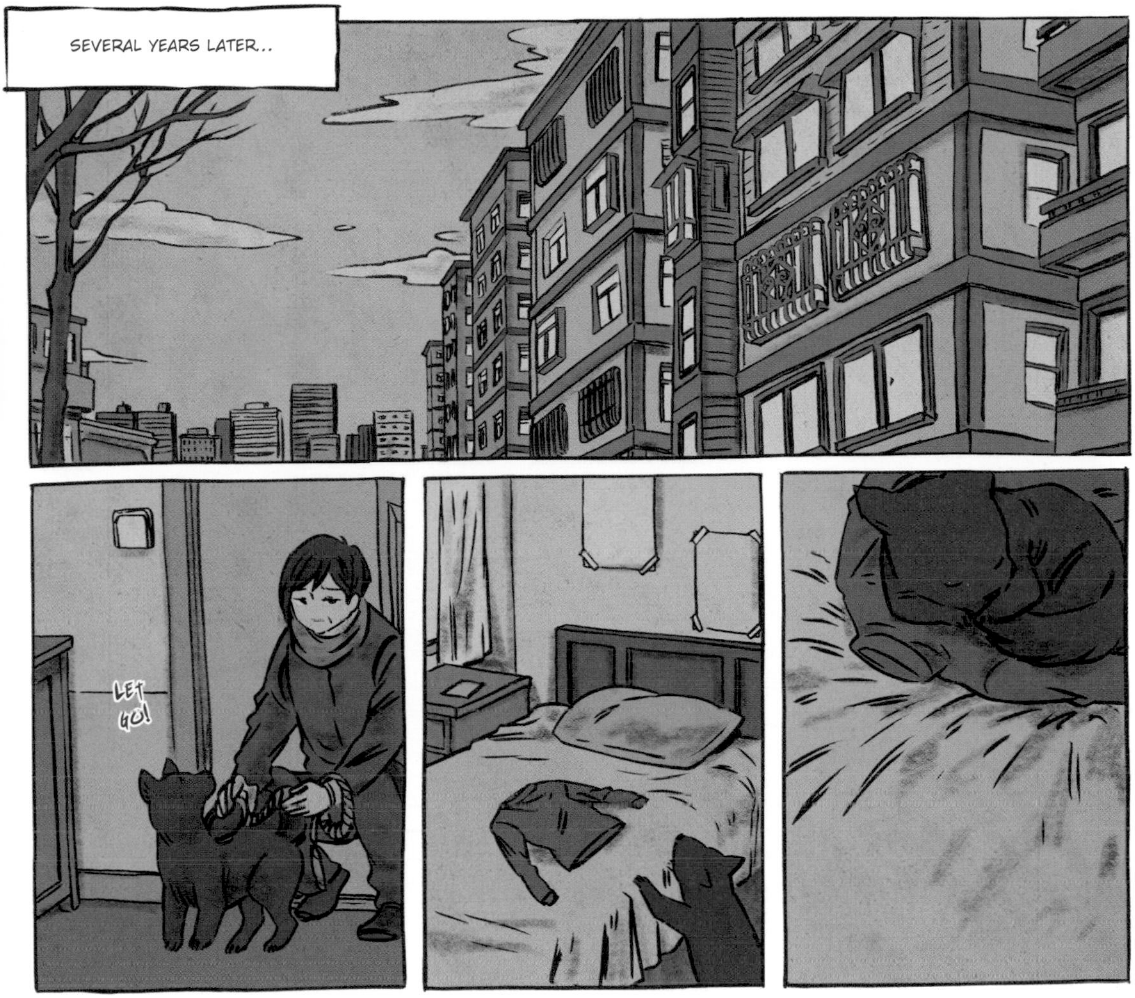
SEVERAL YEARS LATER...
LET GO!

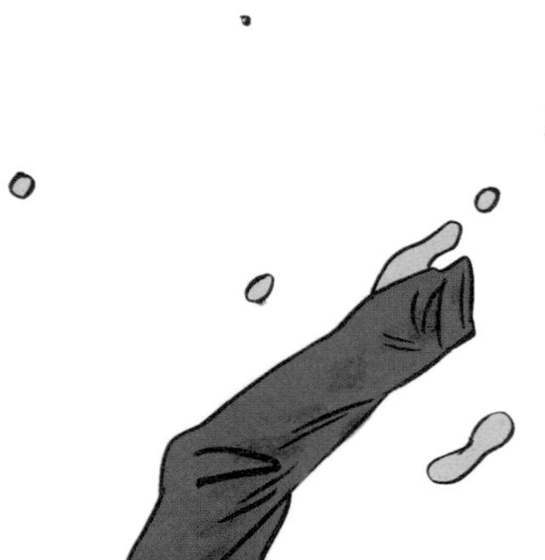

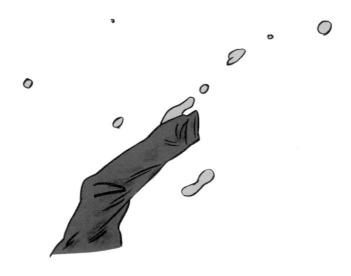

Love Carries On

AUTHOR: WANG NING
ARTIST: XU ZIRAN

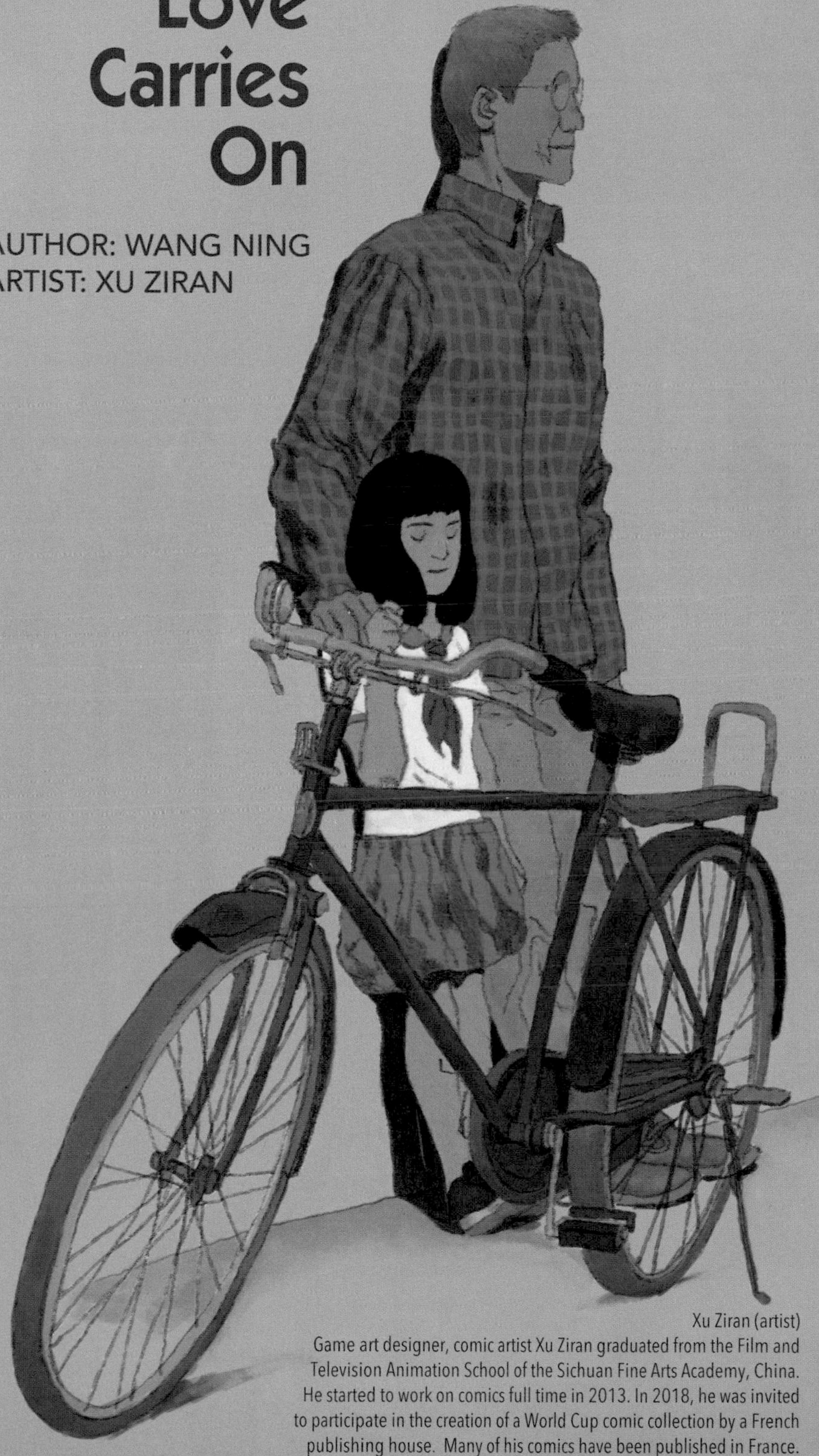

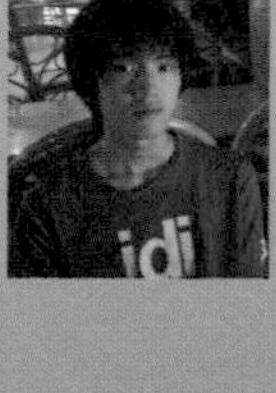

Xu Ziran (artist)
Game art designer, comic artist Xu Ziran graduated from the Film and Television Animation School of the Sichuan Fine Arts Academy, China. He started to work on comics full time in 2013. In 2018, he was invited to participate in the creation of a World Cup comic collection by a French publishing house. Many of his comics have been published in France.

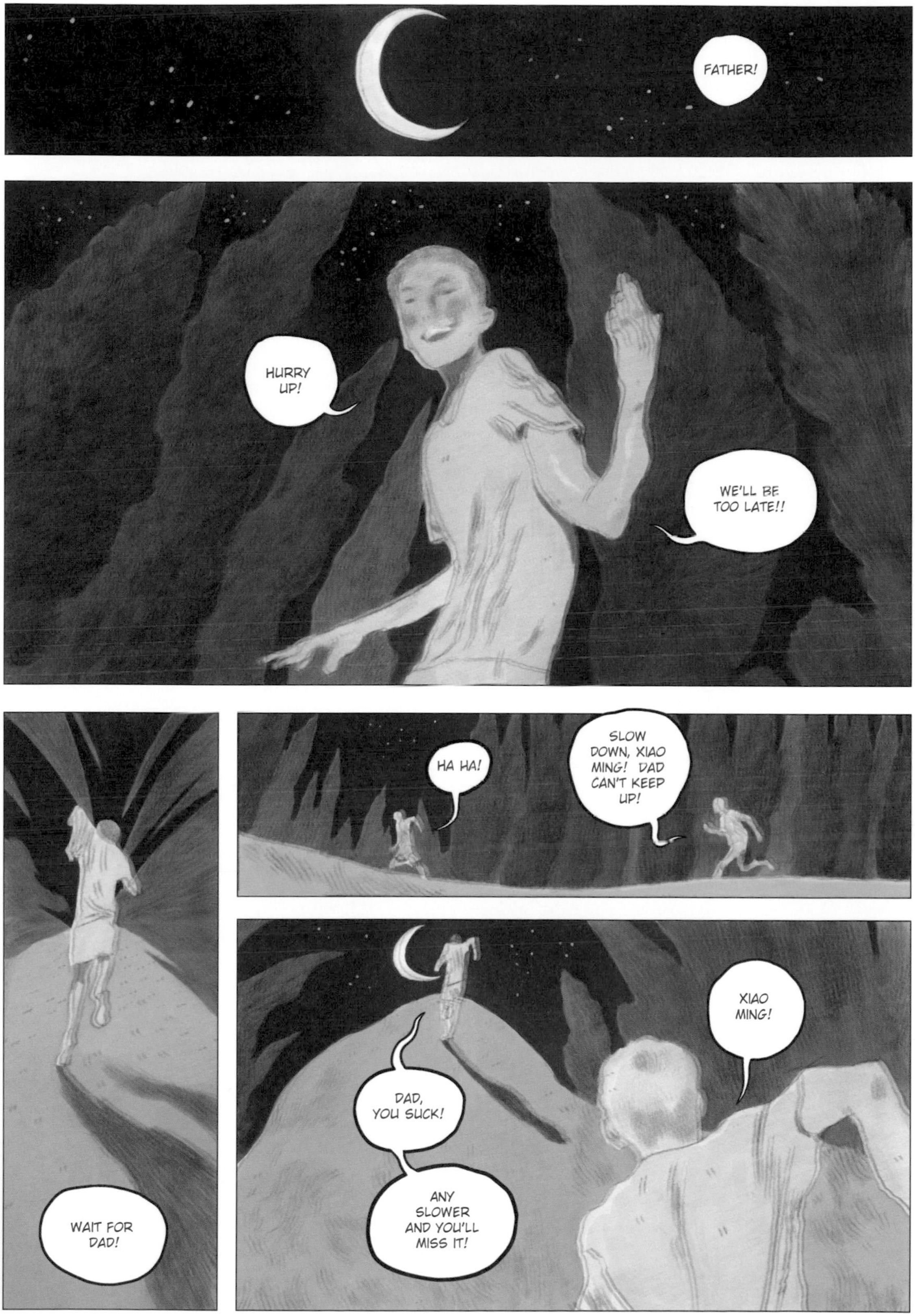
FATHER!
HURRY UP!
WE'LL BE TOO LATE!!
WAIT FOR DAD!
HA HA!
SLOW DOWN, XIAO MING! DAD CAN'T KEEP UP!
DAD, YOU SUCK!
ANY SLOWER AND YOU'LL MISS IT!
XIAO MING!

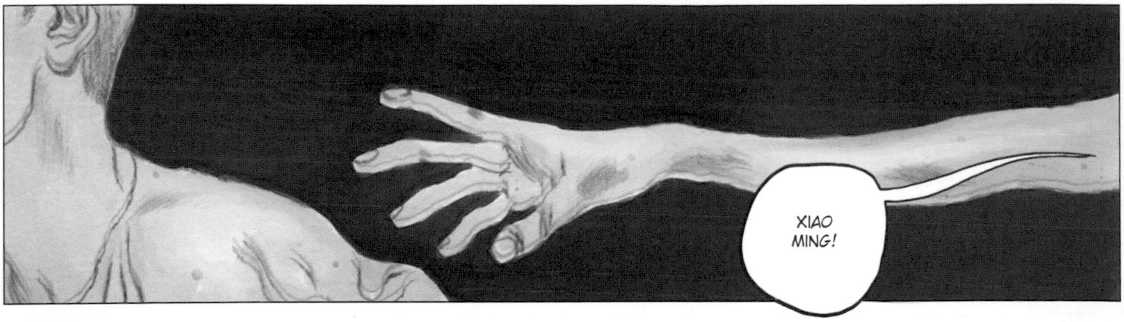
XIAO MING!
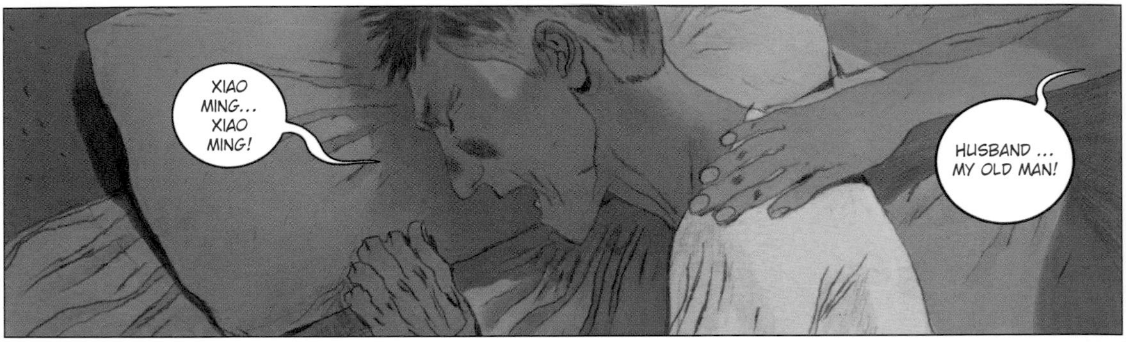
XIAO MING... XIAO MING!
HUSBAND ... MY OLD MAN!
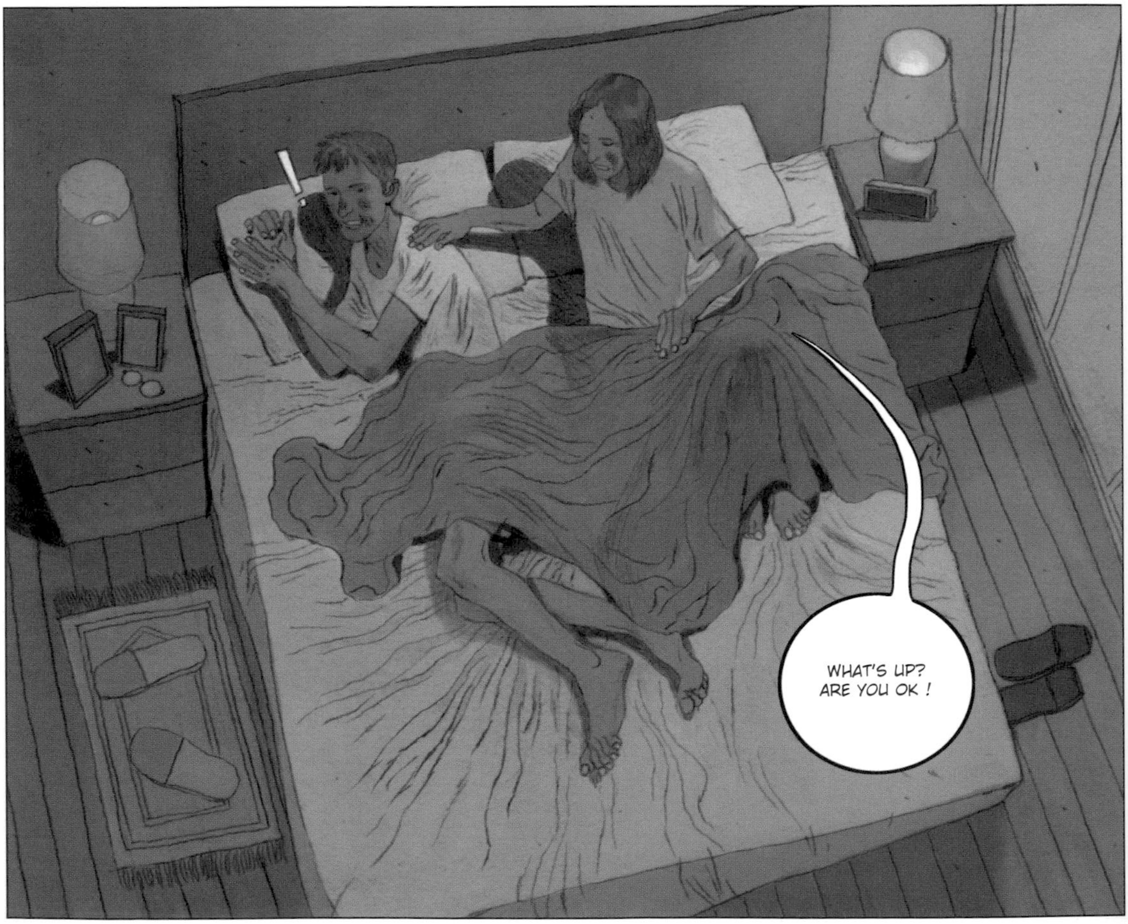
WHAT'S UP? ARE YOU OK !

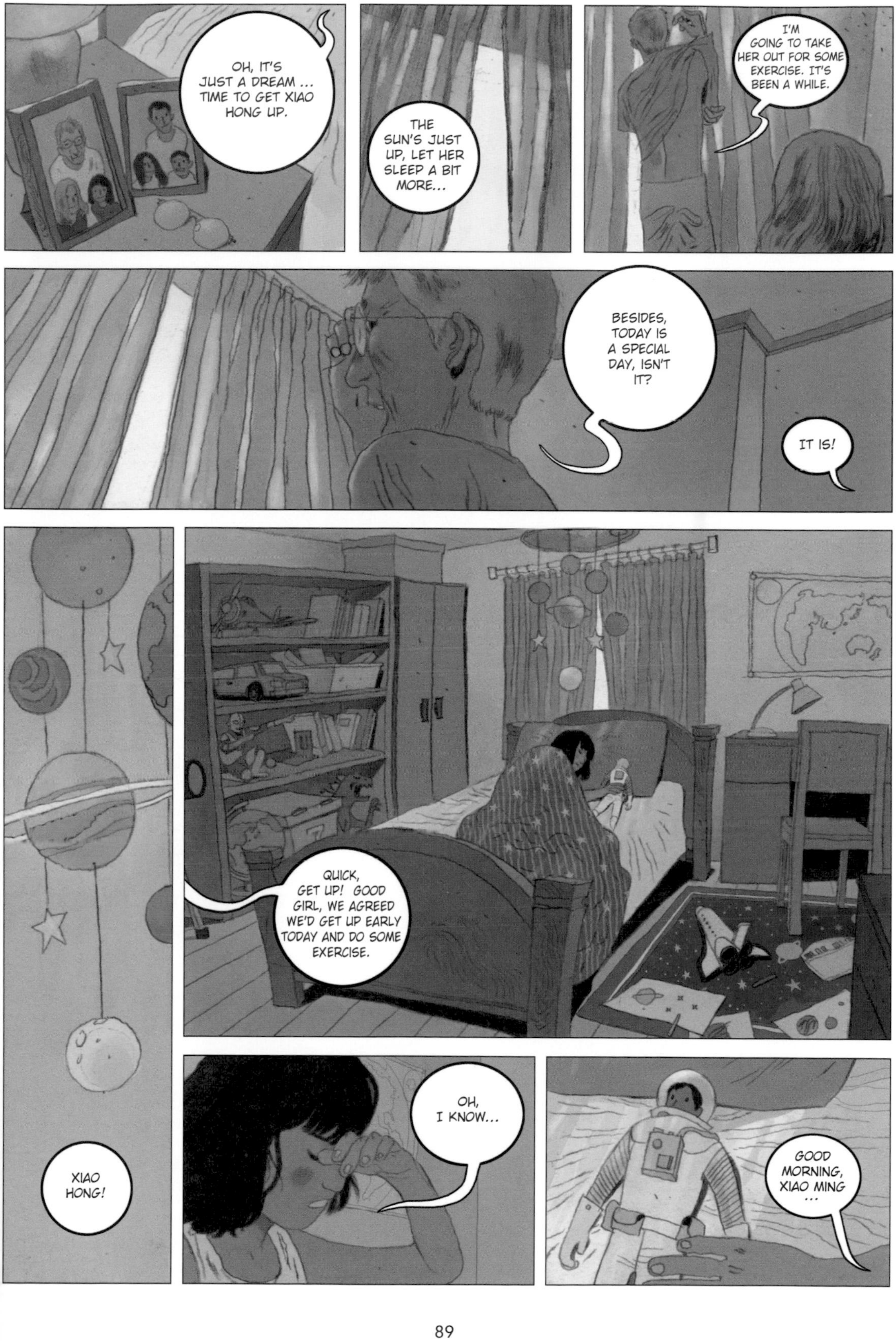

OH, IT'S JUST A DREAM ... TIME TO GET XIAO HONG UP.
THE SUN'S JUST UP, LET HER SLEEP A BIT MORE...
I'M GOING TO TAKE HER OUT FOR SOME EXERCISE. IT'S BEEN A WHILE.
BESIDES, TODAY IS A SPECIAL DAY, ISN'T IT?
IT IS!
XIAO HONG!
QUICK, GET UP! GOOD GIRL, WE AGREED WE'D GET UP EARLY TODAY AND DO SOME EXERCISE.
OH, I KNOW...
GOOD MORNING, XIAO MING ...

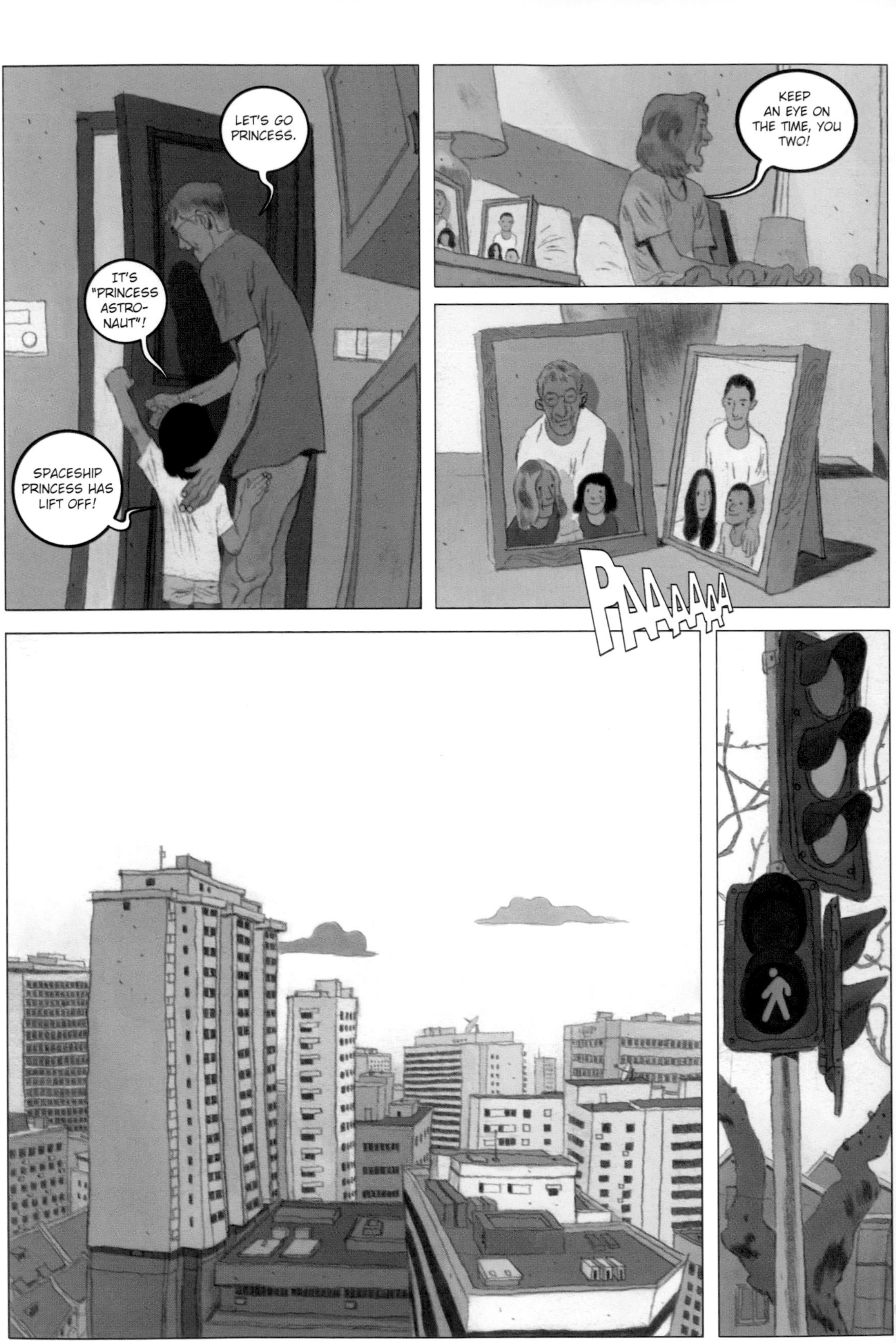
LET'S GO PRINCESS.
IT'S "PRINCESS ASTRO-NAUT"!
SPACESHIP PRINCESS HAS LIFT OFF!
KEEP AN EYE ON THE TIME, YOU TWO!
PAAAAAA

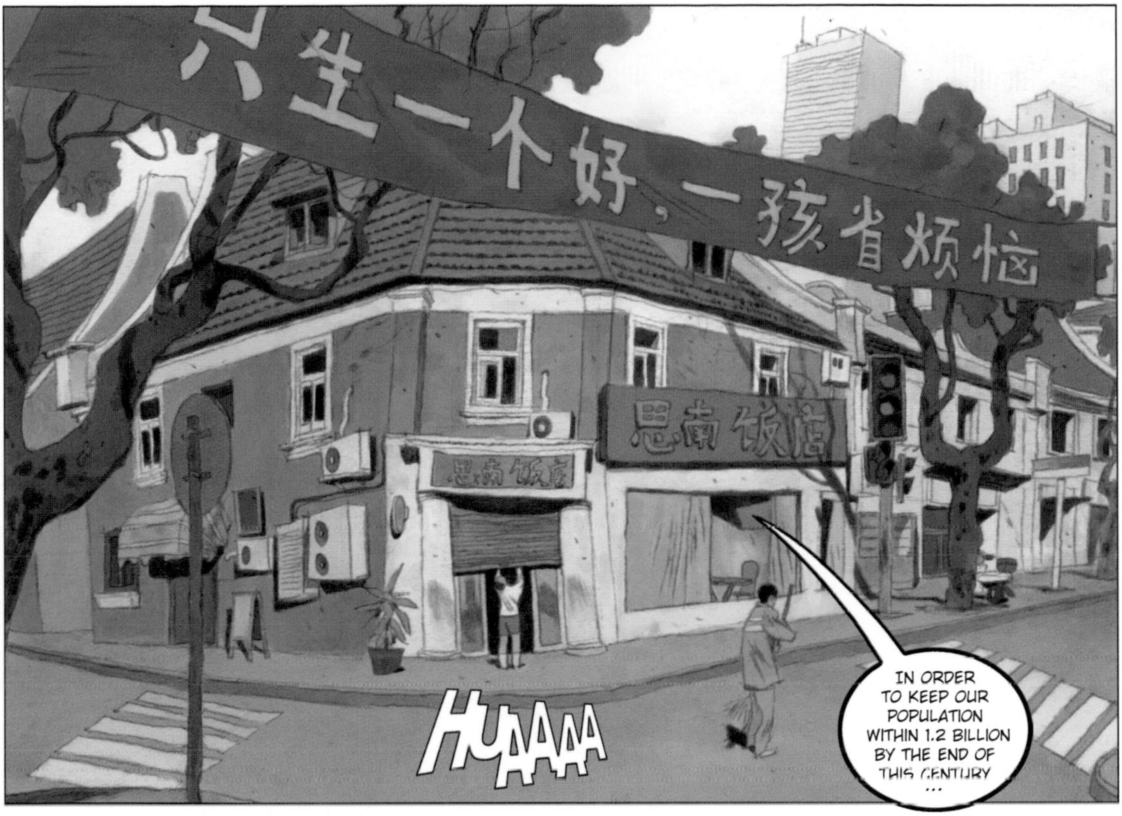
只生一个好，一孩省烦恼
思南饭店
思南饭店
HUAAAA
IN ORDER TO KEEP OUR POPULATION WITHIN 1.2 BILLION BY THE END OF THIS CENTURY ...

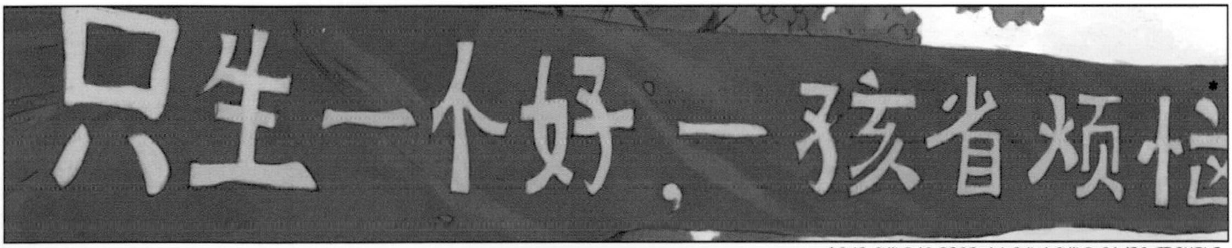
只生一个好，一孩省烦恼*

*ONE CHILD IS BEST. AN ONLY CHILD SAVES TROUBLE.

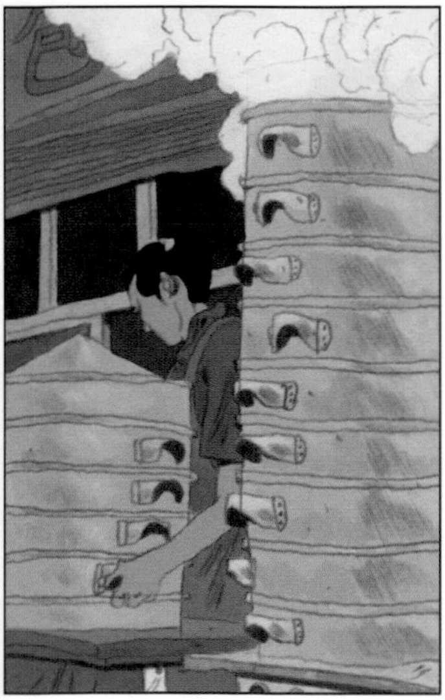

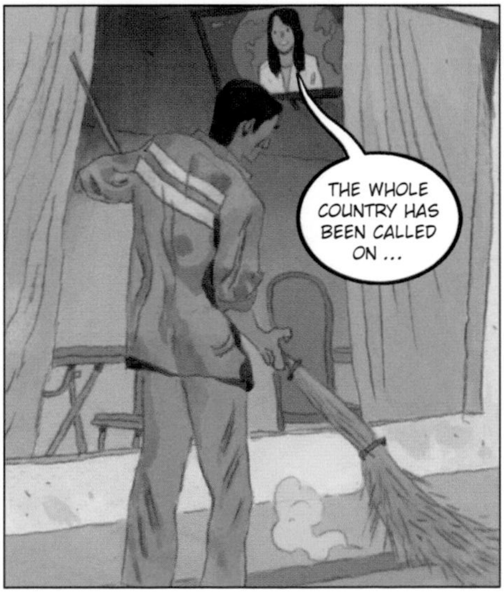
THE WHOLE COUNTRY HAS BEEN CALLED ON ...

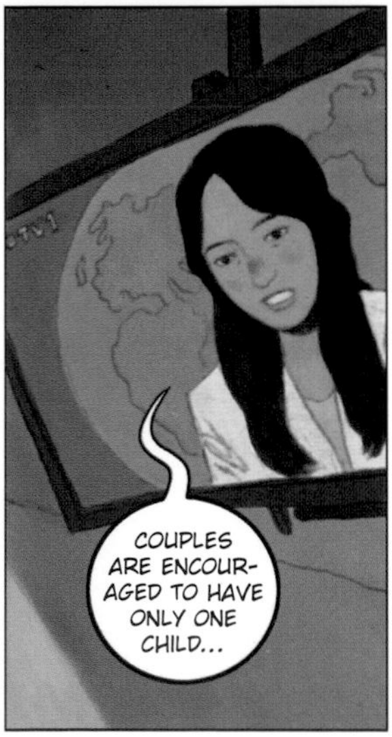
COUPLES ARE ENCOUR-AGED TO HAVE ONLY ONE CHILD...

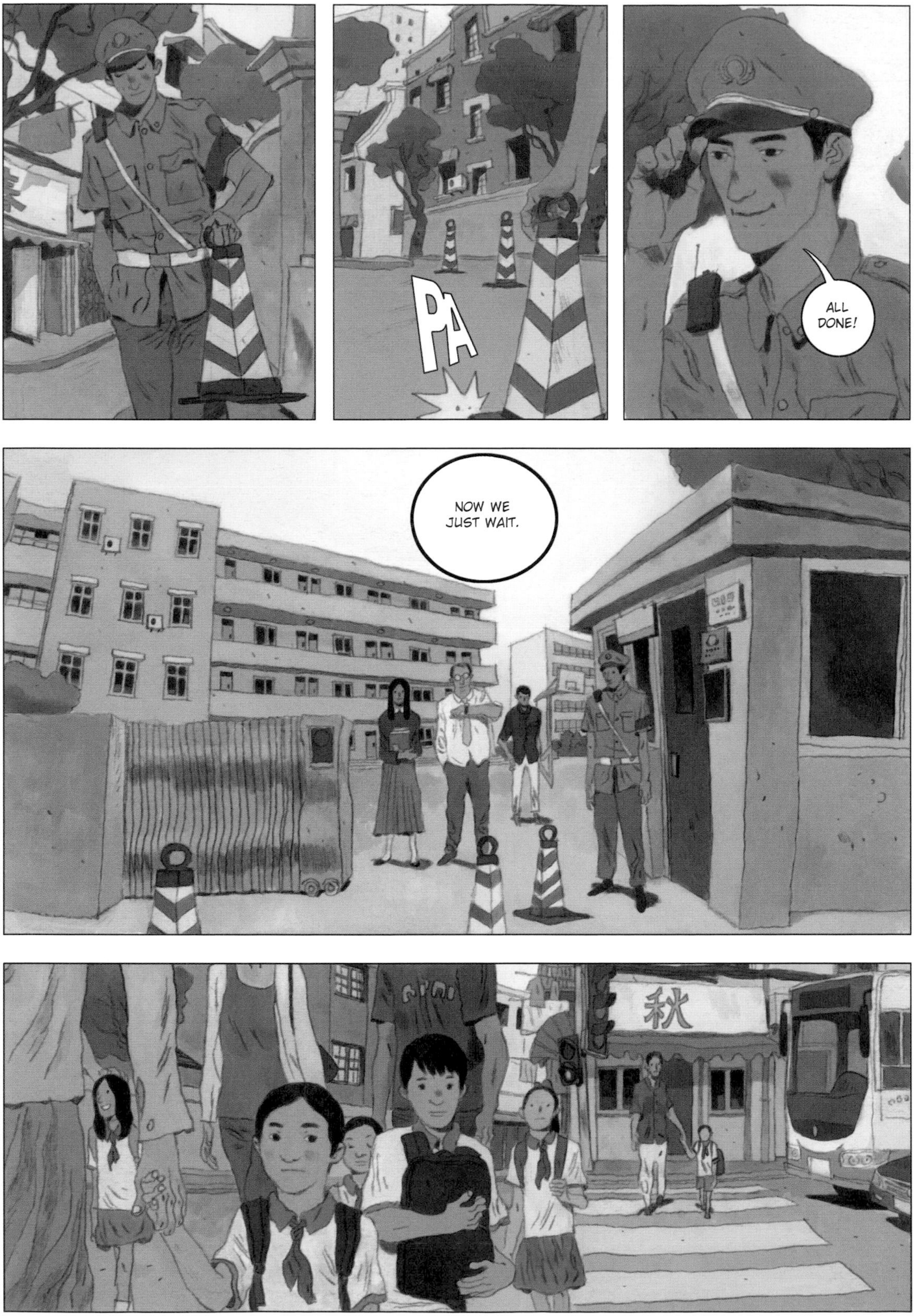
PA
ALL DONE!
NOW WE JUST WAIT.
秋

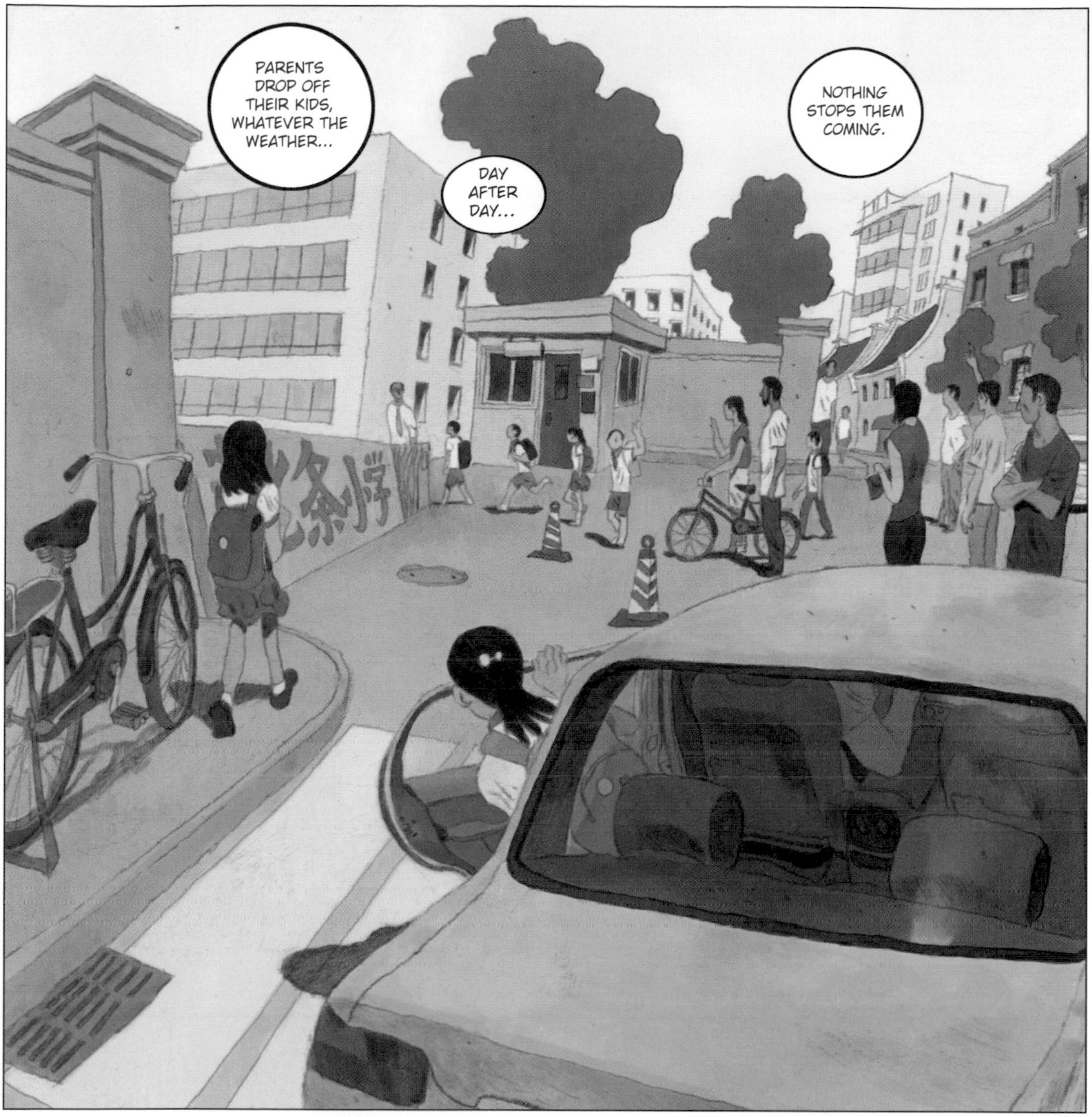
PARENTS DROP OFF THEIR KIDS, WHATEVER THE WEATHER...
DAY AFTER DAY...
NOTHING STOPS THEM COMING.

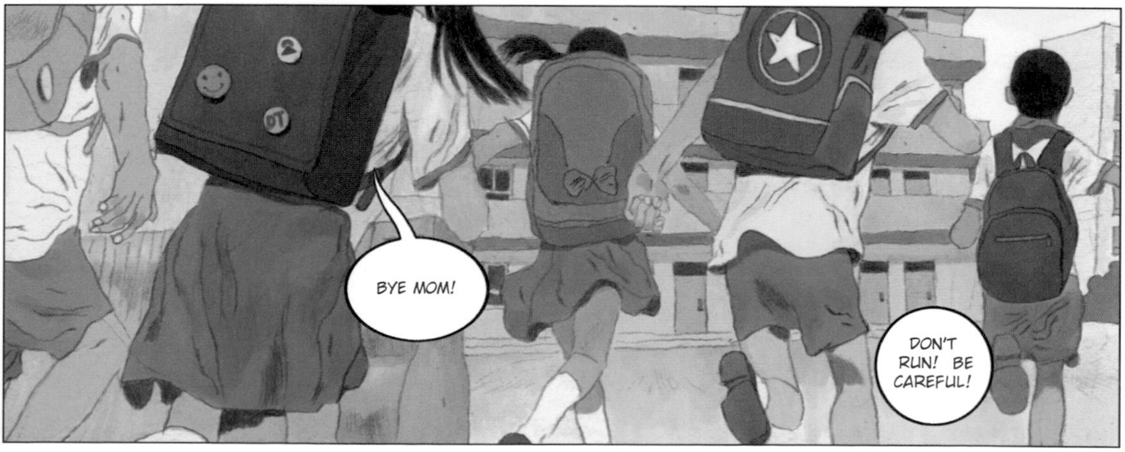
BYE MOM!
DON'T RUN! BE CAREFUL!

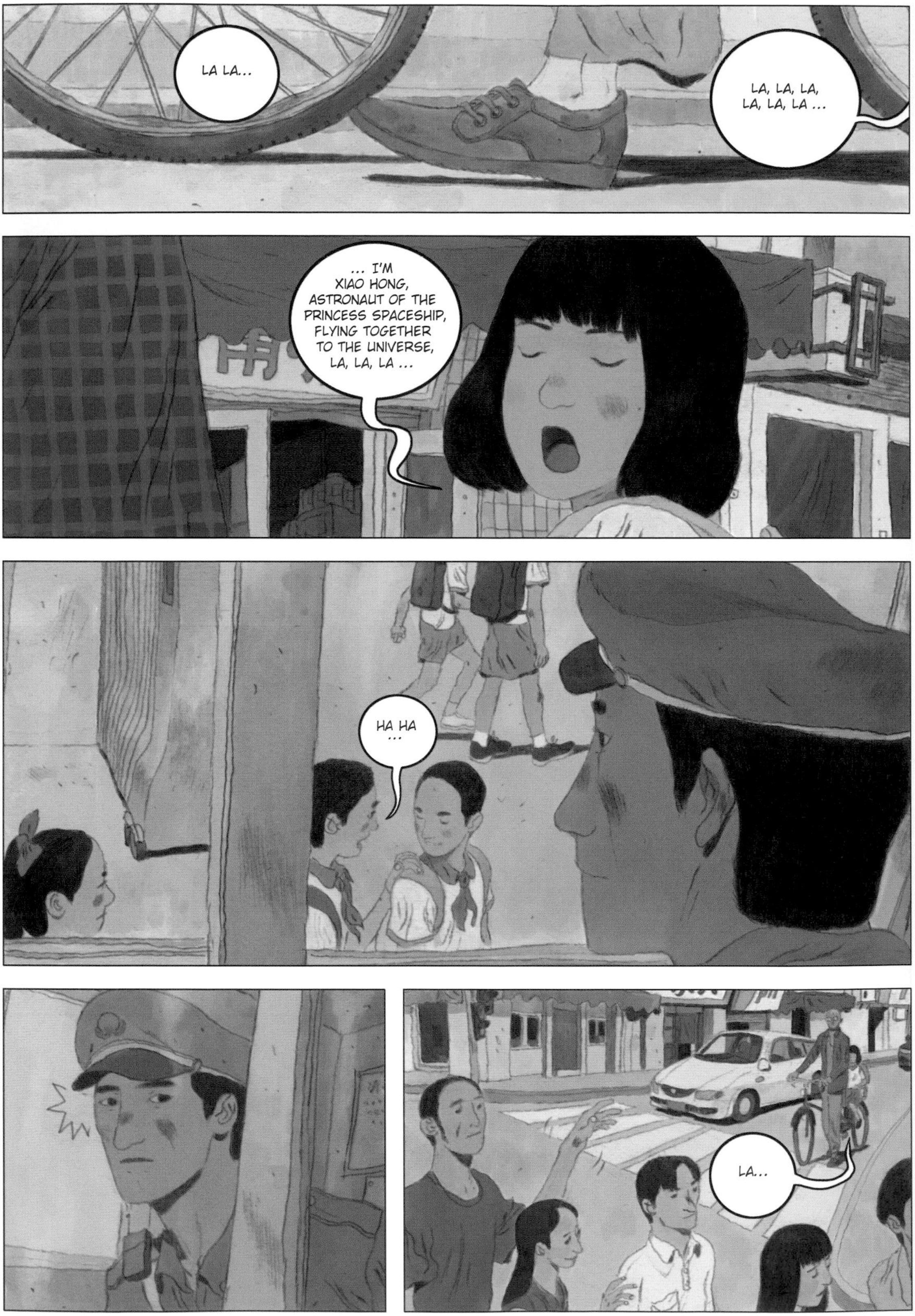
LA LA...
LA, LA, LA, LA, LA, LA ...
... I'M XIAO HONG, ASTRONAUT OF THE PRINCESS SPACESHIP, FLYING TOGETHER TO THE UNIVERSE, LA, LA, LA ...
HA HA ...
LA...

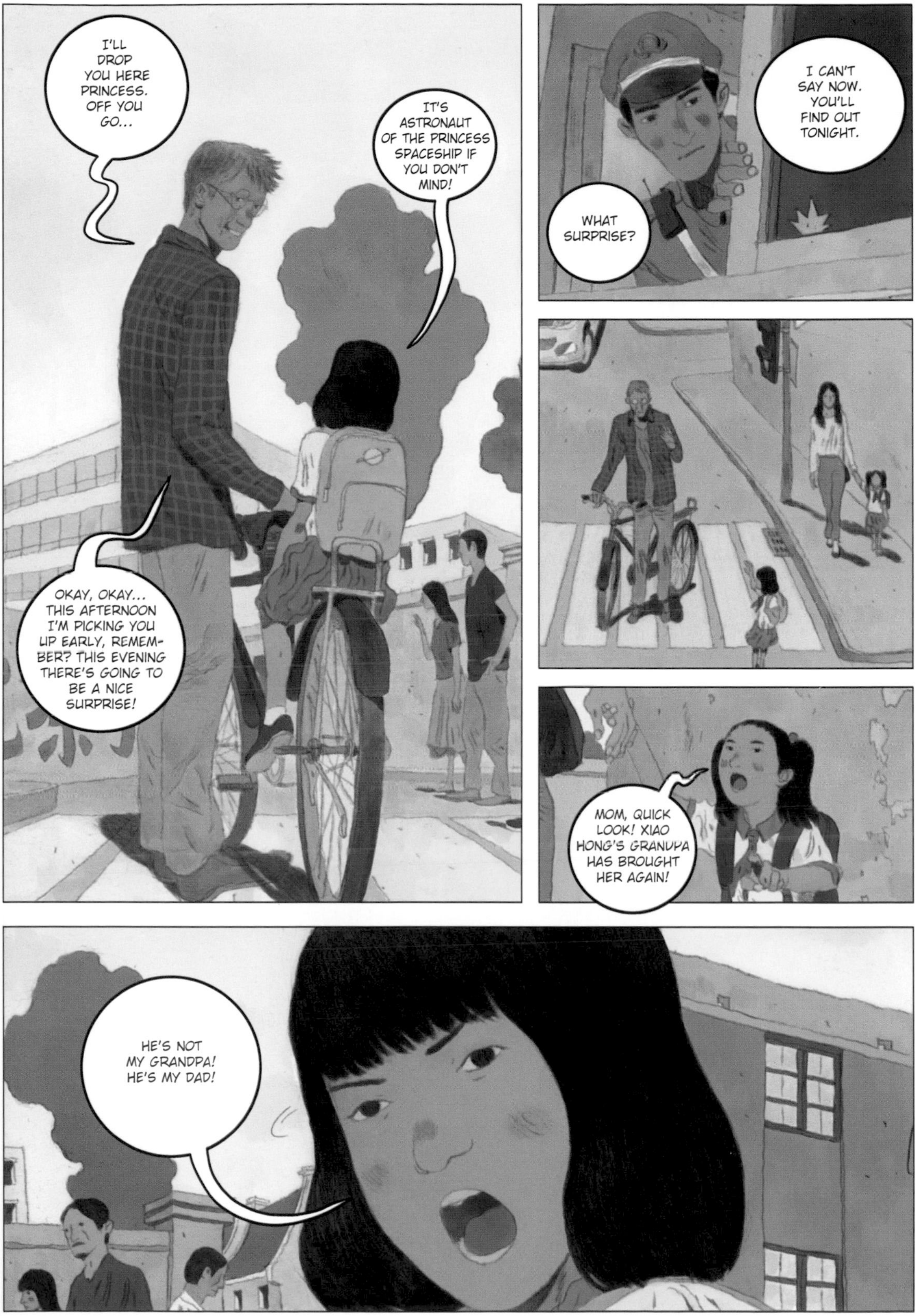
I'LL DROP YOU HERE PRINCESS. OFF YOU GO...
IT'S ASTRONAUT OF THE PRINCESS SPACESHIP IF YOU DON'T MIND!
OKAY, OKAY... THIS AFTERNOON I'M PICKING YOU UP EARLY, REMEMBER? THIS EVENING THERE'S GOING TO BE A NICE SURPRISE!
WHAT SURPRISE?
I CAN'T SAY NOW. YOU'LL FIND OUT TONIGHT.
MOM, QUICK LOOK! XIAO HONG'S GRANDPA HAS BROUGHT HER AGAIN!
HE'S NOT MY GRANDPA! HE'S MY DAD!

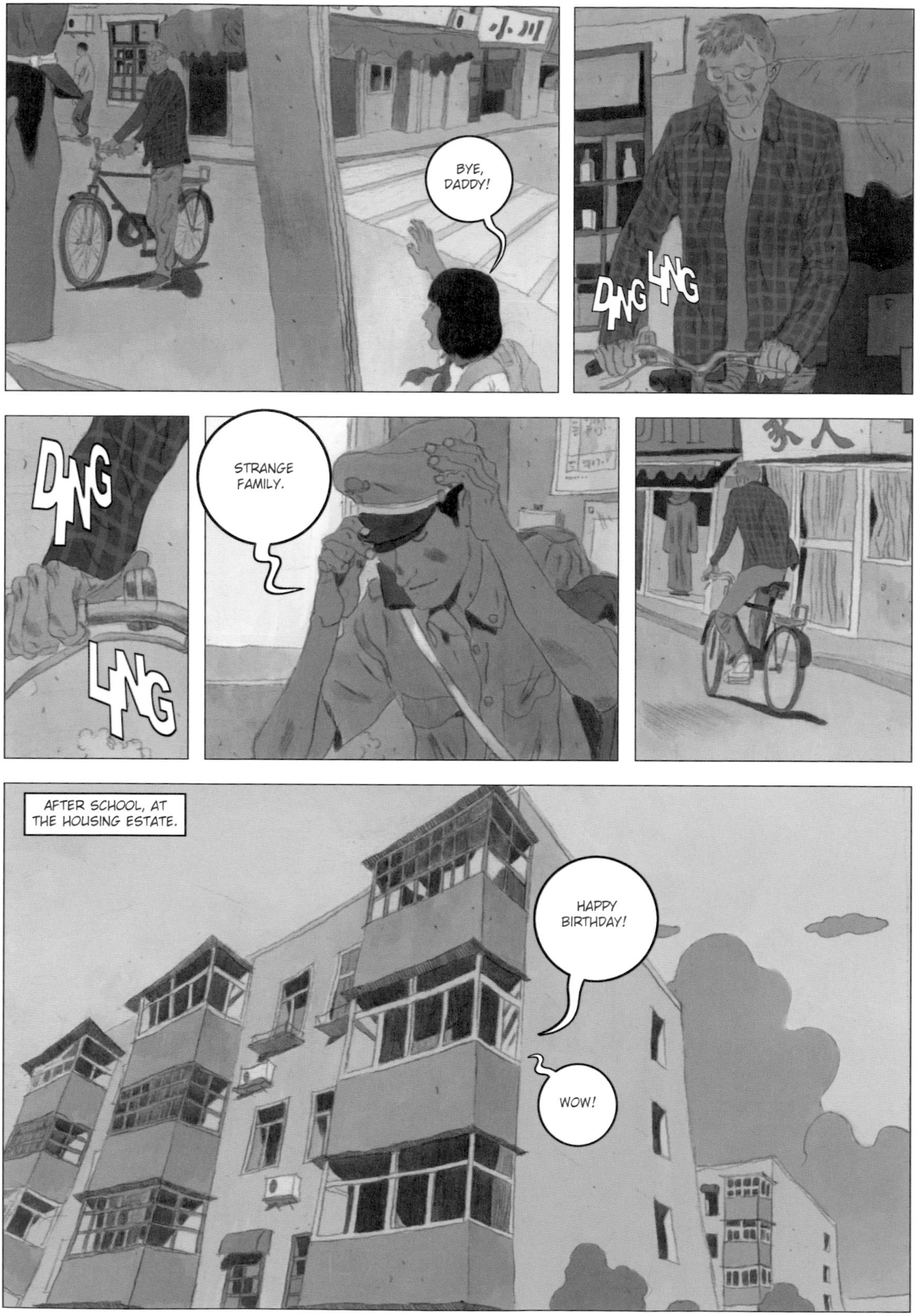

小川
BYE, DADDY!
DING LING
DING
LING
STRANGE FAMILY.
AFTER SCHOOL, AT THE HOUSING ESTATE.
HAPPY BIRTHDAY!
WOW!

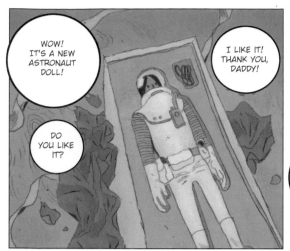

WOW! IT'S A NEW ASTRONAUT DOLL!

DO YOU LIKE IT?

I LIKE IT! THANK YOU, DADDY!

LOOK CLOSELY, IT'S A GIRL!

REALLY!

THIS IS XIAO HONG, WHEN SHE GROWS UP!

COOL! WHEN I GROW UP, I WANT TO BE PARTNERS WITH XIAO MING.

SHALL WE GO INTO SPACE, XIAO HONG?

XIAO MING...

YES – CALLING XIAO MING! HE IS ON THE SPACESHIP MAKING THE FINAL PREPARATIONS ...

CALLING XIAO MING, CALLING XIAO MING, I AM THE PRINCESS SPACESHIP'S NEW ASTRONAUT, XIAO HONG!

XIAO HONG, SPACESHIP TEST RUN COMPLETE. EVERYONE, GET READY FOR THE FINAL COUNT-DOWN!

10

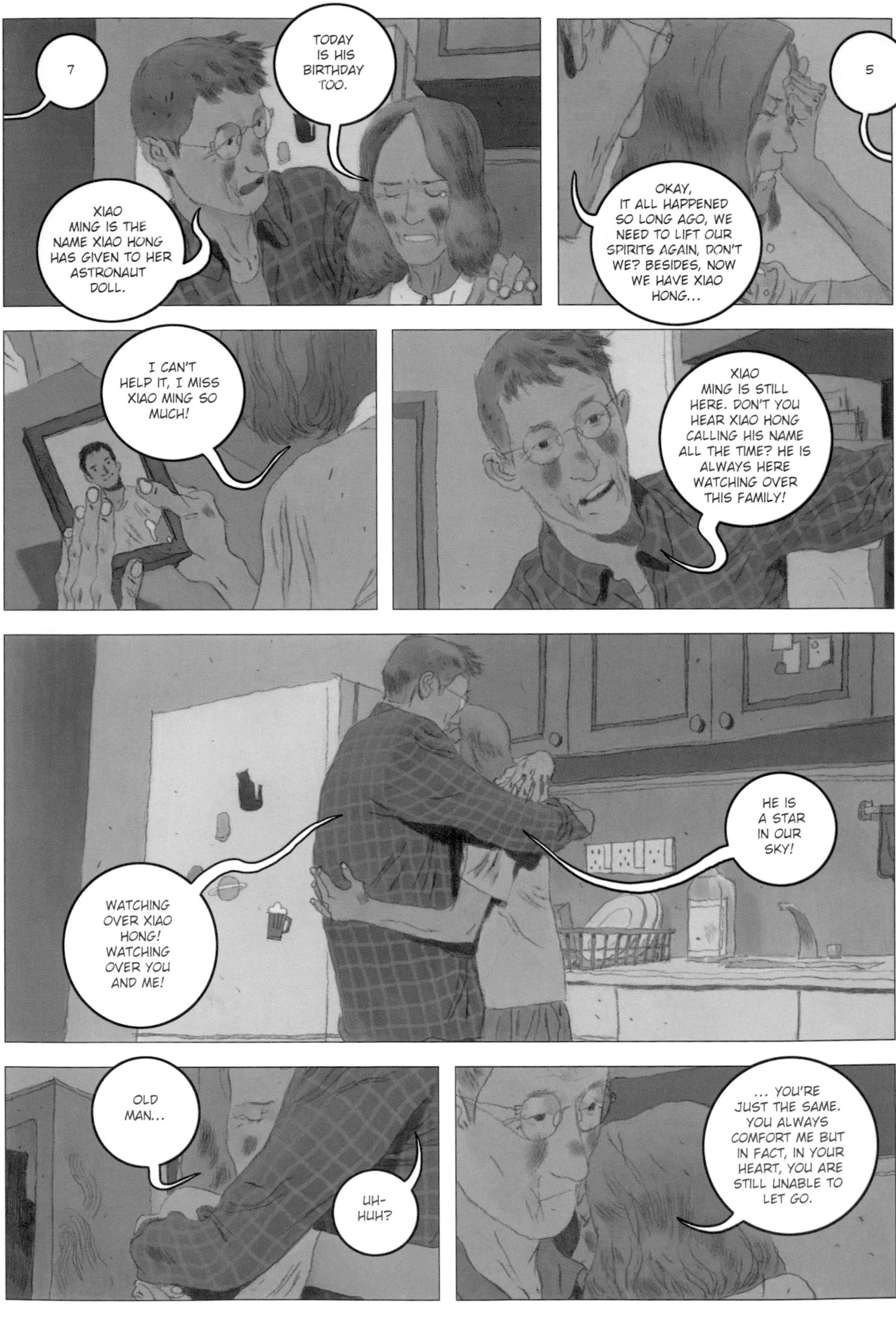
7
TODAY IS HIS BIRTHDAY TOO.
XIAO MING IS THE NAME XIAO HONG HAS GIVEN TO HER ASTRONAUT DOLL.
5
OKAY, IT ALL HAPPENED SO LONG AGO, WE NEED TO LIFT OUR SPIRITS AGAIN, DON'T WE? BESIDES, NOW WE HAVE XIAO HONG...
I CAN'T HELP IT, I MISS XIAO MING SO MUCH!
XIAO MING IS STILL HERE. DON'T YOU HEAR XIAO HONG CALLING HIS NAME ALL THE TIME? HE IS ALWAYS HERE WATCHING OVER THIS FAMILY!
HE IS A STAR IN OUR SKY!
WATCHING OVER XIAO HONG! WATCHING OVER YOU AND ME!
OLD MAN...
UH-HUH?
... YOU'RE JUST THE SAME. YOU ALWAYS COMFORT ME BUT IN FACT, IN YOUR HEART, YOU ARE STILL UNABLE TO LET GO.

3

2

1

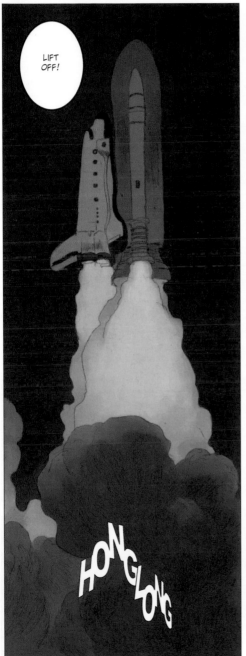

LIFT OFF!

HONG LONG

THE DAY BEFORE YESTERDAY MY DESK MATE XIAO MEI WAS LAUGHING AT ME, ASKING ME WHY I ONLY HAD BOY'S TOYS ...

BECAUSE I LIKE THEM! I DON'T CARE ABOUT BARBIE DOLLS OR DISNEY PRINCESSES!

I'D ONLY JUST BEEN BORN AND I ALREADY OWNED COUNTLESS TOYS. MOMMY AND DADDY SAID THEY WERE PRECIOUS TREASURE LEFT TO ME BY MY BIG BROTHER. MY BIG BROTHER HAS NOW FLOWN INTO OUTER SPACE, THAT WAS THE PLACE HE MOST YEARNED FOR. HE'S WAITING FOR ME TO GROW UP. WE HAVE A PACT TO TRAVEL TO THE STARS! WE'RE ALSO GOING TO TAKE MOMMY AND DADDY...

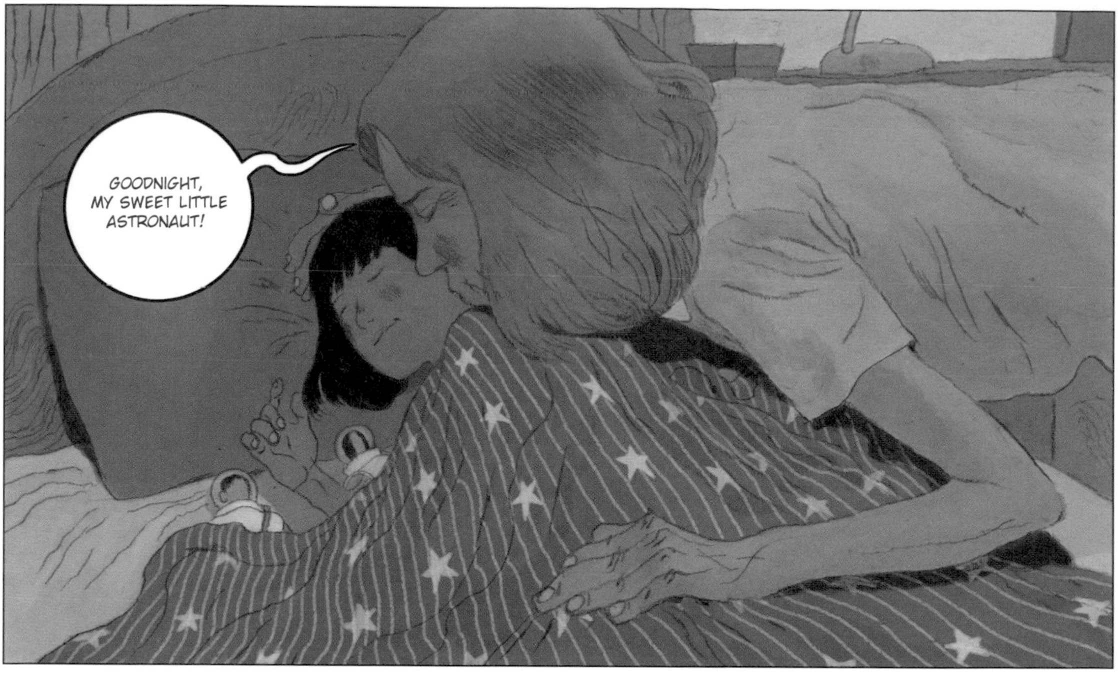
GOODNIGHT, MY SWEET LITTLE ASTRONAUT!

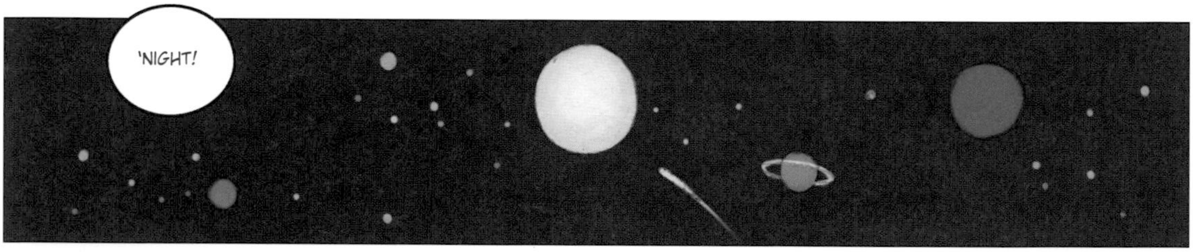
'NIGHT!

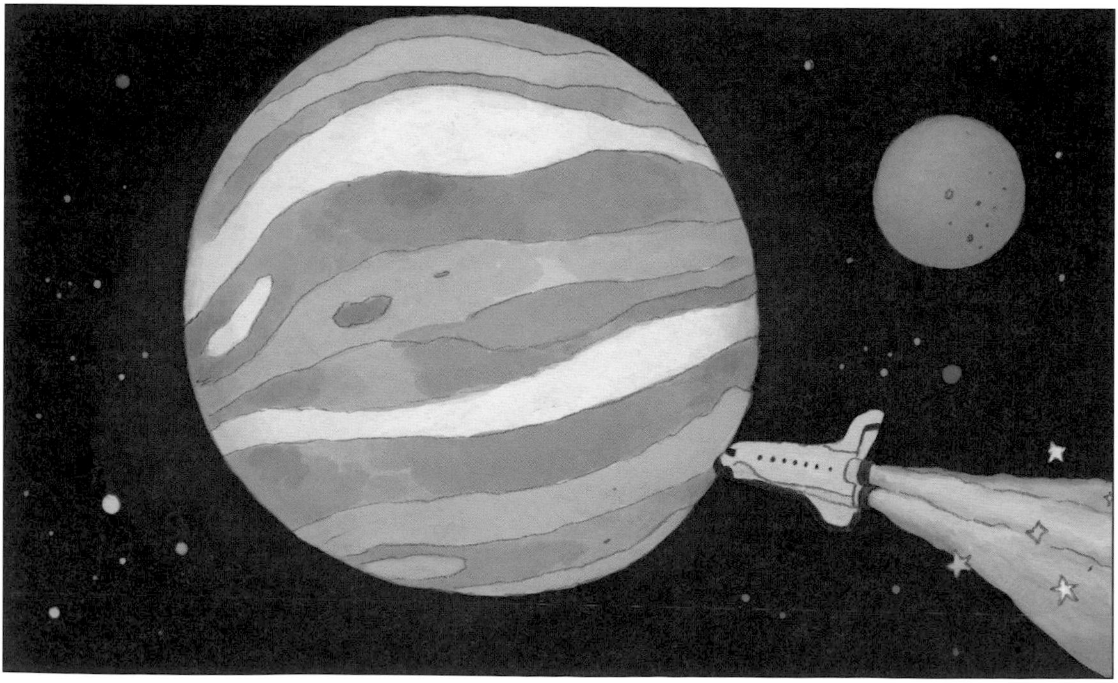

1ST JANUARY 2016

TO PROMOTE THE DEVELOPMENT OF A BALANCED POPULA-TION AND ADHERE TO THE BASIC NATIONAL POLICY OF FAMILY PLANNING, ...

...TO IMPROVE THE POPULATION DEVELOPMENT STRATEGY AND FULLY IMPLEMENT THE POLICY THAT ONE COUPLE CAN HAVE TWO CHILDREN.

DID YOU HEAR, OLD MAN?

TAKE ACTION TO DEAL WITH THE AGING POPULATION. TODAY IS THE FIRST DAY THAT THE NEW FAMILY PLANNING POLICY IS COMPREHENSIVELY PUT INTO ACTION...

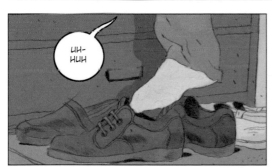

UH-HUH

I'M GOING TO PICK XIAO HONG UP FROM SCHOOL.

HE LEFT.

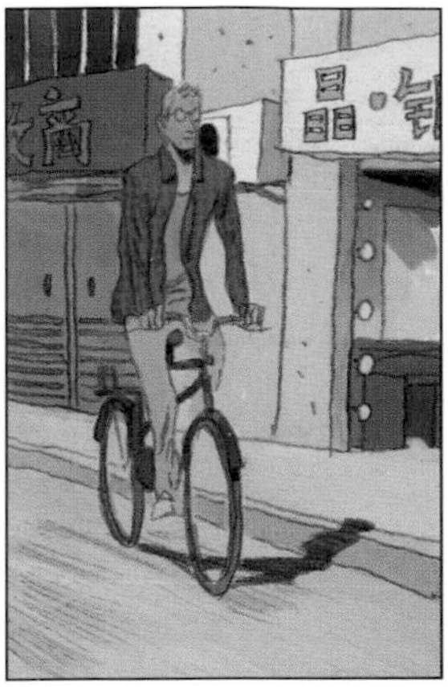

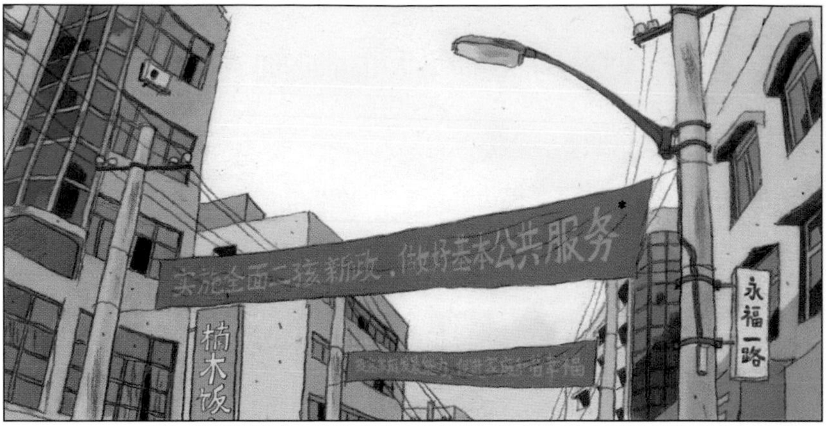

实施全面二孩新政，做好基本公共服务*
永福一路

*FULLY IMPLEMENT THE NEW POLICY TO HAVE TWO CHILDREN AND PROVIDE BASIC PUBLIC SERVICES.

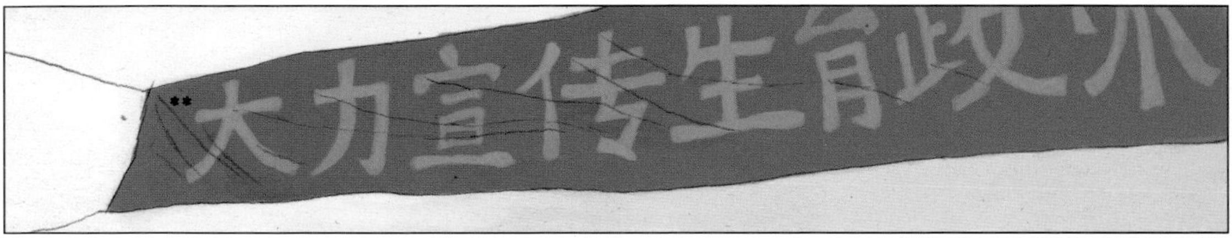

**大力宣传生育政

**VIGOROUSLY PROMOTE THE BIRTH POLICY.

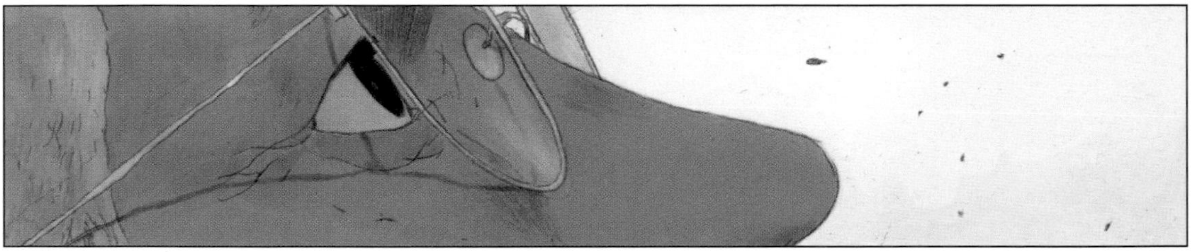

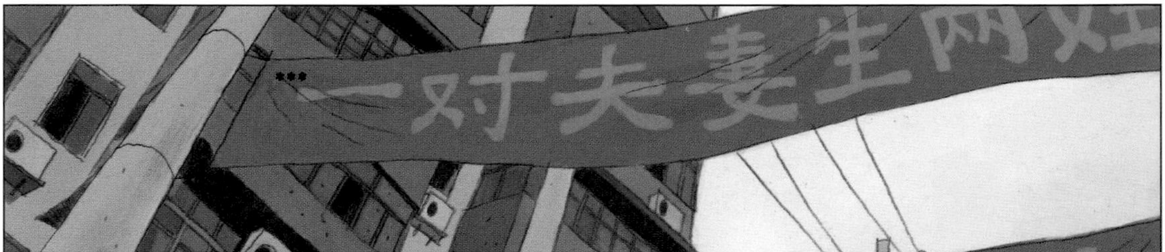

***一对夫妻生
****一儿一女就是好，

***A COUPLE SHOULD HAVE TWO BABIES.

****IT'S BEST TO HAVE A BOY AND A GIRL.

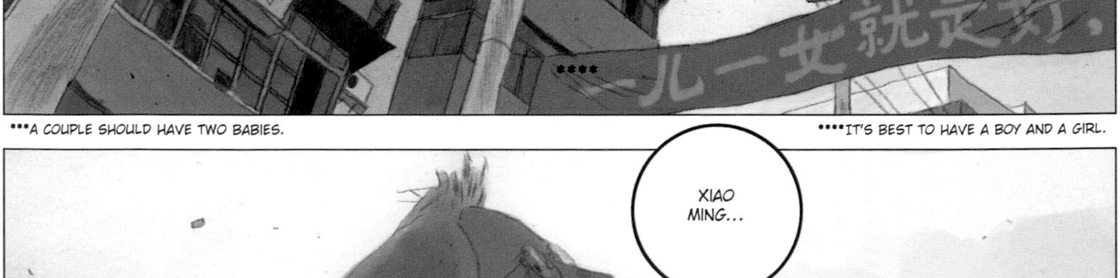

XIAO MING...

XIAO MING!
XIAO MING!
PLEASE! WAKE UP!
XIAO MING! NOOO ...!
KEEP STRONG, CARRY ON.
KEEP
STRONG,
CARRY
ON.
...AT THAT TIME IT WAS THE CONDOLENCE I HEARD THE MOST. BUT I WAS WEAK AND POWERLESS.
奠
奠

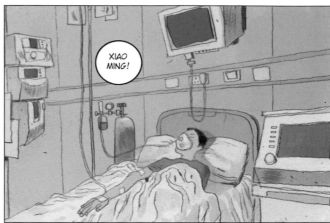

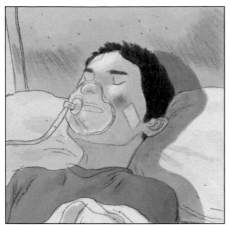

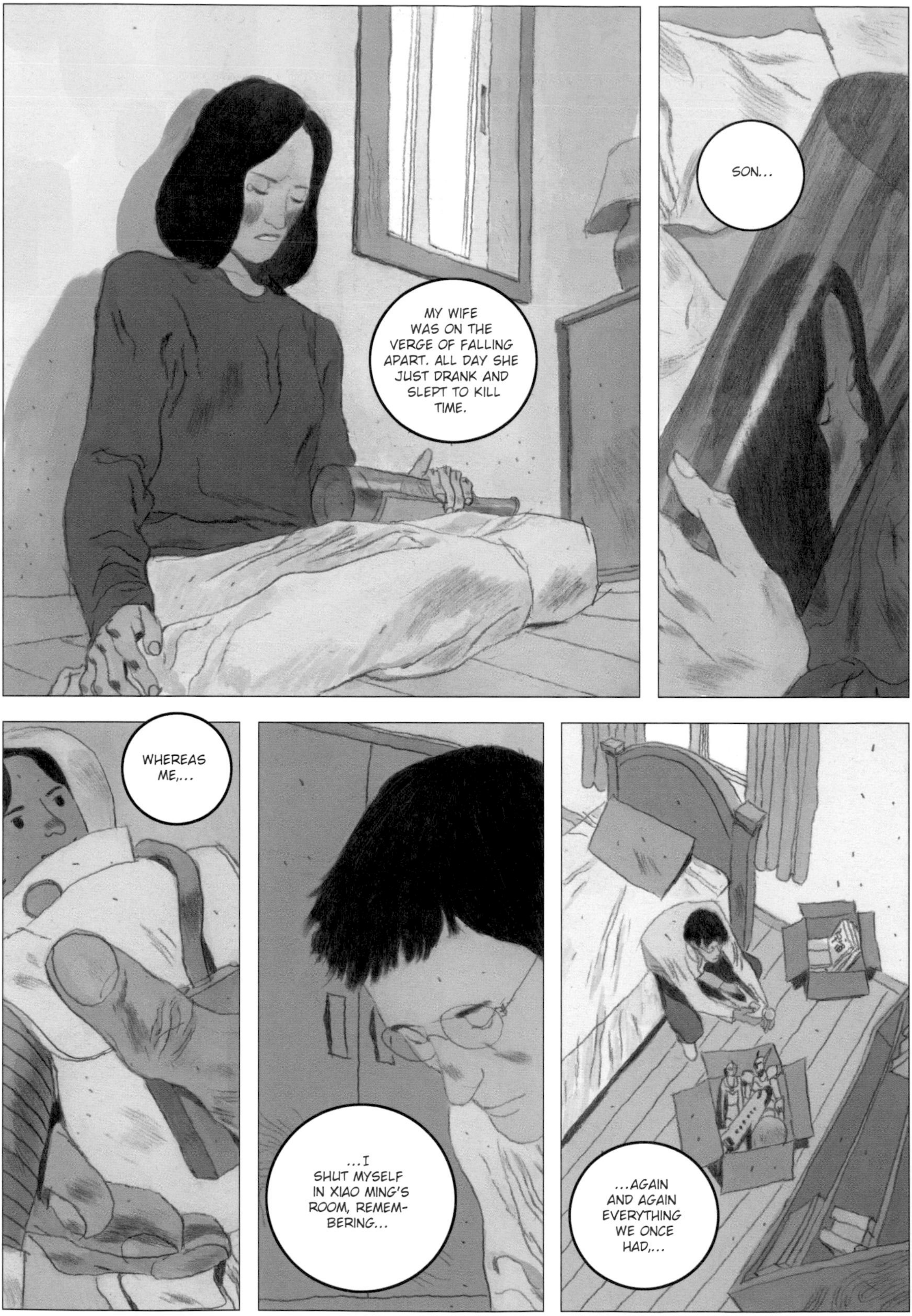
MY WIFE WAS ON THE VERGE OF FALLING APART. ALL DAY SHE JUST DRANK AND SLEPT TO KILL TIME.
SON...
WHEREAS ME,...
...I SHUT MYSELF IN XIAO MING'S ROOM, REMEMBERING...
...AGAIN AND AGAIN EVERYTHING WE ONCE HAD,...

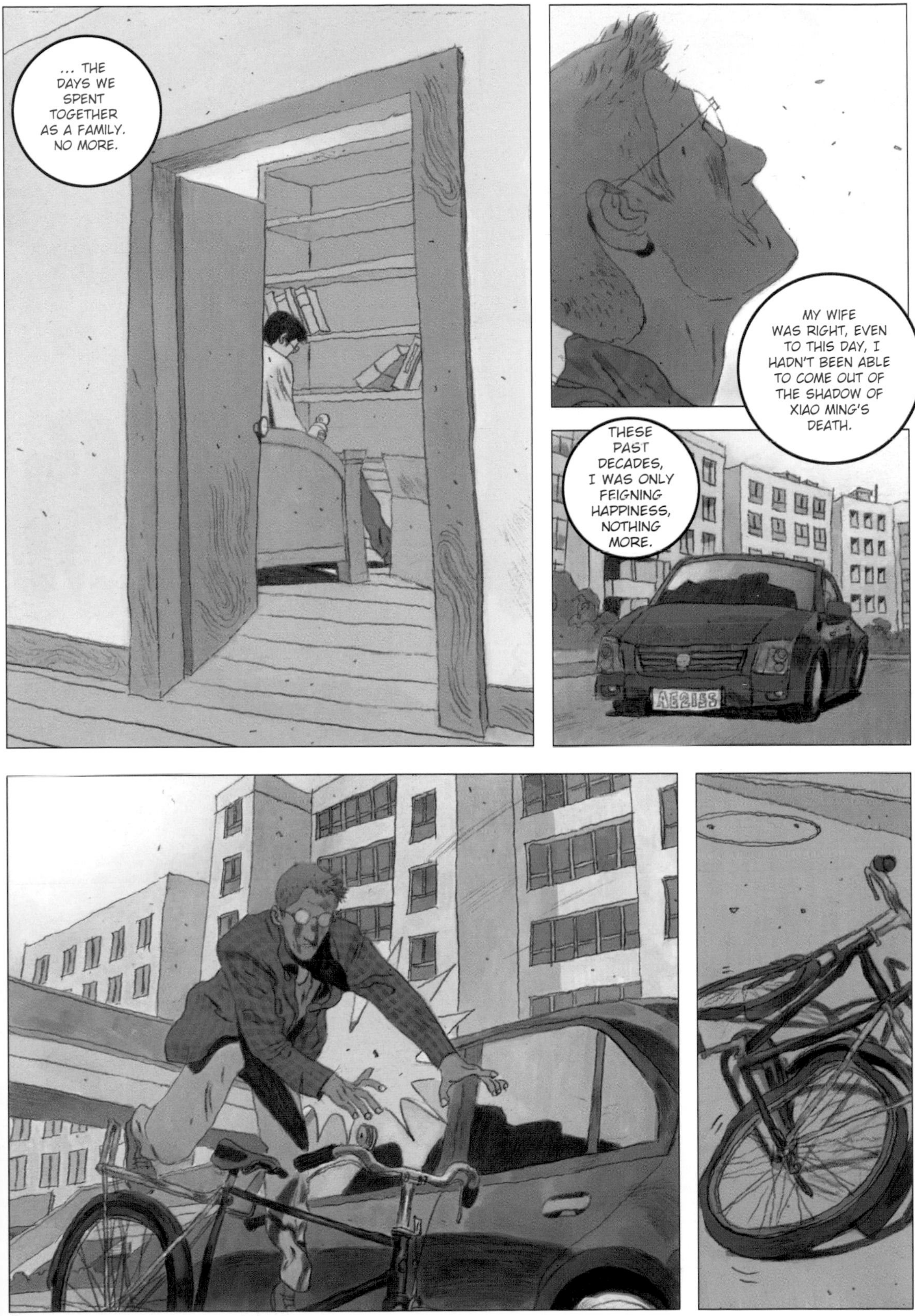
... THE DAYS WE SPENT TOGETHER AS A FAMILY. NO MORE.
MY WIFE WAS RIGHT, EVEN TO THIS DAY, I HADN'T BEEN ABLE TO COME OUT OF THE SHADOW OF XIAO MING'S DEATH.
THESE PAST DECADES, I WAS ONLY FEIGNING HAPPINESS, NOTHING MORE.

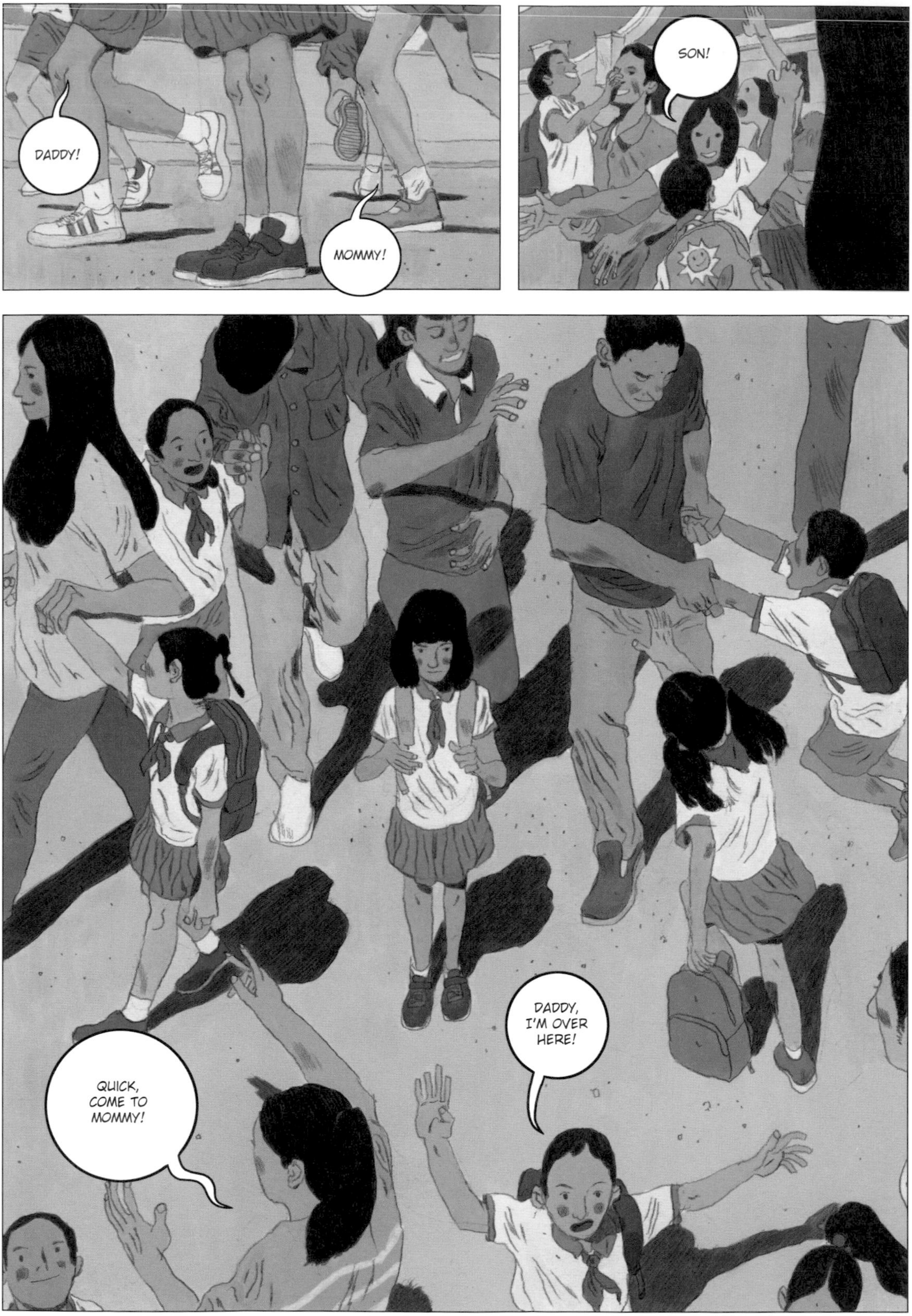
DADDY!
MOMMY!
SON!
QUICK, COME TO MOMMY!
DADDY, I'M OVER HERE!

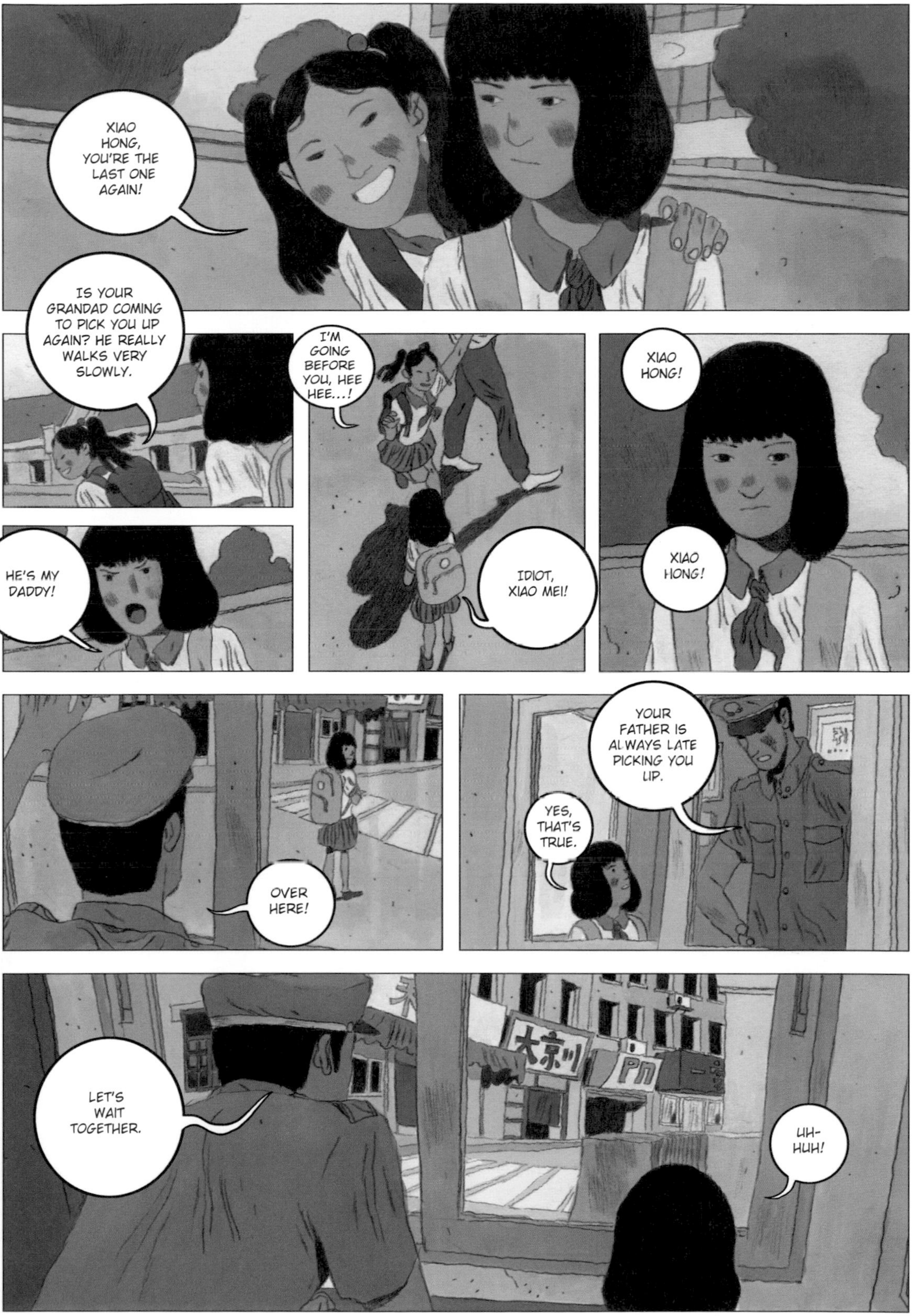
XIAO HONG, YOU'RE THE LAST ONE AGAIN!
IS YOUR GRANDAD COMING TO PICK YOU UP AGAIN? HE REALLY WALKS VERY SLOWLY.
HE'S MY DADDY!
I'M GOING BEFORE YOU, HEE HEE...!
IDIOT, XIAO MEI!
XIAO HONG!
XIAO HONG!
OVER HERE!
YOUR FATHER IS ALWAYS LATE PICKING YOU UP.
YES, THAT'S TRUE.
LET'S WAIT TOGETHER.
UH-HUH!

DAD!
CHEER UP! IF YOU FALL OVER, DON'T START SNIVELING, YOU TAUGHT ME THAT!
XIAO MING... DADDY'S GOTTEN OLD NOW.
TO ME YOU'RE STILL THE WAY YOU WERE WHEN YOU WERE YOUNG!
DADDY!
?

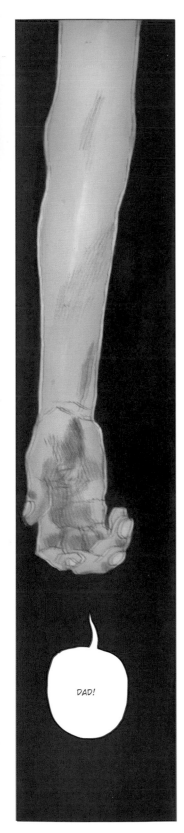

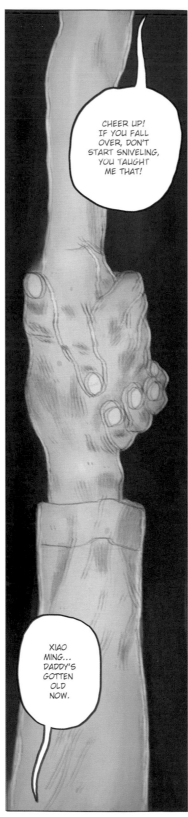

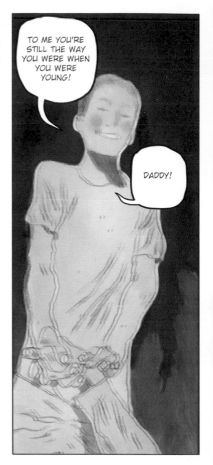

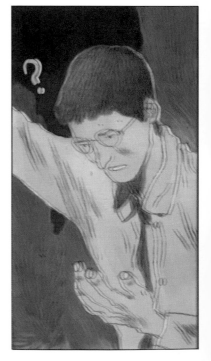

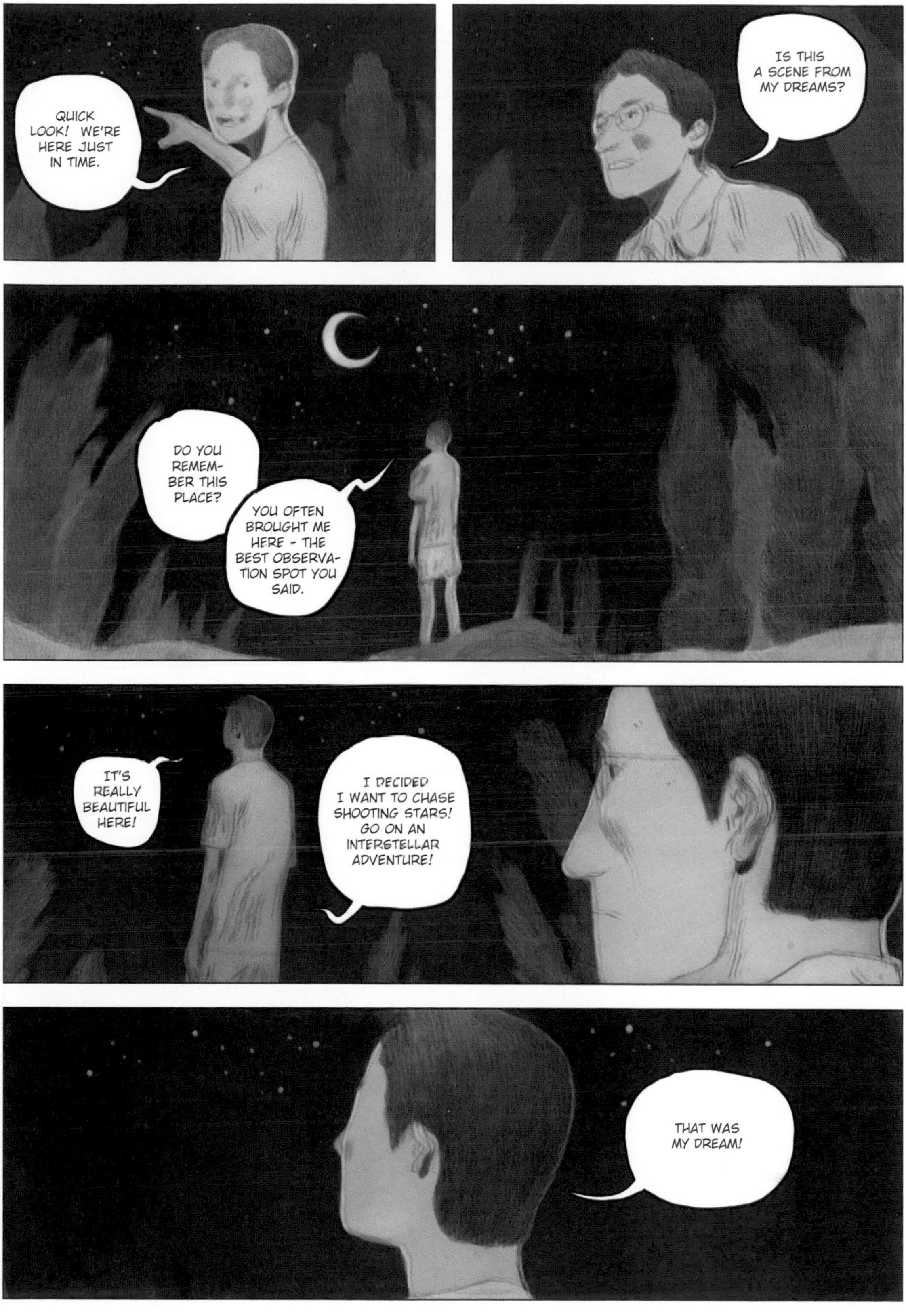
QUICK LOOK! WE'RE HERE JUST IN TIME.
IS THIS A SCENE FROM MY DREAMS?
DO YOU REMEMBER THIS PLACE?
YOU OFTEN BROUGHT ME HERE - THE BEST OBSERVATION SPOT YOU SAID.
IT'S REALLY BEAUTIFUL HERE!
I DECIDED I WANT TO CHASE SHOOTING STARS! GO ON AN INTERSTELLAR ADVENTURE!
THAT WAS MY DREAM!

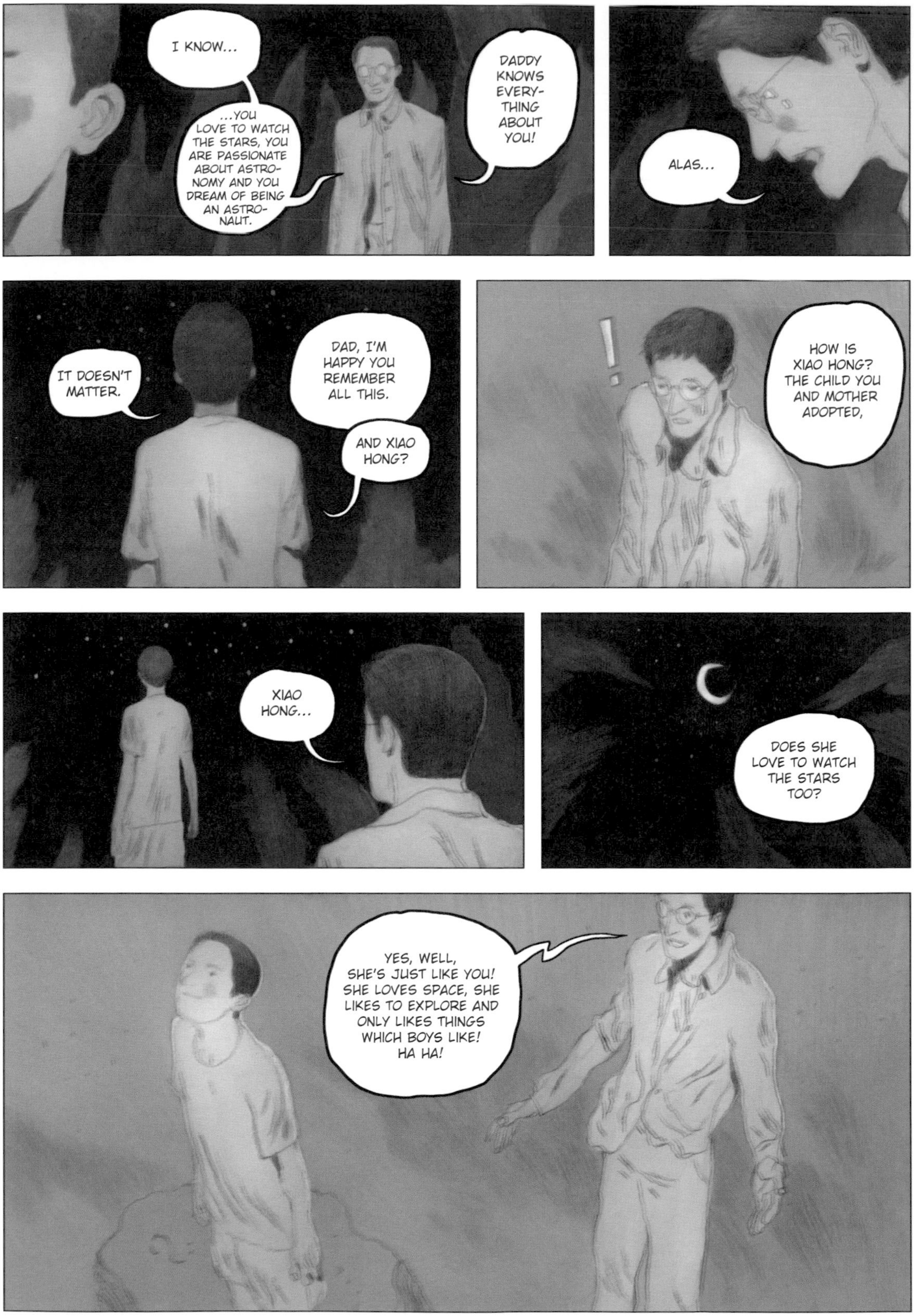
I KNOW...
...YOU LOVE TO WATCH THE STARS, YOU ARE PASSIONATE ABOUT ASTRONOMY AND YOU DREAM OF BEING AN ASTRONAUT.
DADDY KNOWS EVERYTHING ABOUT YOU!
ALAS...
IT DOESN'T MATTER.
DAD, I'M HAPPY YOU REMEMBER ALL THIS.
AND XIAO HONG?
!
HOW IS XIAO HONG? THE CHILD YOU AND MOTHER ADOPTED,
XIAO HONG...
DOES SHE LOVE TO WATCH THE STARS TOO?
YES, WELL, SHE'S JUST LIKE YOU! SHE LOVES SPACE, SHE LIKES TO EXPLORE AND ONLY LIKES THINGS WHICH BOYS LIKE! HA HA!

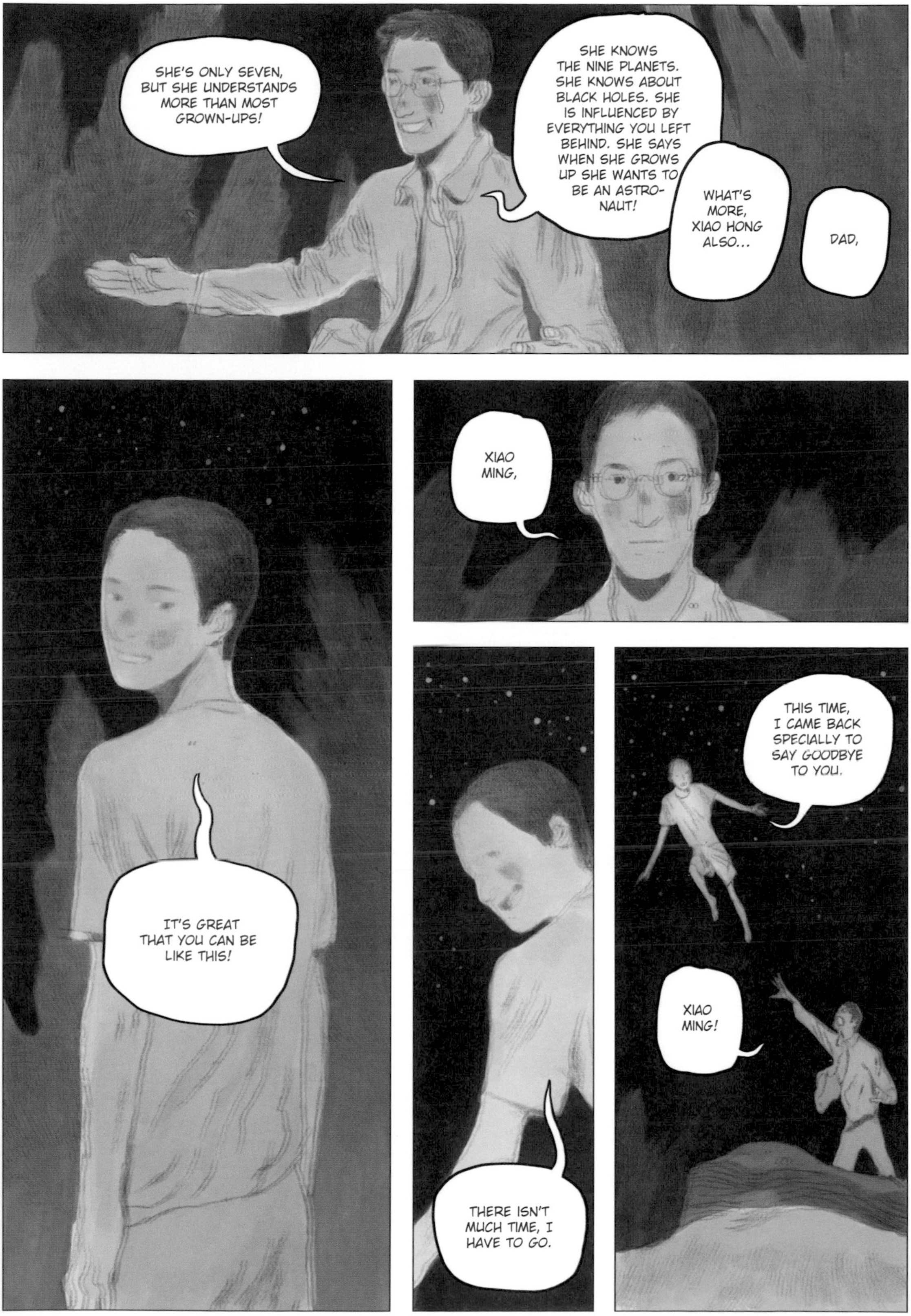
SHE'S ONLY SEVEN, BUT SHE UNDERSTANDS MORE THAN MOST GROWN-UPS!
SHE KNOWS THE NINE PLANETS. SHE KNOWS ABOUT BLACK HOLES. SHE IS INFLUENCED BY EVERYTHING YOU LEFT BEHIND. SHE SAYS WHEN SHE GROWS UP SHE WANTS TO BE AN ASTRO-NAUT!
WHAT'S MORE, XIAO HONG ALSO...
DAD,
IT'S GREAT THAT YOU CAN BE LIKE THIS!
XIAO MING,
THERE ISN'T MUCH TIME, I HAVE TO GO.
THIS TIME, I CAME BACK SPECIALLY TO SAY GOODBYE TO YOU.
XIAO MING!

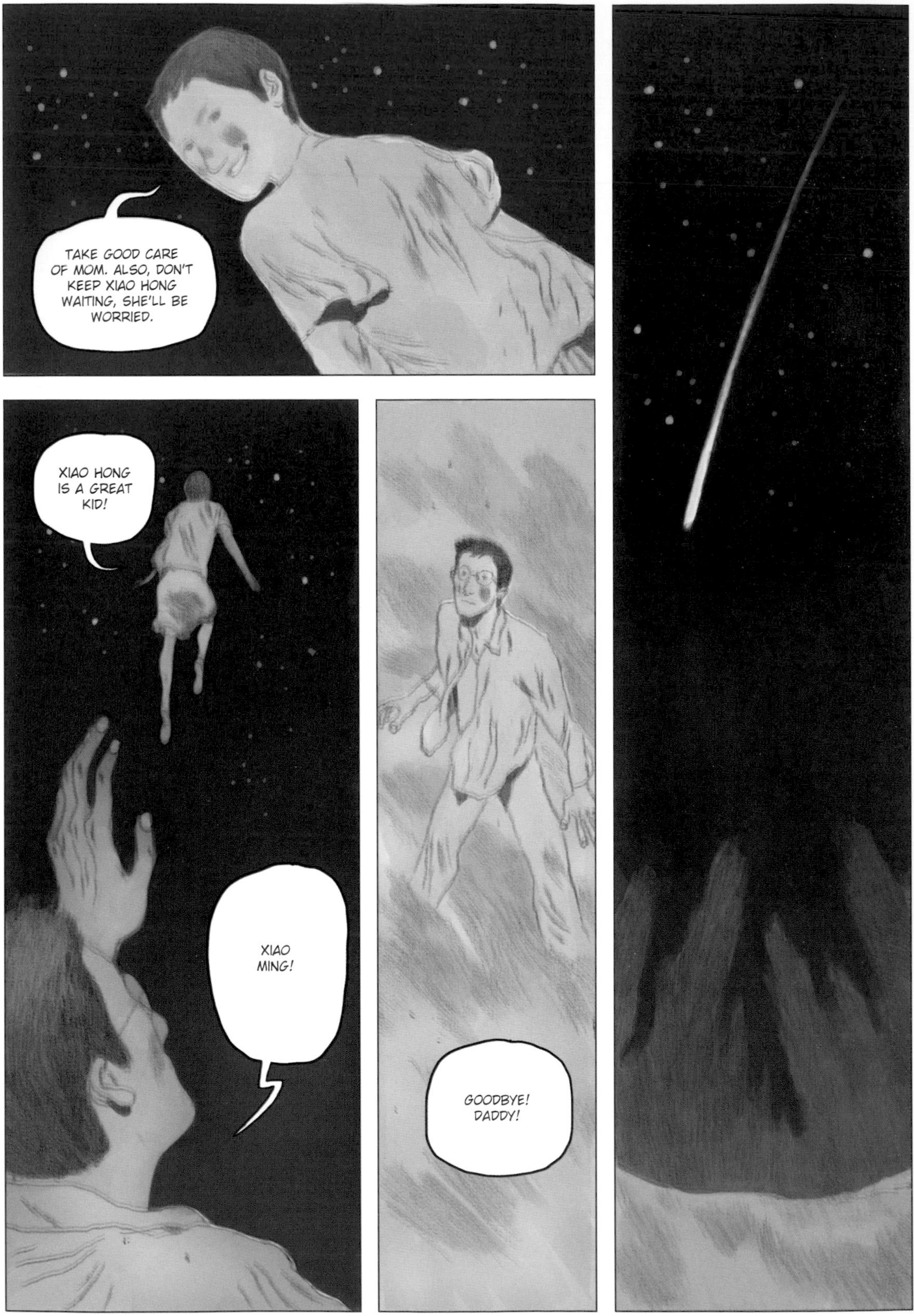
TAKE GOOD CARE OF MOM. ALSO, DON'T KEEP XIAO HONG WAITING, SHE'LL BE WORRIED.
XIAO HONG IS A GREAT KID!
XIAO MING!
GOODBYE! DADDY!

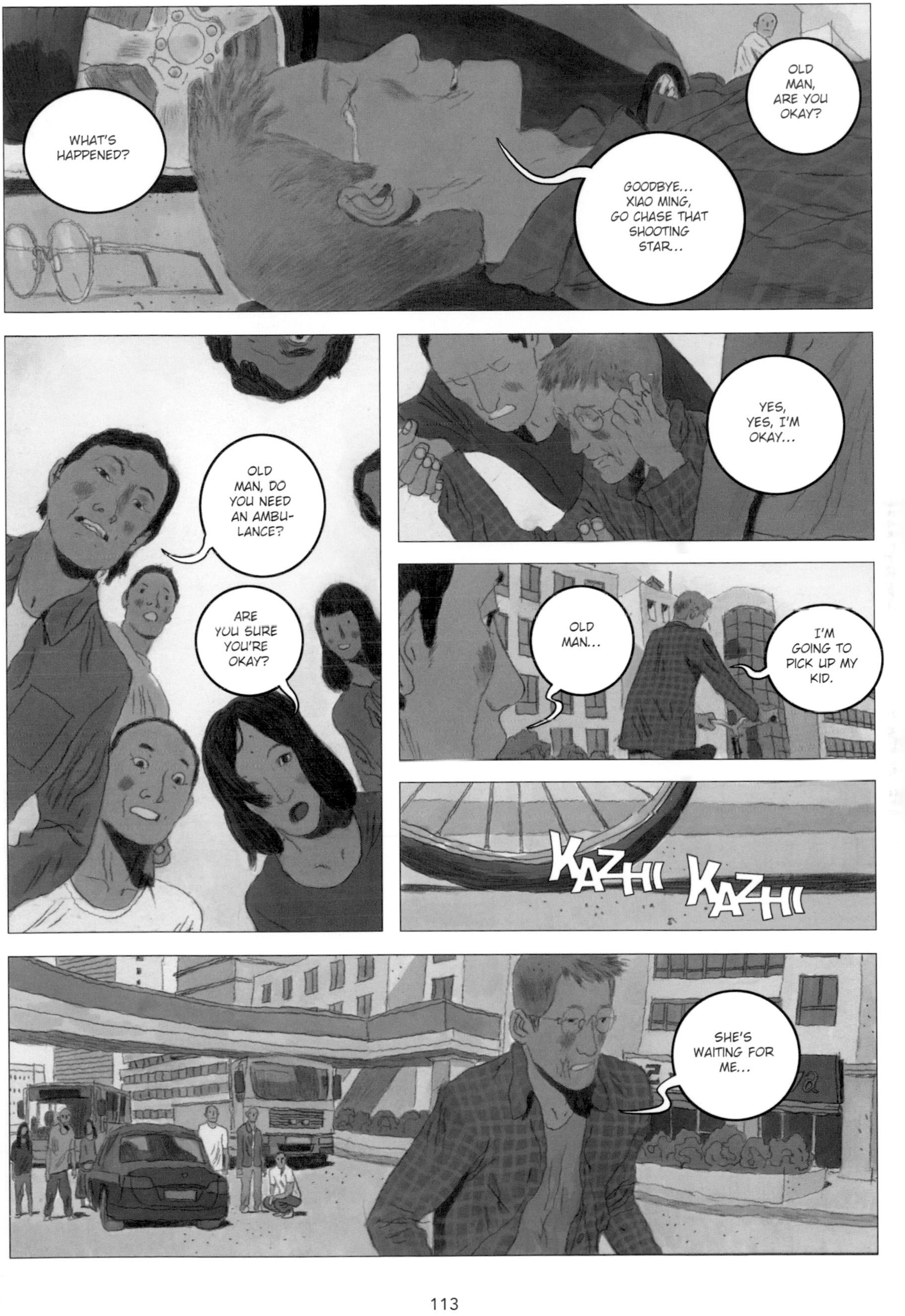
WHAT'S HAPPENED?
OLD MAN, ARE YOU OKAY?
GOODBYE... XIAO MING, GO CHASE THAT SHOOTING STAR...
OLD MAN, DO YOU NEED AN AMBU-LANCE?
ARE YOU SURE YOU'RE OKAY?
YES, YES, I'M OKAY...
OLD MAN...
I'M GOING TO PICK UP MY KID.
KAZHI KAZHI
SHE'S WAITING FOR ME...

WAAAA

WHAT A COINCIDENCE! IT REALLY IS SUCH A COINCIDENCE! TO HAVE THE SAME BIRTHDAY AS OUR XIAO MING! HUSBAND, LOOK! DOESN'T THIS CHILD REALLY LOOK LIKE OUR XIAO MING?

SO ADORABLE AND HELPLESS! POOR LITTLE THING...

ALL BABIES LOOK SIMILAR, BUT SHE IS ADORABLE!

SO YOU ARE HAPPY TO PROCEED WITH HER ADOPTION?

OH! DEFINITELY! I FEEL LIKE SHE IS A GIFT FROM ABOVE...

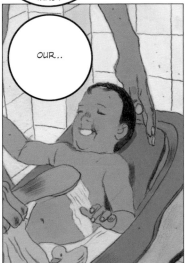

OUR...

...NEW...

...HOPE!

114

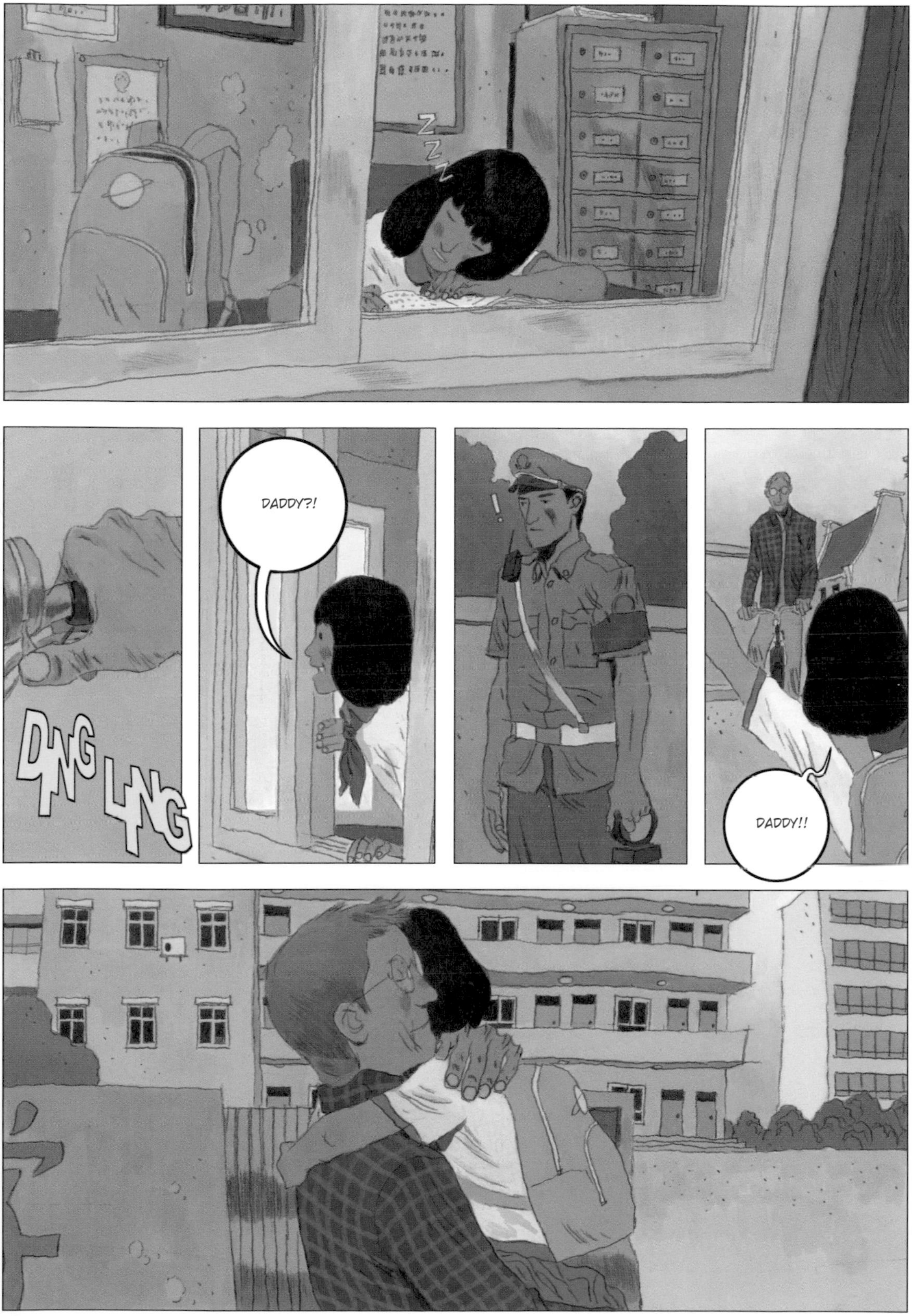
ZZZ
DING LING
DADDY?!
!
DADDY!!

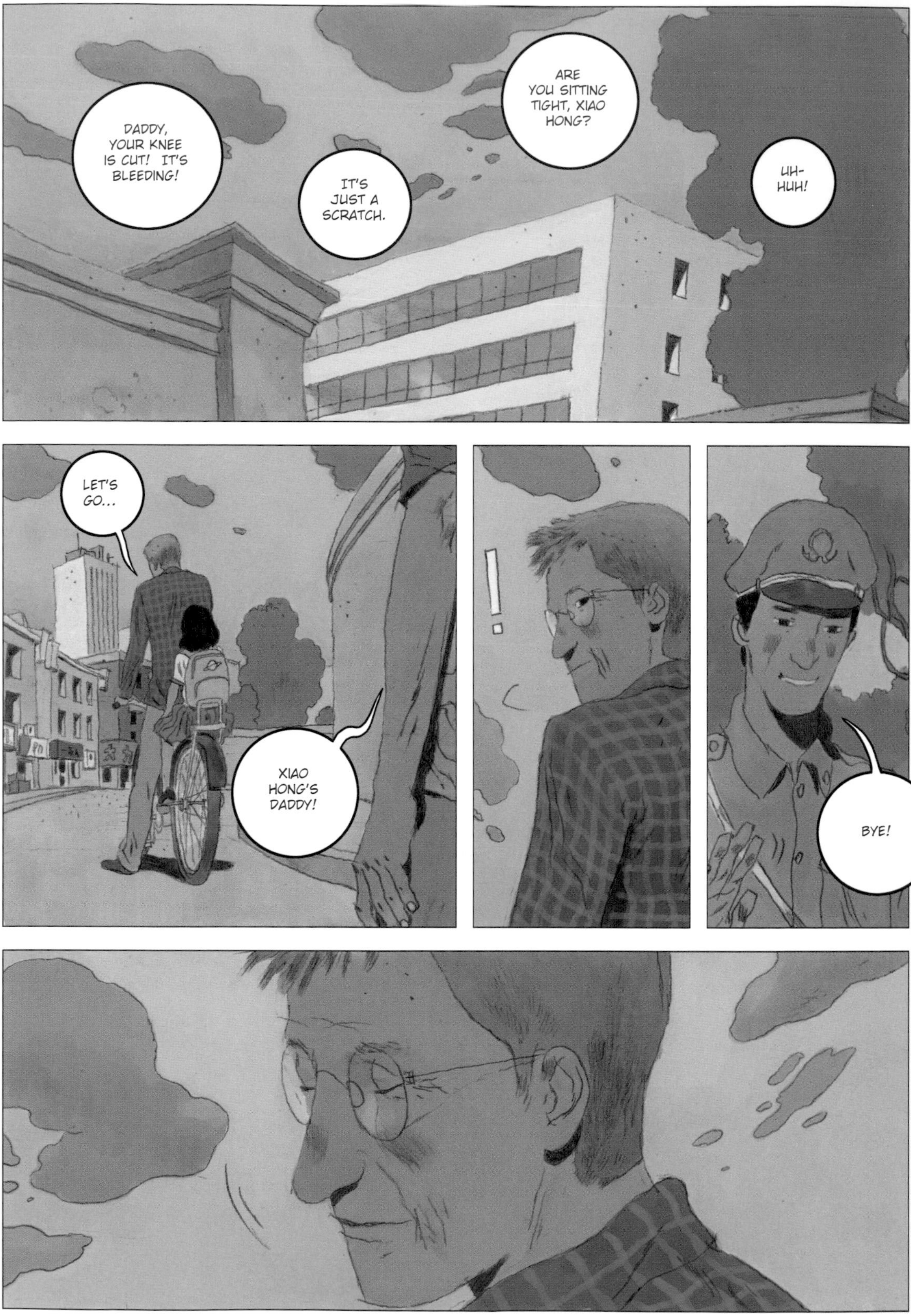
DADDY, YOUR KNEE IS CUT! IT'S BLEEDING!
IT'S JUST A SCRATCH.
ARE YOU SITTING TIGHT, XIAO HONG?
UH-HUH!
LET'S GO...
XIAO HONG'S DADDY!
!
BYE!

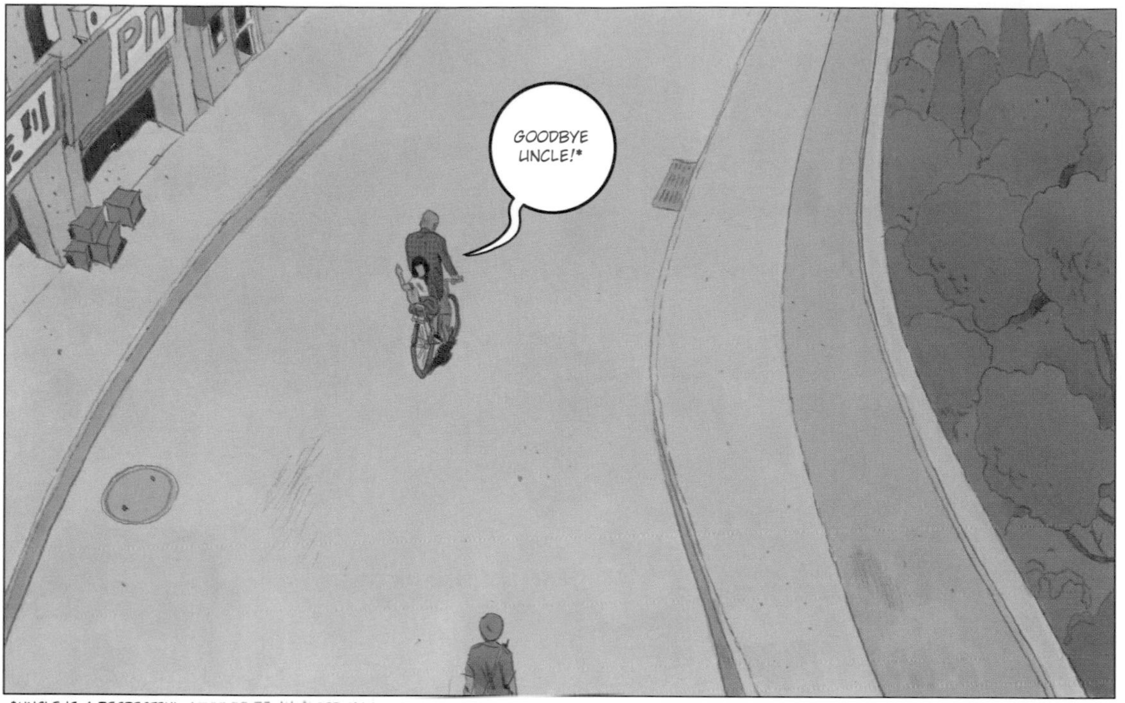
GOODBYE UNCLE!*

*UNCLE IS A RESPECTFUL ADDRESS TO AN OLDER MAN

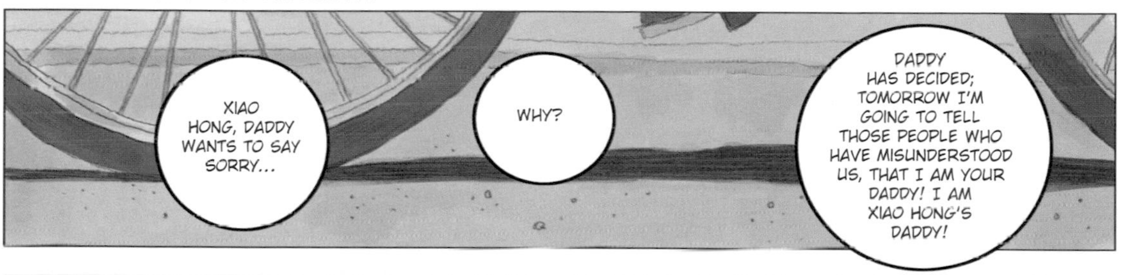
XIAO HONG, DADDY WANTS TO SAY SORRY...
WHY?
DADDY HAS DECIDED; TOMORROW I'M GOING TO TELL THOSE PEOPLE WHO HAVE MISUNDERSTOOD US, THAT I AM YOUR DADDY! I AM XIAO HONG'S DADDY!

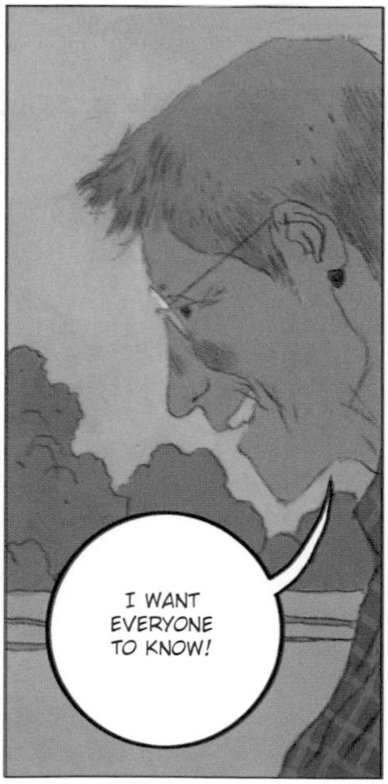
I WANT EVERYONE TO KNOW!

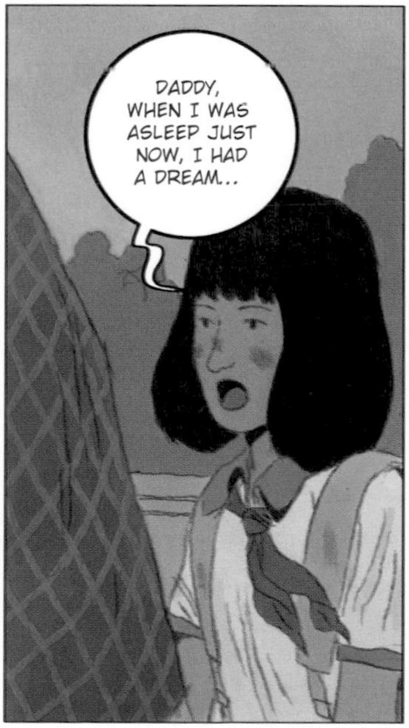
DADDY, WHEN I WAS ASLEEP JUST NOW, I HAD A DREAM...

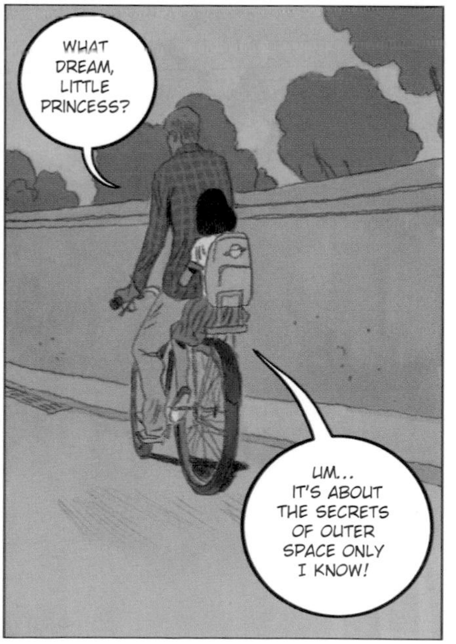
WHAT DREAM, LITTLE PRINCESS?
UM... IT'S ABOUT THE SECRETS OF OUTER SPACE ONLY I KNOW!

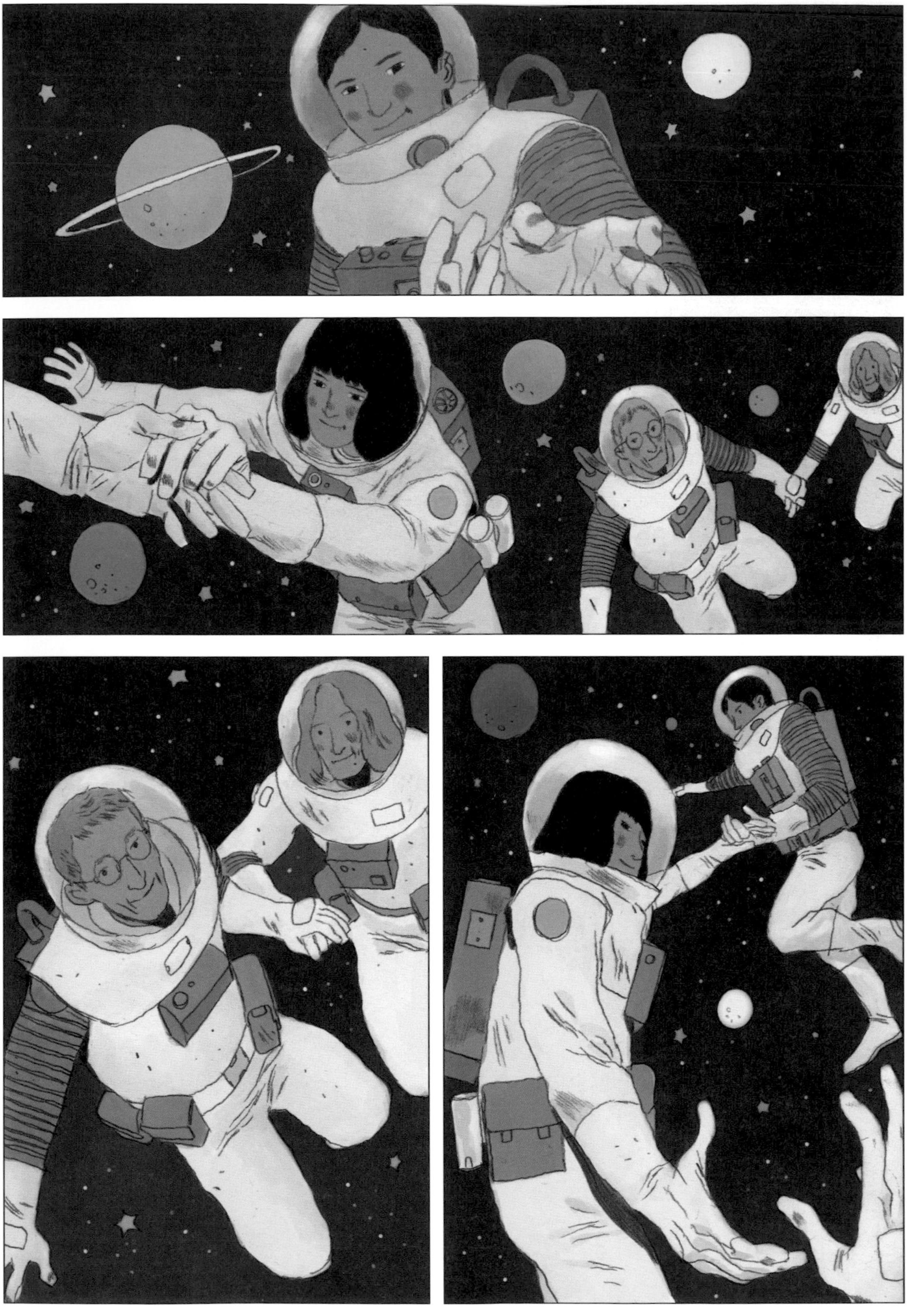

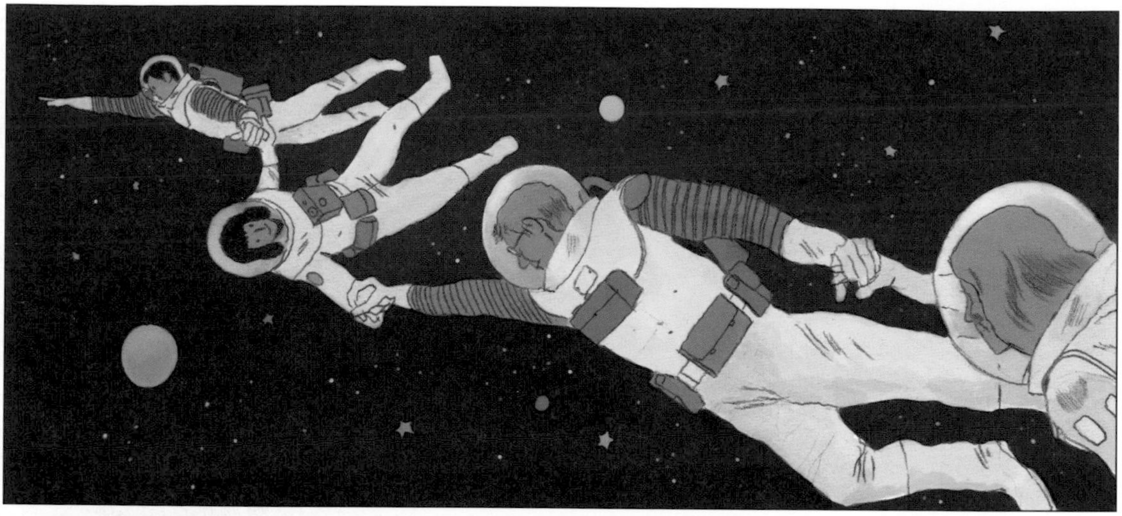

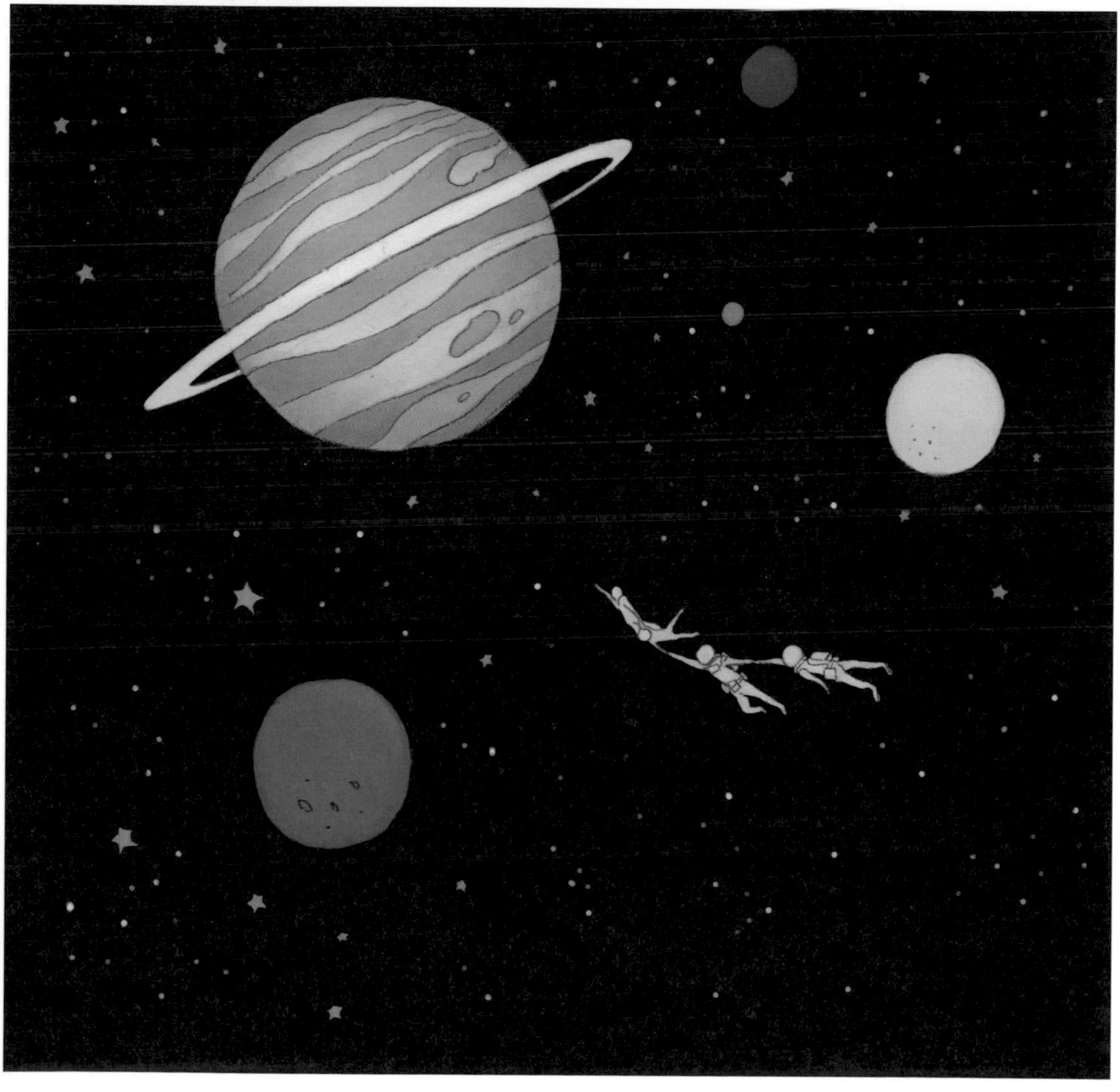

Last Wish

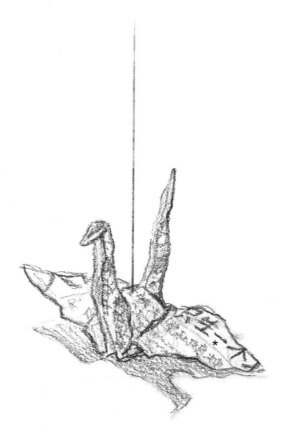

AUTHOR: WANG NING   ARTIST: QIN CHANG

Qin Chang (artist)
Born in 1990, Qin Chang graduated from Tianjin University Animation Department. He used to work in games, film and TV design for many years. He created the 'White Pupil Series' collection. In 2018, he participated in the National Culture and Art Fund training project. He was also invited to create the back cover of the French master of manhua, Edmond Baudoin's, French language comic book, "China notebook".

*Just give birth to one

Translator's note: In China, the crane symbolizes longevity and peace.
Some Chinese people believe that cranes carry their spirit to heaven after they die.

BEIJING, 34 YEARS AGO

THIS IS A LARGE HOUSING COMPLEX WHERE MORE THAN 60 FAMILIES LIVE. IT IS DIVIDED INTO FOUR PARALLEL ROWS. OUR HOUSE IS IN THE LAST ROW AND THERE IS ONLY A WALL SEPARATING THE LANE FROM THE OUTSIDE.

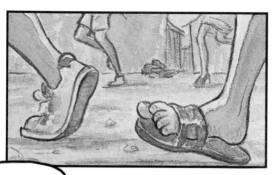

OH! SHE'S ABOUT TO GIVE BIRTH! WHAT FOOD SHALL I PRE-PARE?!

JRRY! HURRY! E AMBULANCE IS HERE!

*FINE ARTS PUBLISHING GROUP FAMILY AREA

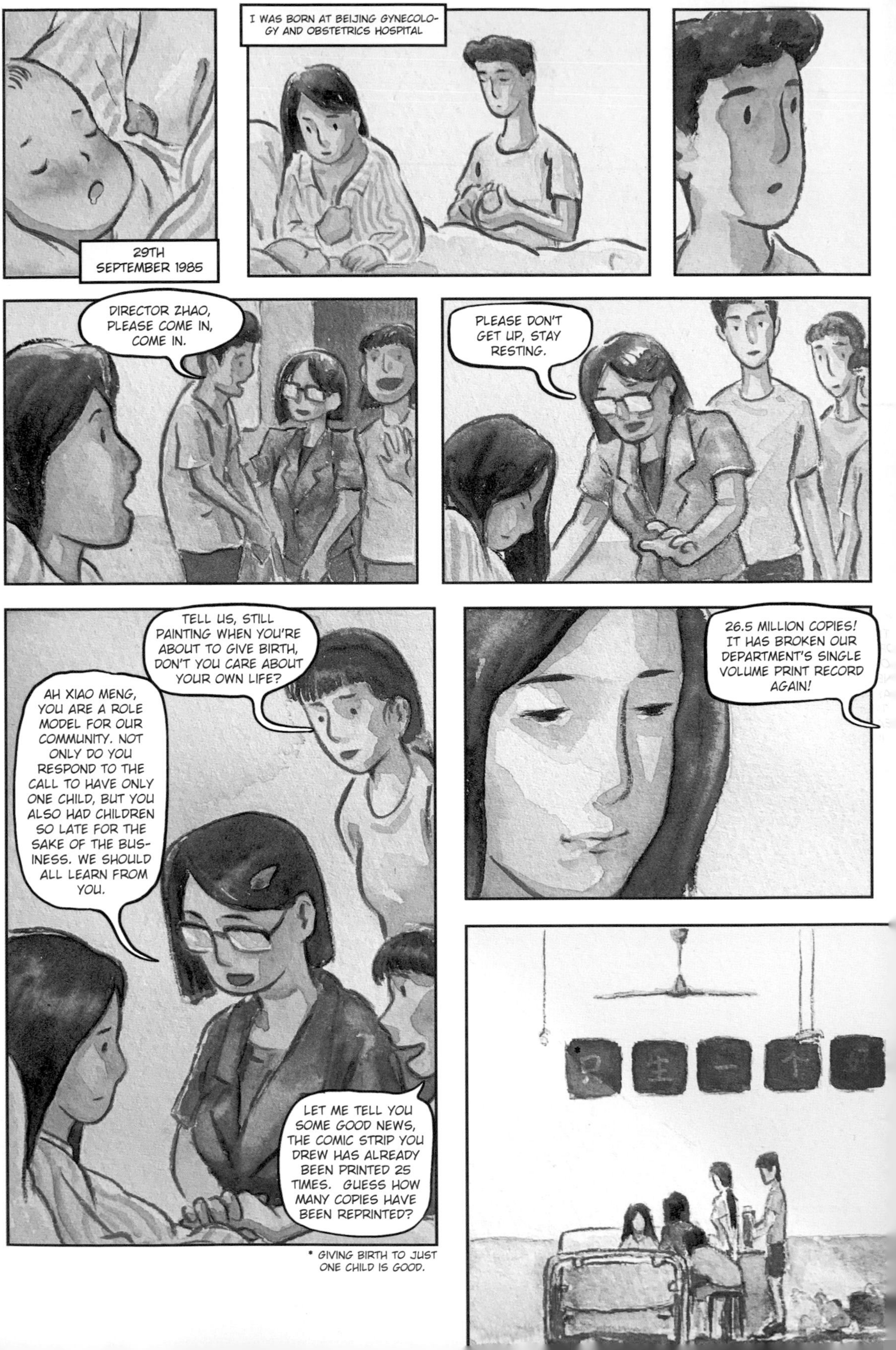

29TH SEPTEMBER 1985
I WAS BORN AT BEIJING GYNECOLOGY AND OBSTETRICS HOSPITAL
DIRECTOR ZHAO, PLEASE COME IN, COME IN.
PLEASE DON'T GET UP, STAY RESTING.
TELL US, STILL PAINTING WHEN YOU'RE ABOUT TO GIVE BIRTH, DON'T YOU CARE ABOUT YOUR OWN LIFE?
AH XIAO MENG, YOU ARE A ROLE MODEL FOR OUR COMMUNITY. NOT ONLY DO YOU RESPOND TO THE CALL TO HAVE ONLY ONE CHILD, BUT YOU ALSO HAD CHILDREN SO LATE FOR THE SAKE OF THE BUSINESS. WE SHOULD ALL LEARN FROM YOU.
LET ME TELL YOU SOME GOOD NEWS, THE COMIC STRIP YOU DREW HAS ALREADY BEEN PRINTED 25 TIMES. GUESS HOW MANY COPIES HAVE BEEN REPRINTED?
26.5 MILLION COPIES! IT HAS BROKEN OUR DEPARTMENT'S SINGLE VOLUME PRINT RECORD AGAIN!
*

* GIVING BIRTH TO JUST ONE CHILD IS GOOD.

I'LL SEE THEM OUT.

OKAY, GOODBYE, DIRECTOR ZHAO, TAKE CARE.

WHAT HAVE WE DONE TO DESERVE THIS...

WHY? WHAT DID THE DOCTORS SAY?

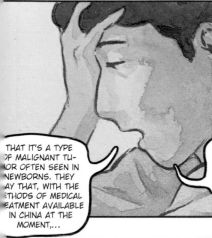

THAT IT'S A TYPE OF MALIGNANT TU-MOR OFTEN SEEN IN NEWBORNS. THEY SAY THAT, WITH THE METHODS OF MEDICAL TREATMENT AVAILABLE IN CHINA AT THE MOMENT,...

...ONCE THE ILLNESS HAS TAKEN EFFECT IT CAN ALL HAPPEN VERY QUICKLY, EVEN IF IT IS HANDLED WELL. IT'S PROBABLE THAT THE LONGEST SHE'LL LIVE IS 25 YEARS.

DARLING LEILEI, WHAT IS YOUR LAST WISH?

AT THAT AGE OF COURSE I HAD NO THOUGHT OF WHAT AWAITED ME.

I ONLY KNOW THAT, FROM AS FAR BACK AS I CAN REMEMBER, MY MOM CRIED EVERY DAY.

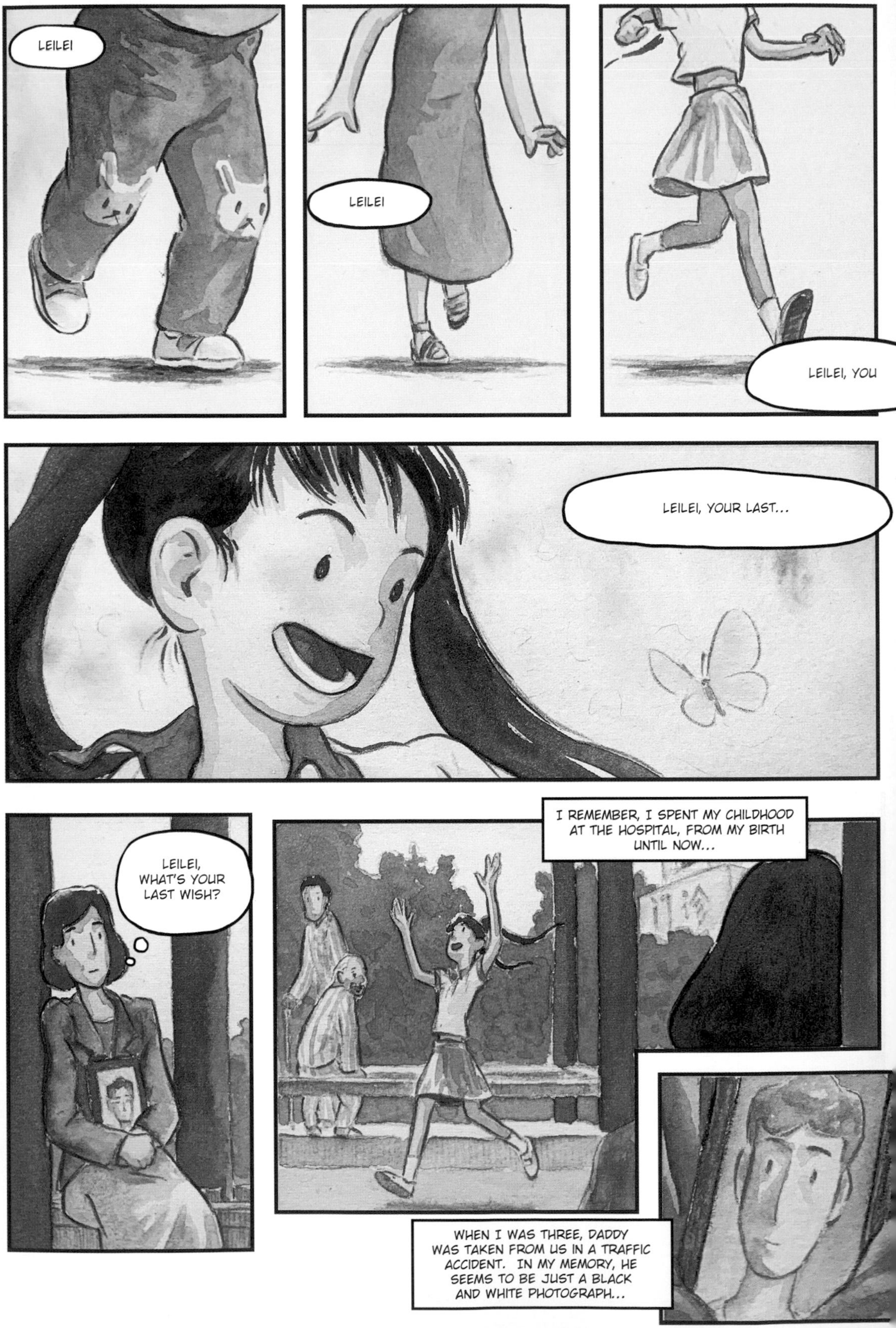
LEILEI
LEILEI
LEILEI, YOU
LEILEI, YOUR LAST...
LEILEI, WHAT'S YOUR LAST WISH?
I REMEMBER, I SPENT MY CHILDHOOD AT THE HOSPITAL, FROM MY BIRTH UNTIL NOW...
WHEN I WAS THREE, DADDY WAS TAKEN FROM US IN A TRAFFIC ACCIDENT. IN MY MEMORY, HE SEEMS TO BE JUST A BLACK AND WHITE PHOTOGRAPH...

SPRING, 1998

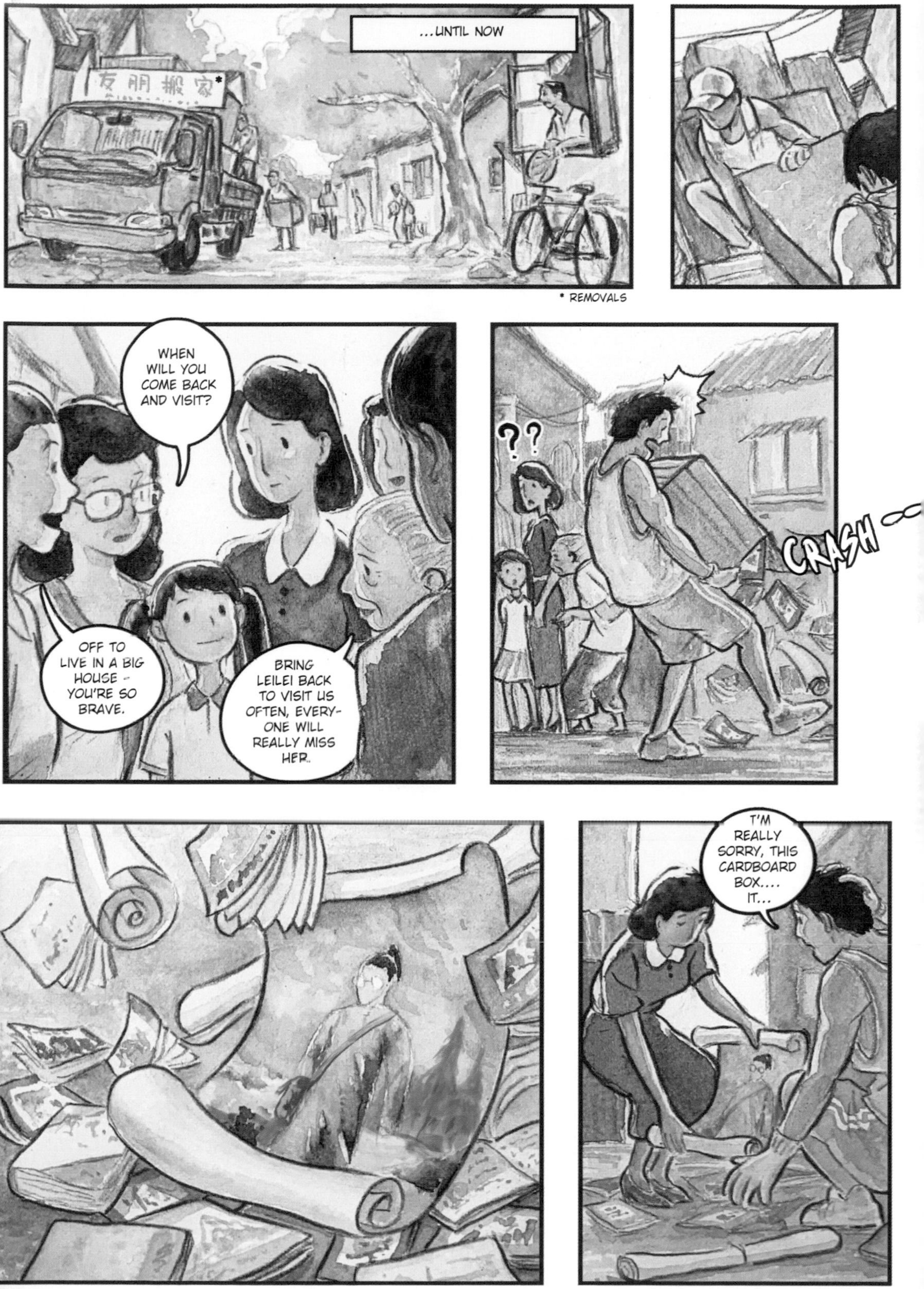
...UNTIL NOW
友朋搬家*
* REMOVALS
WHEN WILL YOU COME BACK AND VISIT?
OFF TO LIVE IN A BIG HOUSE - YOU'RE SO BRAVE.
BRING LEILEI BACK TO VISIT US OFTEN, EVERY-ONE WILL REALLY MISS HER..
??
CRASH
I'M REALLY SORRY, THIS CARDBOARD BOX.... IT...

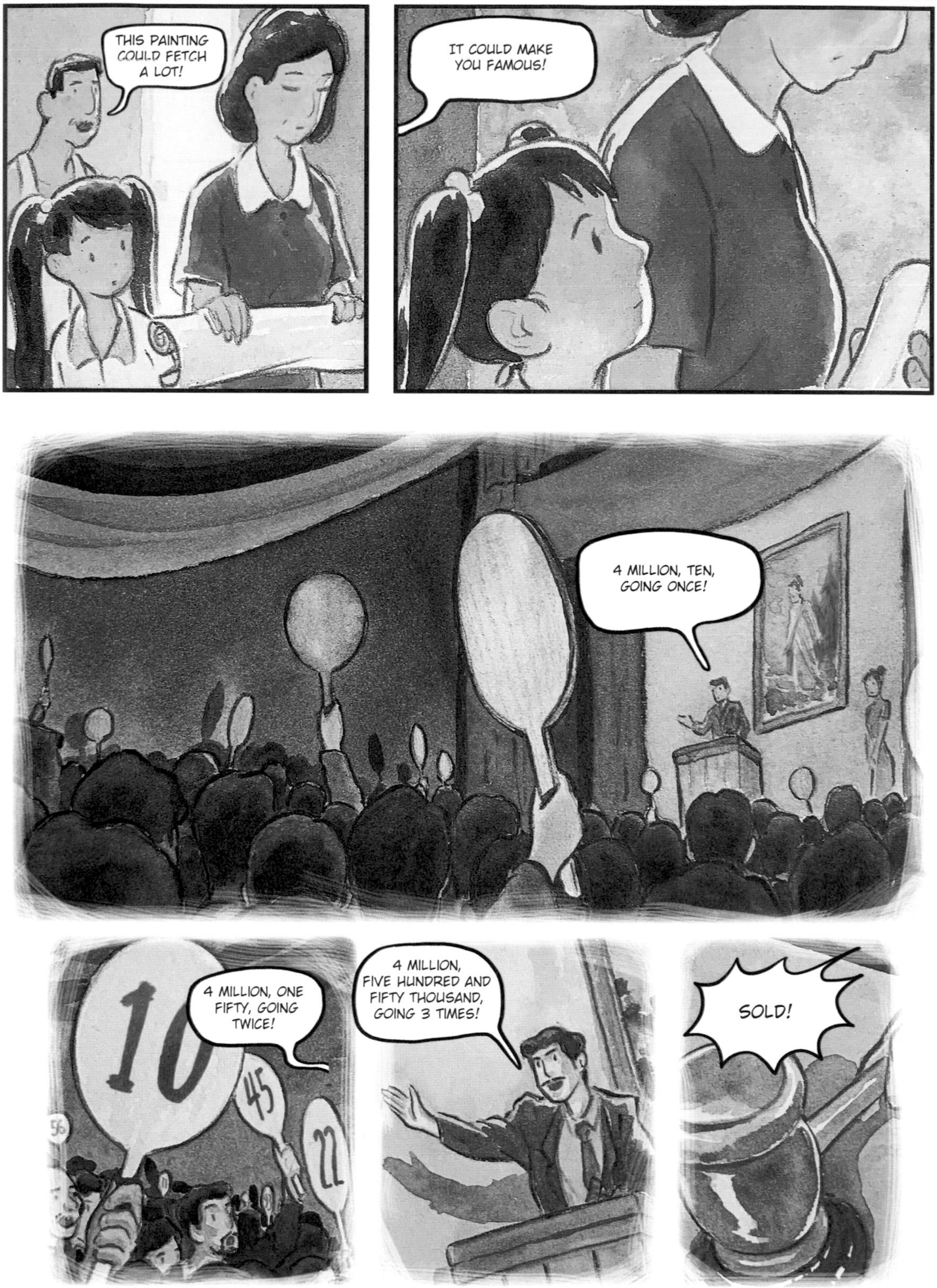
THIS PAINTING COULD FETCH A LOT!
IT COULD MAKE YOU FAMOUS!
4 MILLION, TEN, GOING ONCE!
4 MILLION, ONE FIFTY, GOING TWICE!
4 MILLION, FIVE HUNDRED AND FIFTY THOUSAND, GOING 3 TIMES!
SOLD!

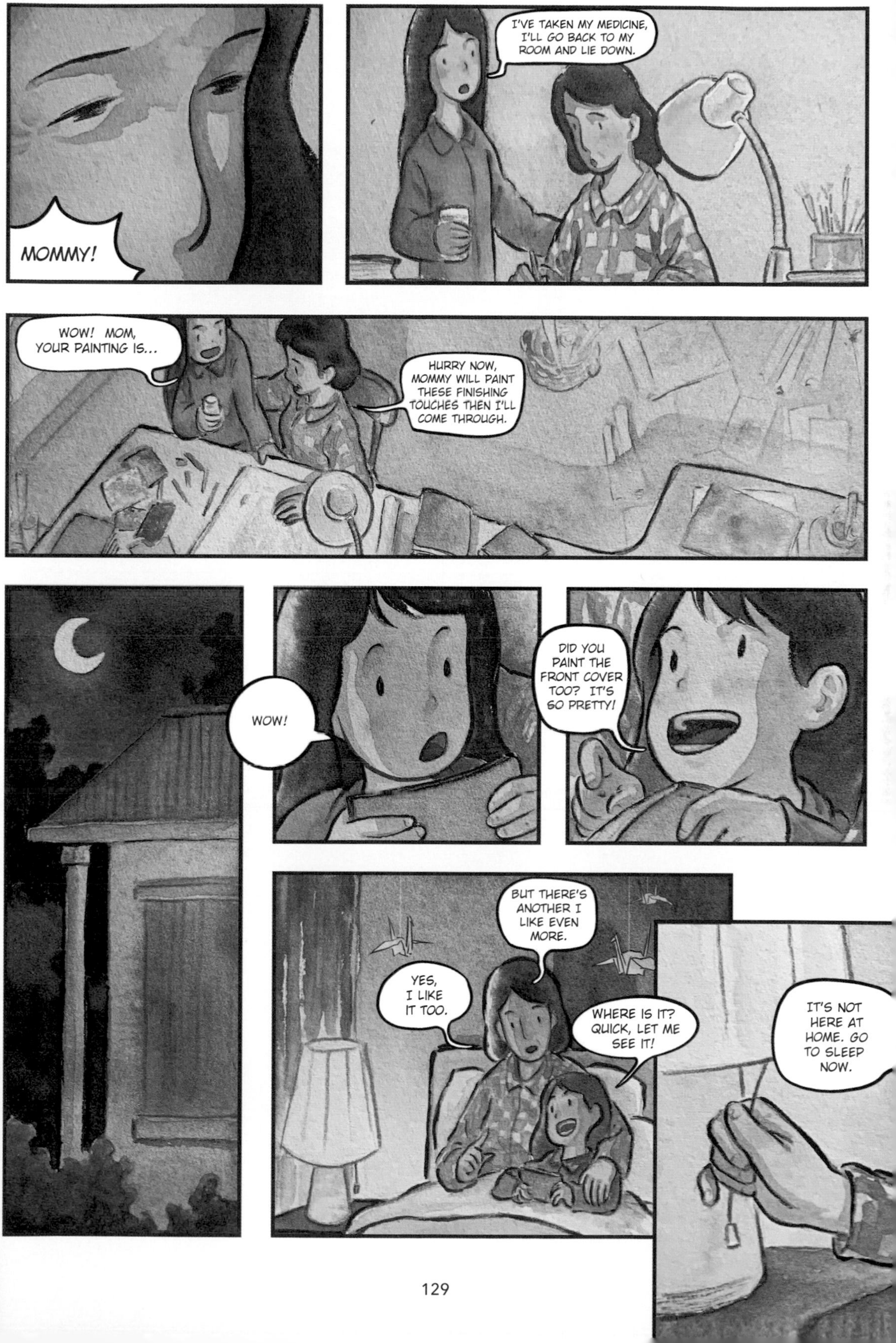
MOMMY!
I'VE TAKEN MY MEDICINE, I'LL GO BACK TO MY ROOM AND LIE DOWN.
WOW! MOM, YOUR PAINTING IS...
HURRY NOW, MOMMY WILL PAINT THESE FINISHING TOUCHES THEN I'LL COME THROUGH.
WOW!
DID YOU PAINT THE FRONT COVER TOO? IT'S SO PRETTY!
BUT THERE'S ANOTHER I LIKE EVEN MORE.
YES, I LIKE IT TOO.
WHERE IS IT? QUICK, LET ME SEE IT!
IT'S NOT HERE AT HOME. GO TO SLEEP NOW.

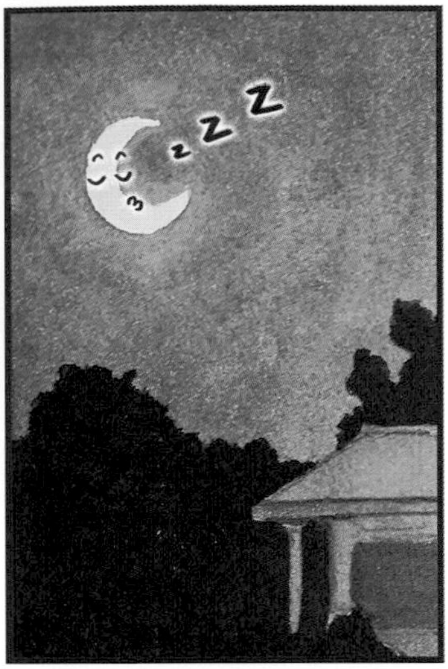

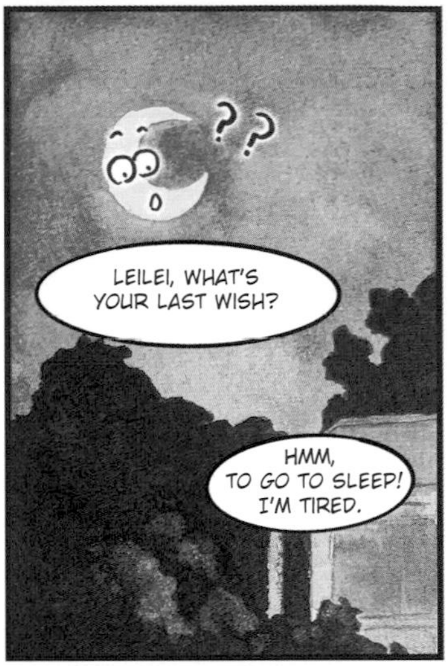
LEILEI, WHAT'S YOUR LAST WISH?
HMM, TO GO TO SLEEP! I'M TIRED.

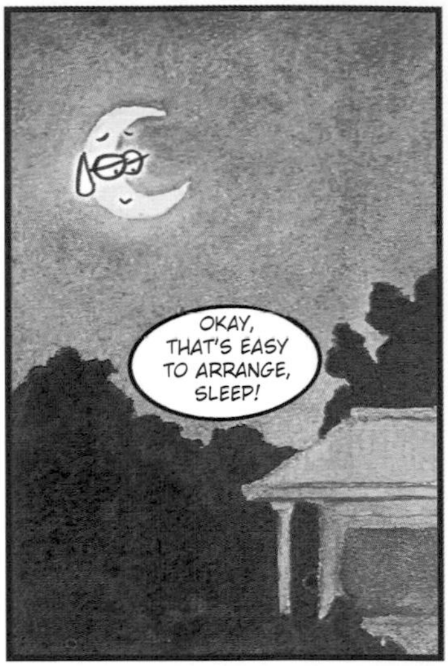
OKAY, THAT'S EASY TO ARRANGE, SLEEP!

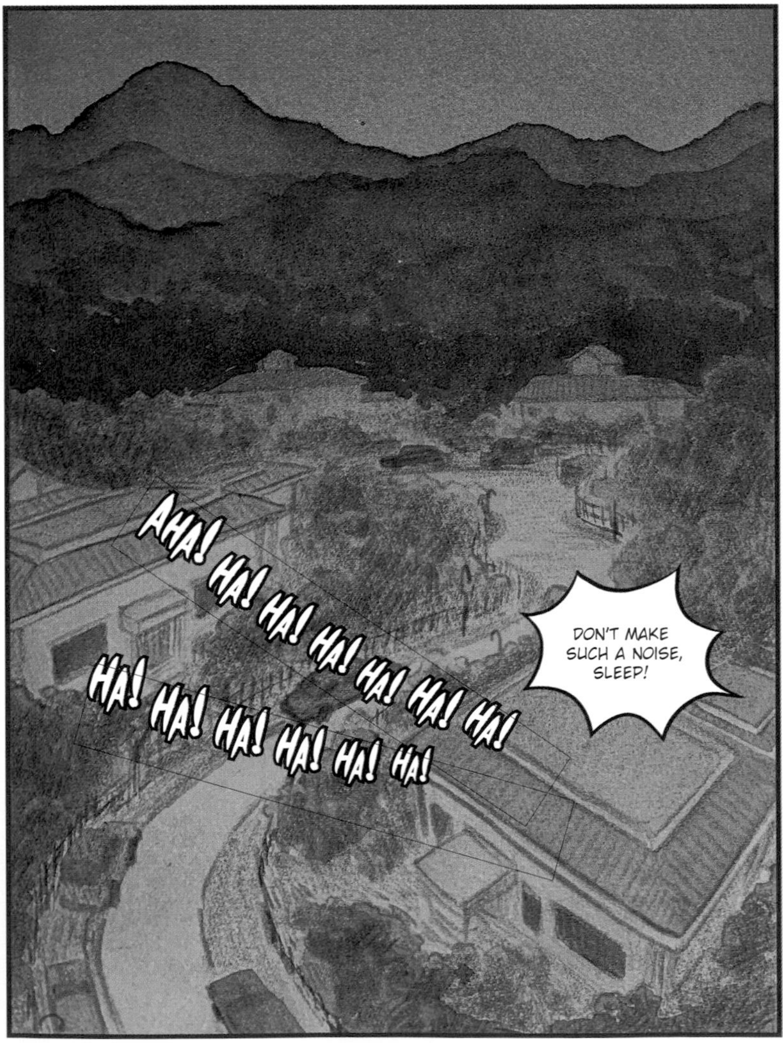
AHA! HA! HA! HA! HA! HA! HA!
HA! HA! HA! HA! HA! HA!
DON'T MAKE SUCH A NOISE, SLEEP!

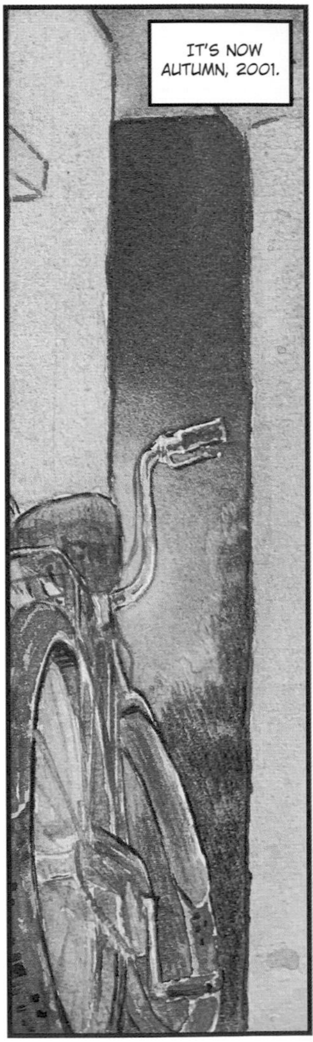
IT'S NOW AUTUMN, 2001.

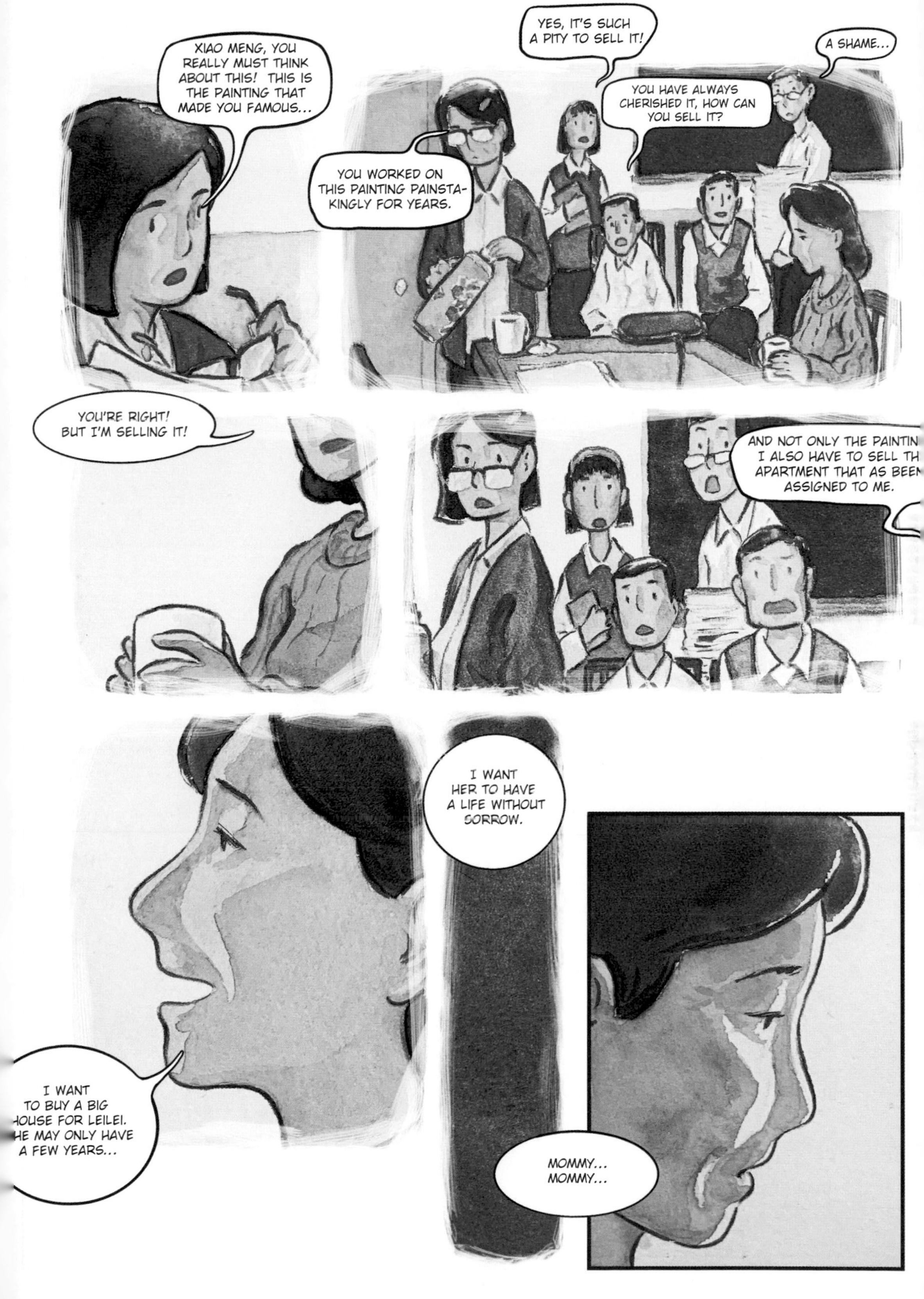

XIAO MENG, YOU REALLY MUST THINK ABOUT THIS! THIS IS THE PAINTING THAT MADE YOU FAMOUS...
YES, IT'S SUCH A PITY TO SELL IT!
A SHAME...
YOU HAVE ALWAYS CHERISHED IT, HOW CAN YOU SELL IT?
YOU WORKED ON THIS PAINTING PAINSTAKINGLY FOR YEARS.
YOU'RE RIGHT! BUT I'M SELLING IT!
AND NOT ONLY THE PAINTIN I ALSO HAVE TO SELL TH APARTMENT THAT AS BEEN ASSIGNED TO ME.
I WANT TO BUY A BIG HOUSE FOR LEILEI. HE MAY ONLY HAVE A FEW YEARS...
I WANT HER TO HAVE A LIFE WITHOUT SORROW.
MOMMY... MOMMY...

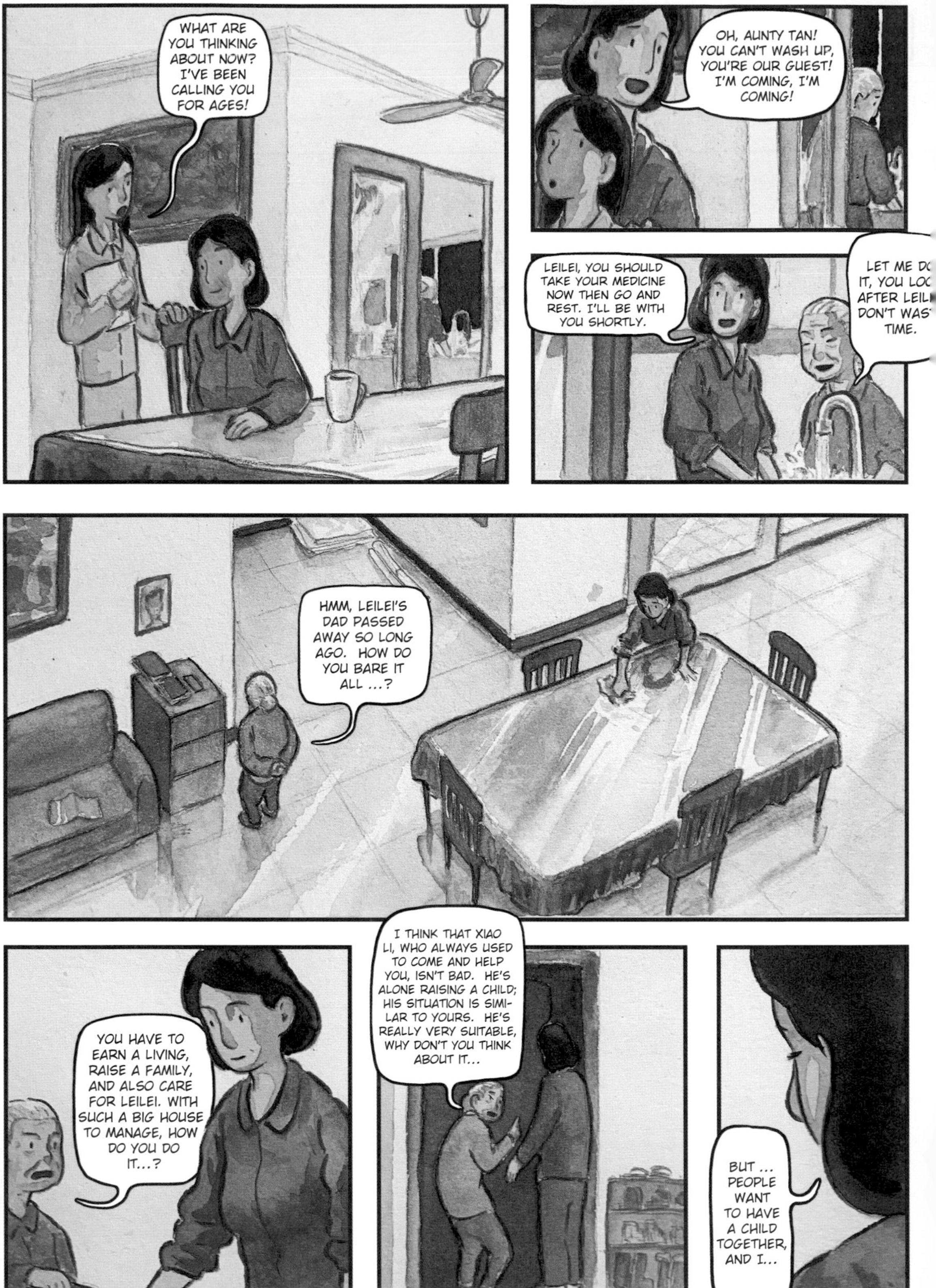
WHAT ARE YOU THINKING ABOUT NOW? I'VE BEEN CALLING YOU FOR AGES!
OH, AUNTY TAN! YOU CAN'T WASH UP, YOU'RE OUR GUEST! I'M COMING, I'M COMING!
LEILEI, YOU SHOULD TAKE YOUR MEDICINE NOW THEN GO AND REST. I'LL BE WITH YOU SHORTLY.
LET ME DO IT, YOU LOO AFTER LEIL DON'T WAS TIME.
HMM, LEILEI'S DAD PASSED AWAY SO LONG AGO. HOW DO YOU BARE IT ALL ...?
YOU HAVE TO EARN A LIVING, RAISE A FAMILY, AND ALSO CARE FOR LEILEI. WITH SUCH A BIG HOUSE TO MANAGE, HOW DO YOU DO IT...?
I THINK THAT XIAO LI, WHO ALWAYS USED TO COME AND HELP YOU, ISN'T BAD. HE'S ALONE RAISING A CHILD; HIS SITUATION IS SIMI-LAR TO YOURS. HE'S REALLY VERY SUITABLE, WHY DON'T YOU THINK ABOUT IT...
BUT ... PEOPLE WANT TO HAVE A CHILD TOGETHER, AND I...

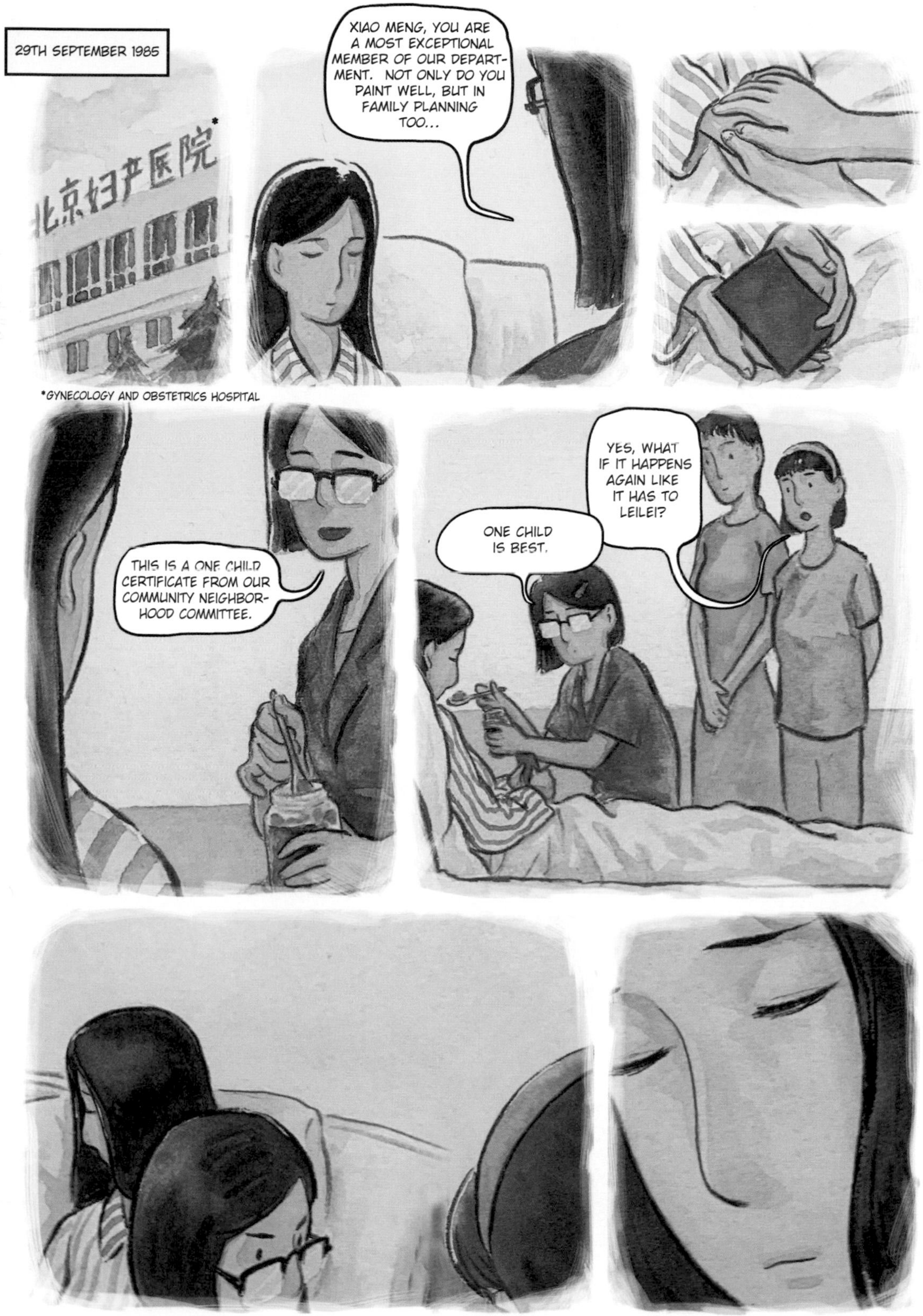

29TH SEPTEMBER 1985
北京妇产医院*
XIAO MENG, YOU ARE A MOST EXCEPTIONAL MEMBER OF OUR DEPARTMENT. NOT ONLY DO YOU PAINT WELL, BUT IN FAMILY PLANNING TOO...
*GYNECOLOGY AND OBSTETRICS HOSPITAL
THIS IS A ONE CHILD CERTIFICATE FROM OUR COMMUNITY NEIGHBORHOOD COMMITTEE.
ONE CHILD IS BEST.
YES, WHAT IF IT HAPPENS AGAIN LIKE IT HAS TO LEILEI?

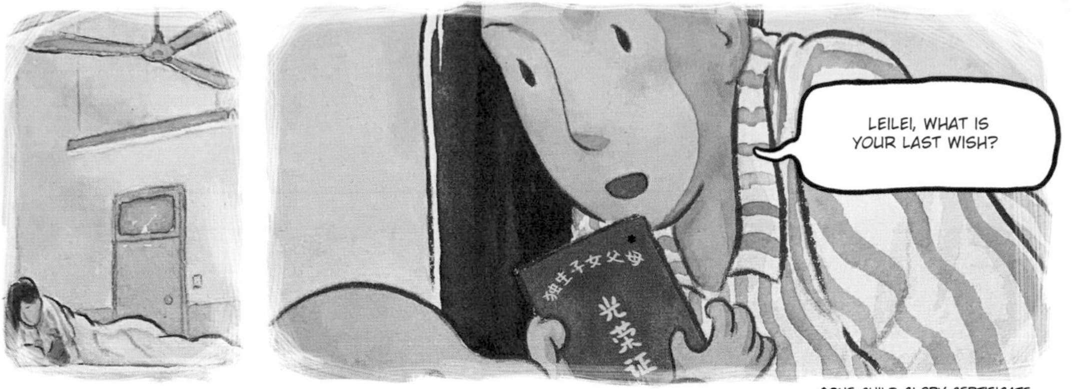
独生子女父母*
光荣证
LEILEI, WHAT IS YOUR LAST WISH?

*ONE CHILD GLORY CERTIFICATE

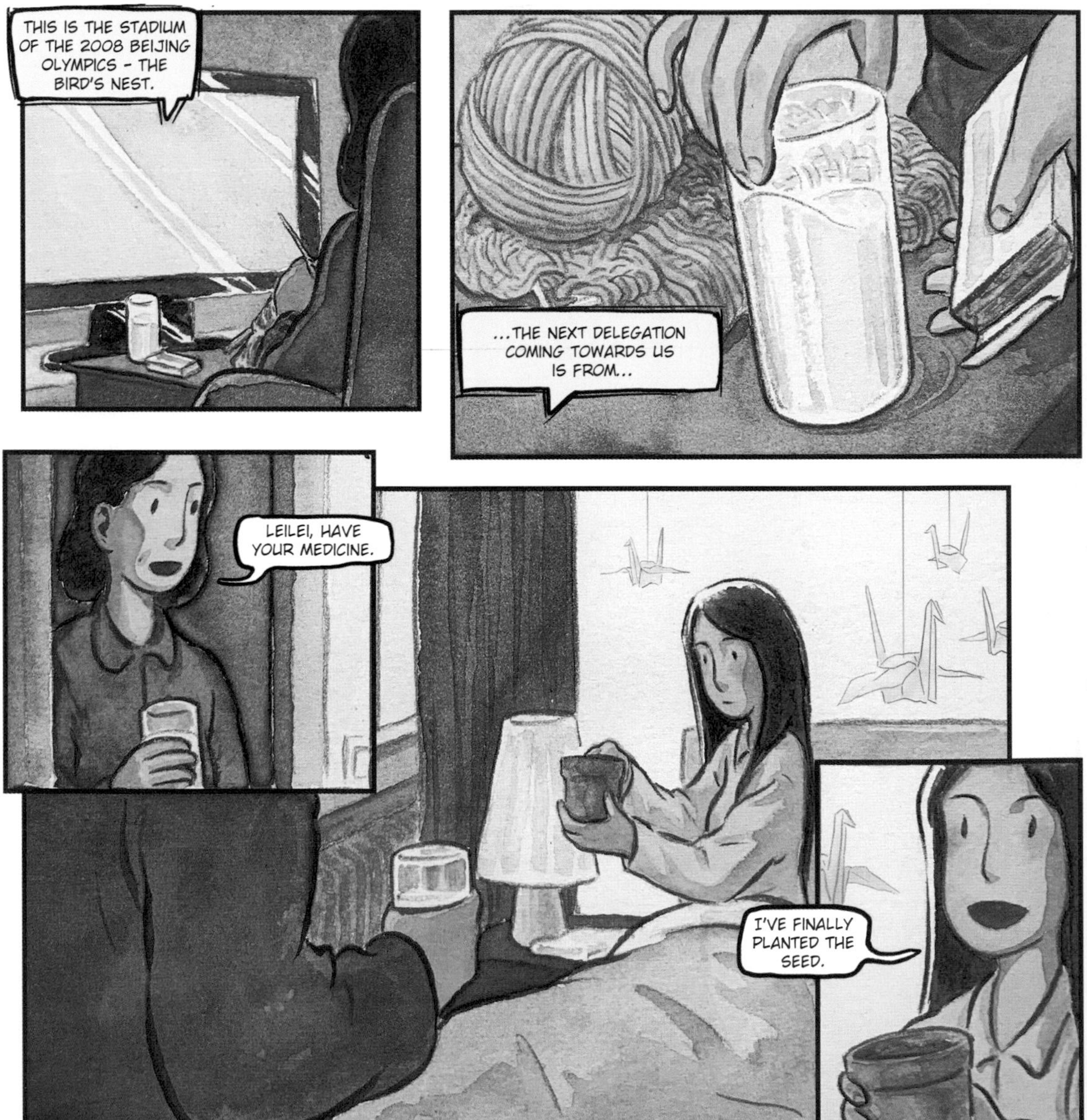
THIS IS THE STADIUM OF THE 2008 BEIJING OLYMPICS - THE BIRD'S NEST.
...THE NEXT DELEGATION COMING TOWARDS US IS FROM...
LEILEI, HAVE YOUR MEDICINE.
I'VE FINALLY PLANTED THE SEED.

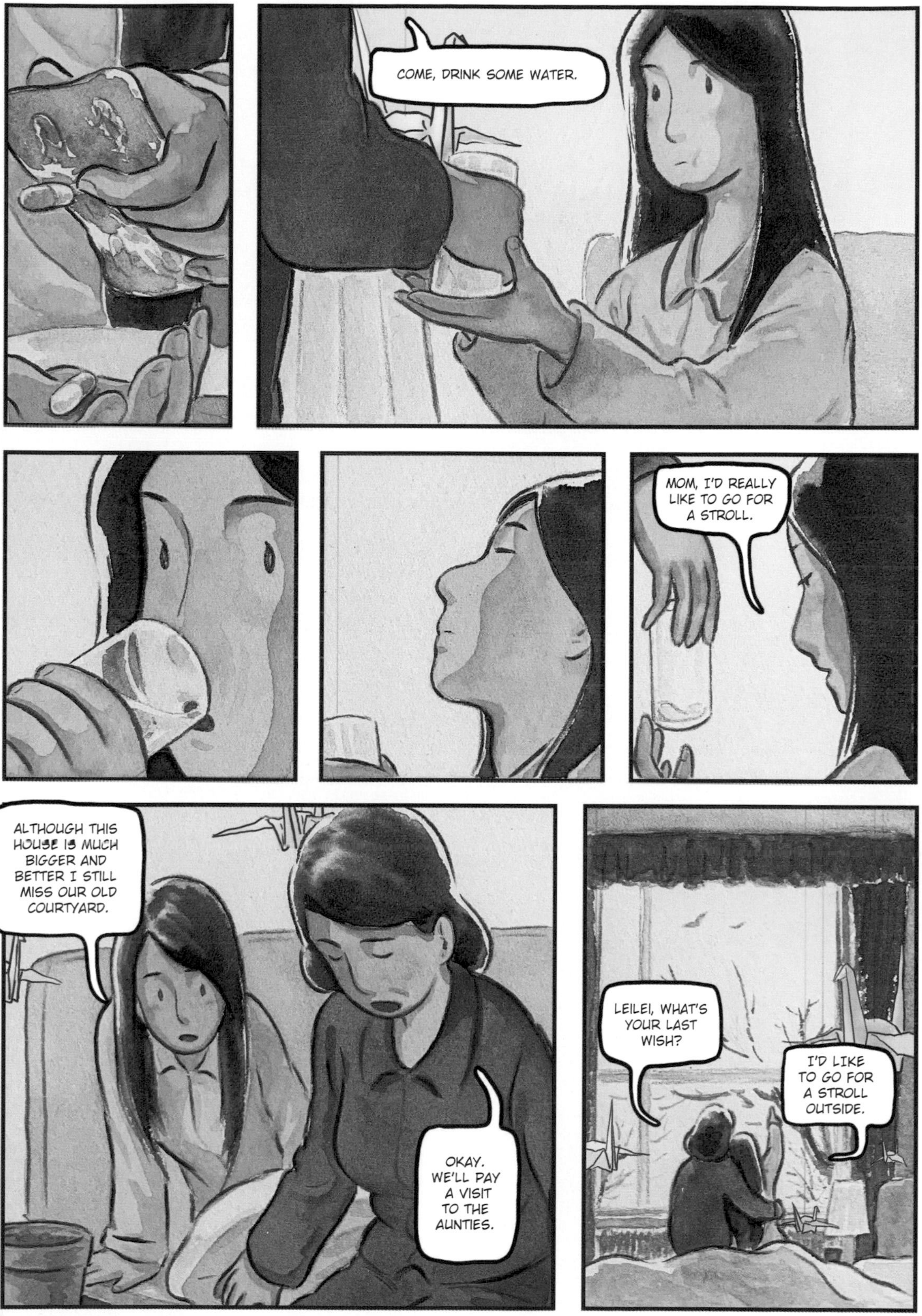
COME, DRINK SOME WATER.
MOM, I'D REALLY LIKE TO GO FOR A STROLL.
ALTHOUGH THIS HOUSE IS MUCH BIGGER AND BETTER I STILL MISS OUR OLD COURTYARD.
OKAY. WE'LL PAY A VISIT TO THE AUNTIES.
LEILEI, WHAT'S YOUR LAST WISH?
I'D LIKE TO GO FOR A STROLL OUTSIDE.

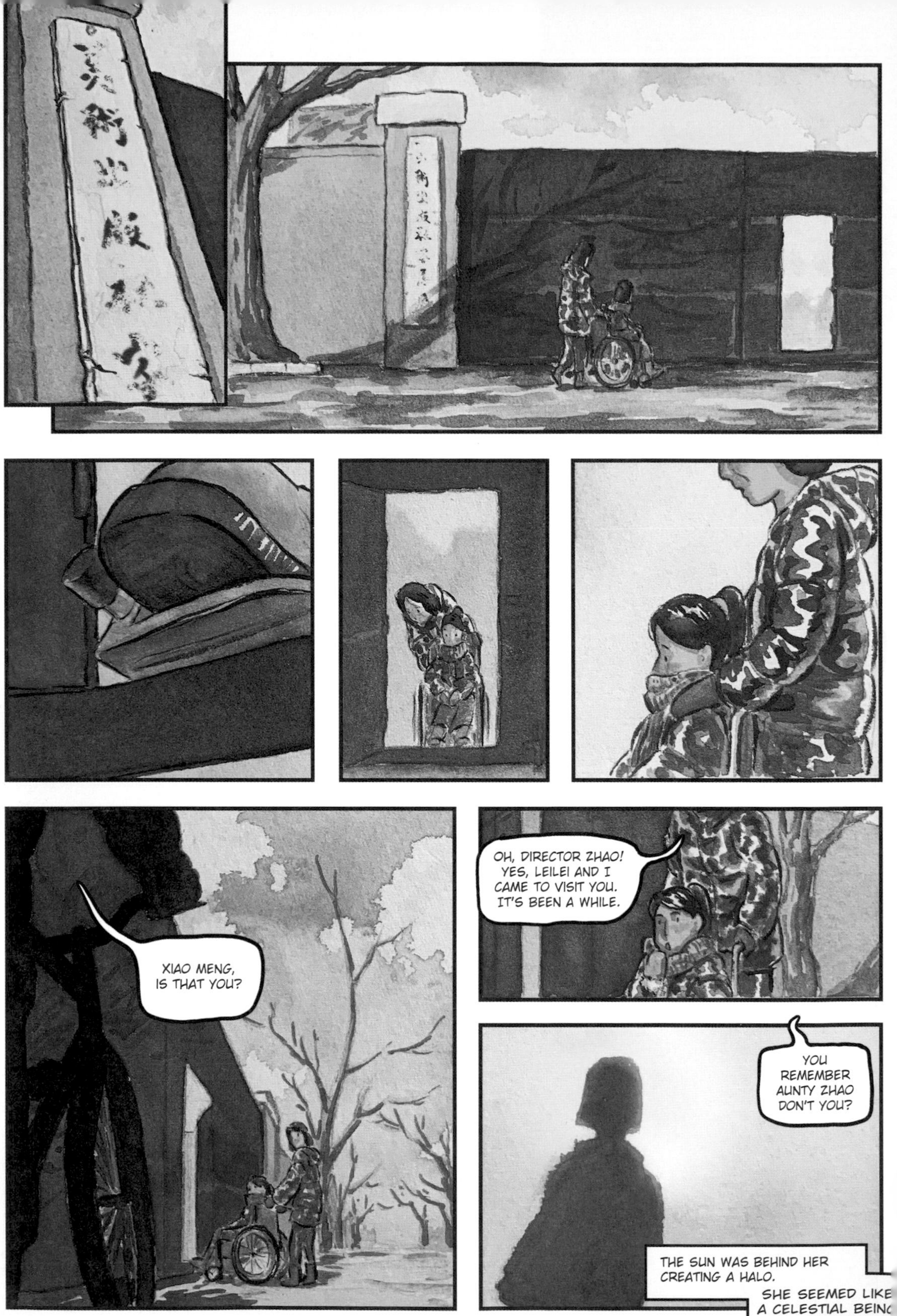
XIAO MENG, IS THAT YOU?
OH, DIRECTOR ZHAO! YES, LEILEI AND I CAME TO VISIT YOU. IT'S BEEN A WHILE.
YOU REMEMBER AUNTY ZHAO DON'T YOU?
THE SUN WAS BEHIND HER CREATING A HALO.
SHE SEEMED LIKE A CELESTIAL BEING IN A PAINTING.

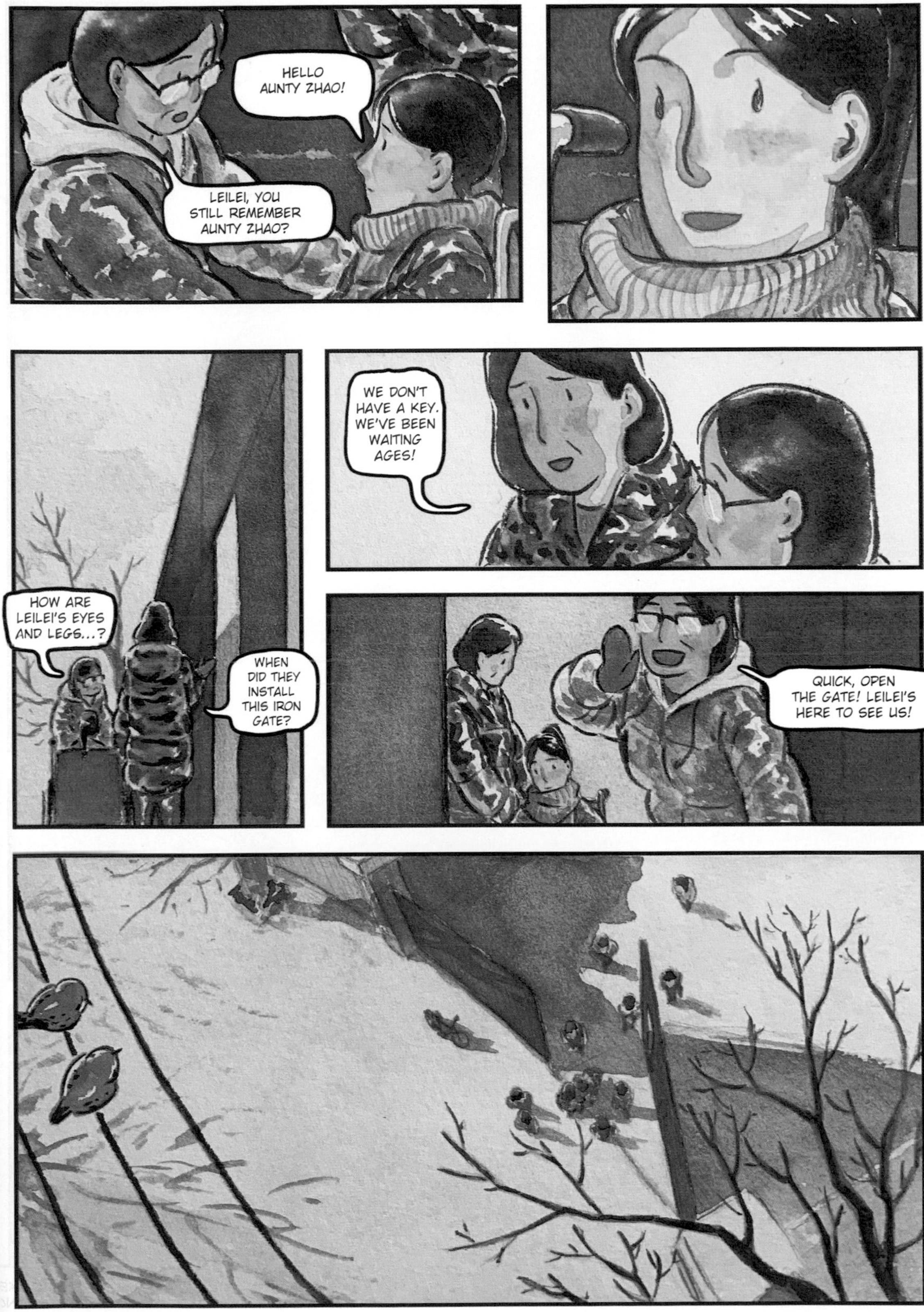
HELLO AUNTY ZHAO!
LEILEI, YOU STILL REMEMBER AUNTY ZHAO?
HOW ARE LEILEI'S EYES AND LEGS...?
WHEN DID THEY INSTALL THIS IRON GATE?
WE DON'T HAVE A KEY. WE'VE BEEN WAITING AGES!
QUICK, OPEN THE GATE! LEILEI'S HERE TO SEE US!

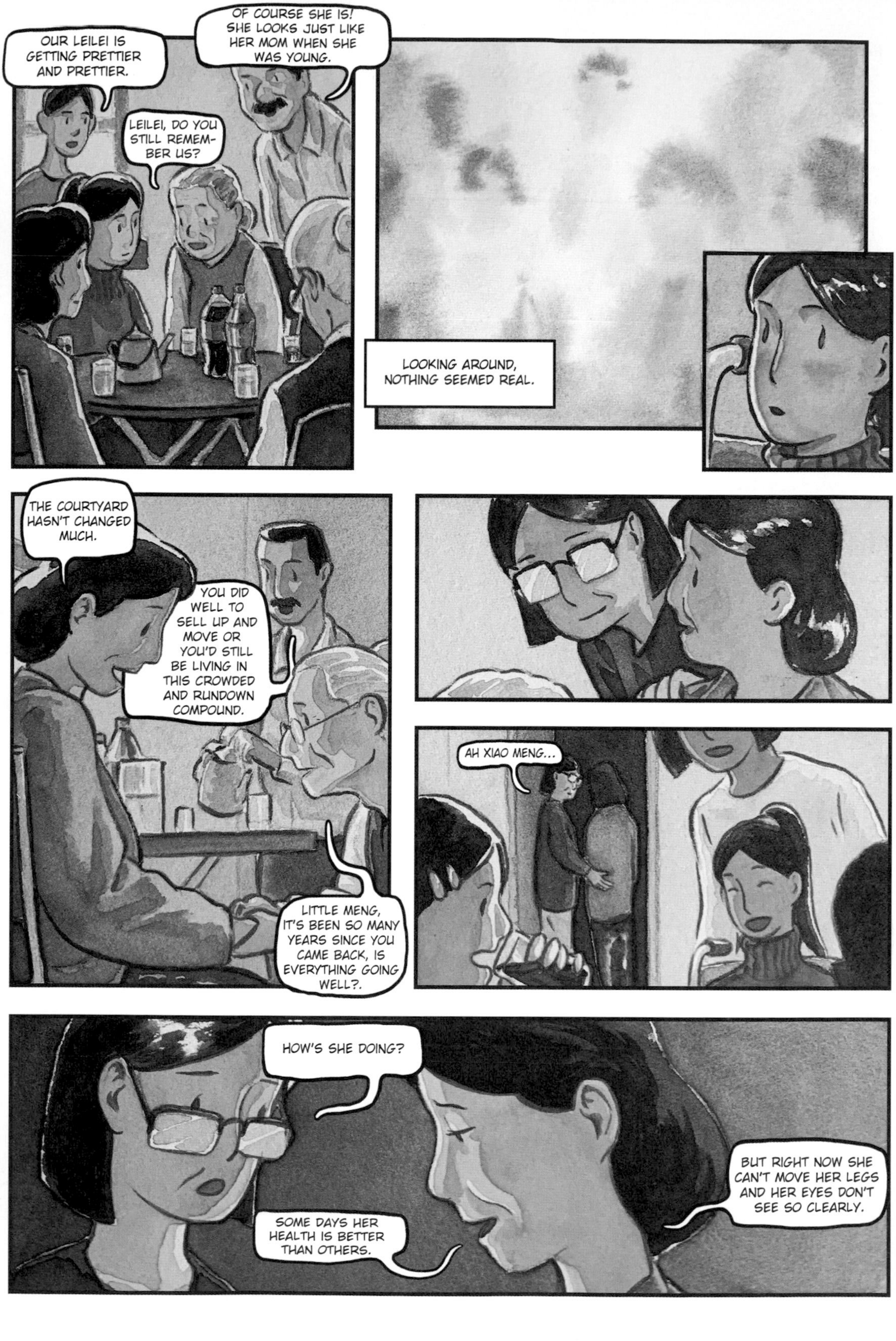
OUR LEILEI IS GETTING PRETTIER AND PRETTIER.
OF COURSE SHE IS! SHE LOOKS JUST LIKE HER MOM WHEN SHE WAS YOUNG.
LEILEI, DO YOU STILL REMEM-BER US?
LOOKING AROUND, NOTHING SEEMED REAL.
THE COURTYARD HASN'T CHANGED MUCH.
YOU DID WELL TO SELL UP AND MOVE OR YOU'D STILL BE LIVING IN THIS CROWDED AND RUNDOWN COMPOUND.
LITTLE MENG, IT'S BEEN SO MANY YEARS SINCE YOU CAME BACK, IS EVERYTHING GOING WELL?.
AH XIAO MENG...
HOW'S SHE DOING?
SOME DAYS HER HEALTH IS BETTER THAN OTHERS.
BUT RIGHT NOW SHE CAN'T MOVE HER LEGS AND HER EYES DON'T SEE SO CLEARLY.

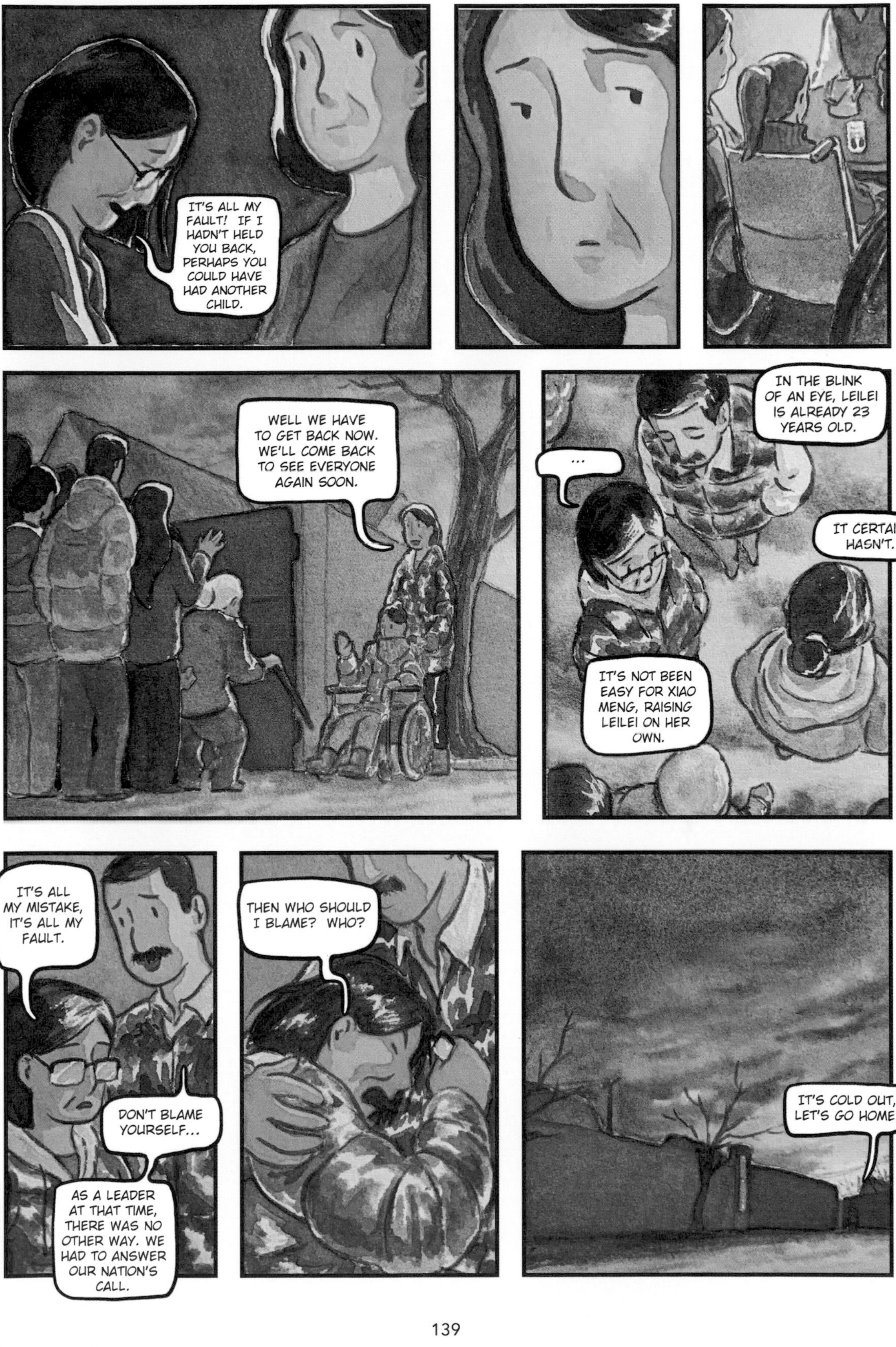
IT'S ALL MY FAULT! IF I HADN'T HELD YOU BACK, PERHAPS YOU COULD HAVE HAD ANOTHER CHILD.
WELL WE HAVE TO GET BACK NOW. WE'LL COME BACK TO SEE EVERYONE AGAIN SOON.
IN THE BLINK OF AN EYE, LEILEI IS ALREADY 23 YEARS OLD.
...
IT CERTAIN HASN'T...
IT'S NOT BEEN EASY FOR XIAO MENG, RAISING LEILEI ON HER OWN.
IT'S ALL MY MISTAKE, IT'S ALL MY FAULT.
DON'T BLAME YOURSELF...
AS A LEADER AT THAT TIME, THERE WAS NO OTHER WAY. WE HAD TO ANSWER OUR NATION'S CALL.
THEN WHO SHOULD I BLAME? WHO?
IT'S COLD OUT, LET'S GO HOME.

WHAT'S YOUR LAST WISH?

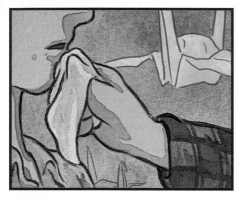

MOM, I'D LIKE TO GET **MARRIED**.

I KNOW THIS IS AN EXTRAVAGANT REQUEST...

WITH ME LIKE THIS, HOW CAN I FIND MYSELF SOMEONE TO LOVE...?

IT'S JUST... I'D REALLY LIKE TO MAKE MY LIFE A LITTLE BIT MORE PERFECT. MOMMY, EVEN IF YOU HELPED ME TO FIND SOMEONE TO MARRY, I WOULDN'T MIND

THAT GIRL I WAS TALKING TO TODAY, XIAO HUI, HAS HAD A CHILD. WHEN WE WERE YOUNG WE HAD AN AGREEMENT, WHEN ONE OF US GOT MARRIED, THE OTHER WOULD BE THE BRIDESMAID...

...SO I'D LIKE TO ASK HER TO BE MY BRIDESMAID.

OKAY, WE'LL INVITE HER.

MOMMY...

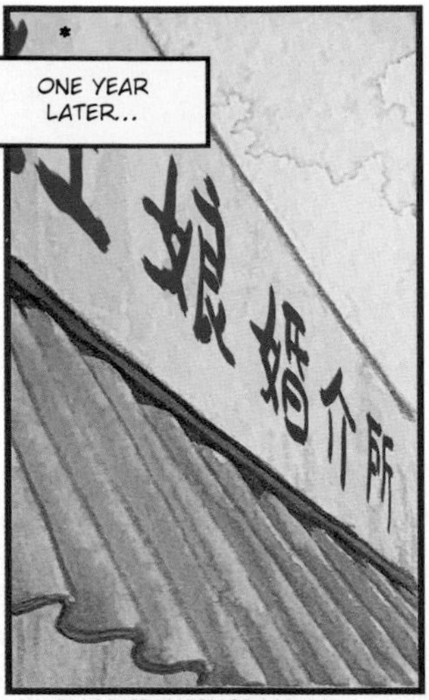
*
ONE YEAR LATER...
娘婚介所

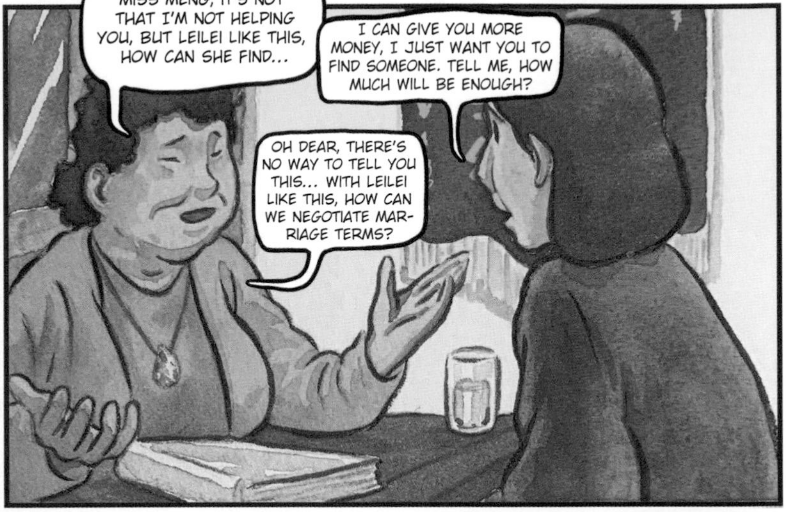
MISS MENG, IT'S NOT THAT I'M NOT HELPING YOU, BUT LEILEI LIKE THIS, HOW CAN SHE FIND...
I CAN GIVE YOU MORE MONEY, I JUST WANT YOU TO FIND SOMEONE. TELL ME, HOW MUCH WILL BE ENOUGH?
OH DEAR, THERE'S NO WAY TO TELL YOU THIS... WITH LEILEI LIKE THIS, HOW CAN WE NEGOTIATE MARRIAGE TERMS?

*MATCHMAKER MARRIAGE AGENCY.

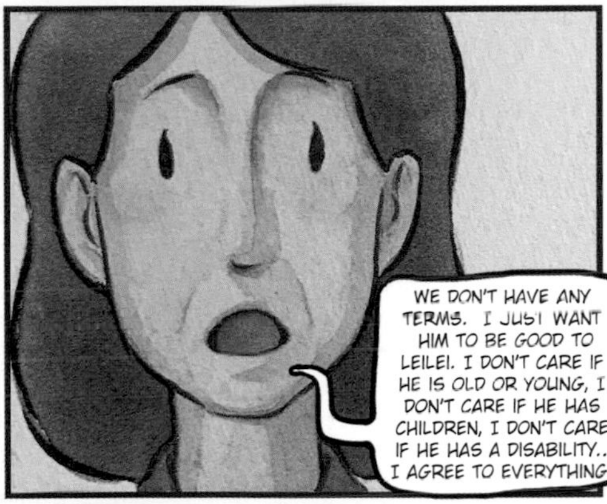
WE DON'T HAVE ANY TERMS. I JUST WANT HIM TO BE GOOD TO LEILEI. I DON'T CARE IF HE IS OLD OR YOUNG, I DON'T CARE IF HE HAS CHILDREN, I DON'T CARE IF HE HAS A DISABILITY... I AGREE TO EVERYTHING!

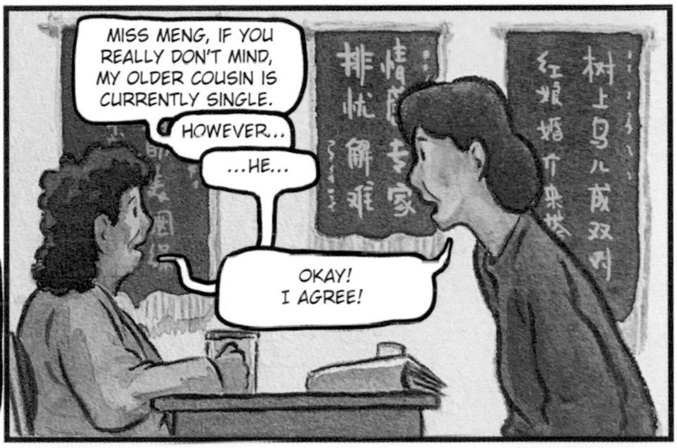
MISS MENG, IF YOU REALLY DON'T MIND, MY OLDER COUSIN IS CURRENTLY SINGLE.
HOWEVER...
...HE...
OKAY! I AGREE!
情感专家
排忧解难
树上鸟儿成双对

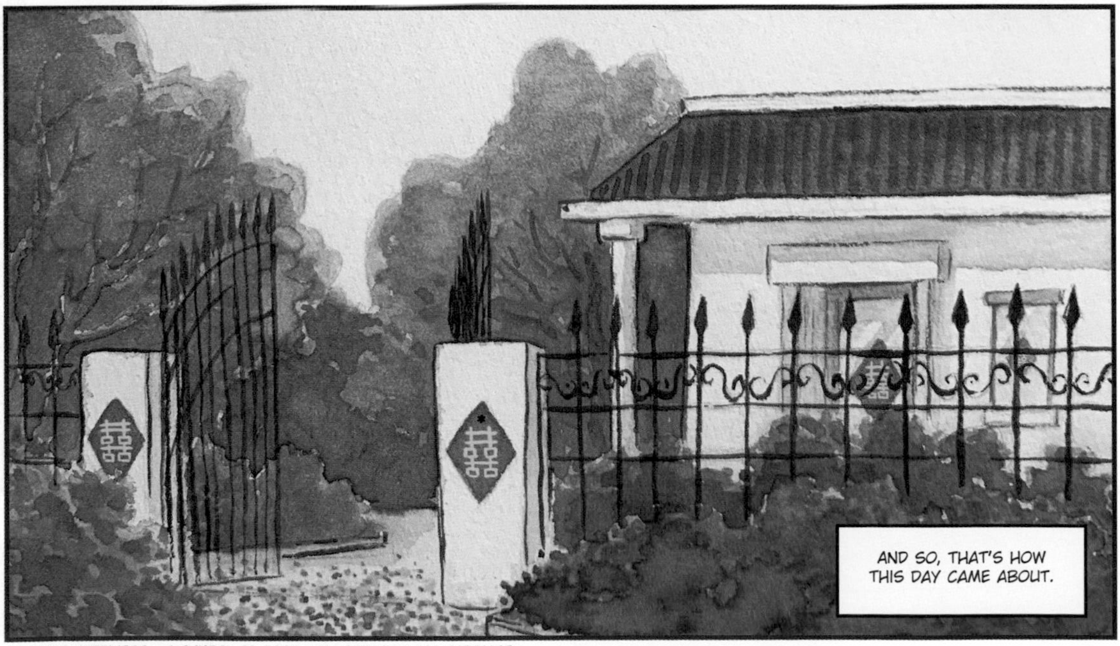
*
AND SO, THAT'S HOW THIS DAY CAME ABOUT.

*DOUBLE HAPPINESS - A SYMBOL OF GOOD LUCK ESPECIALLY IN MARRIAGE

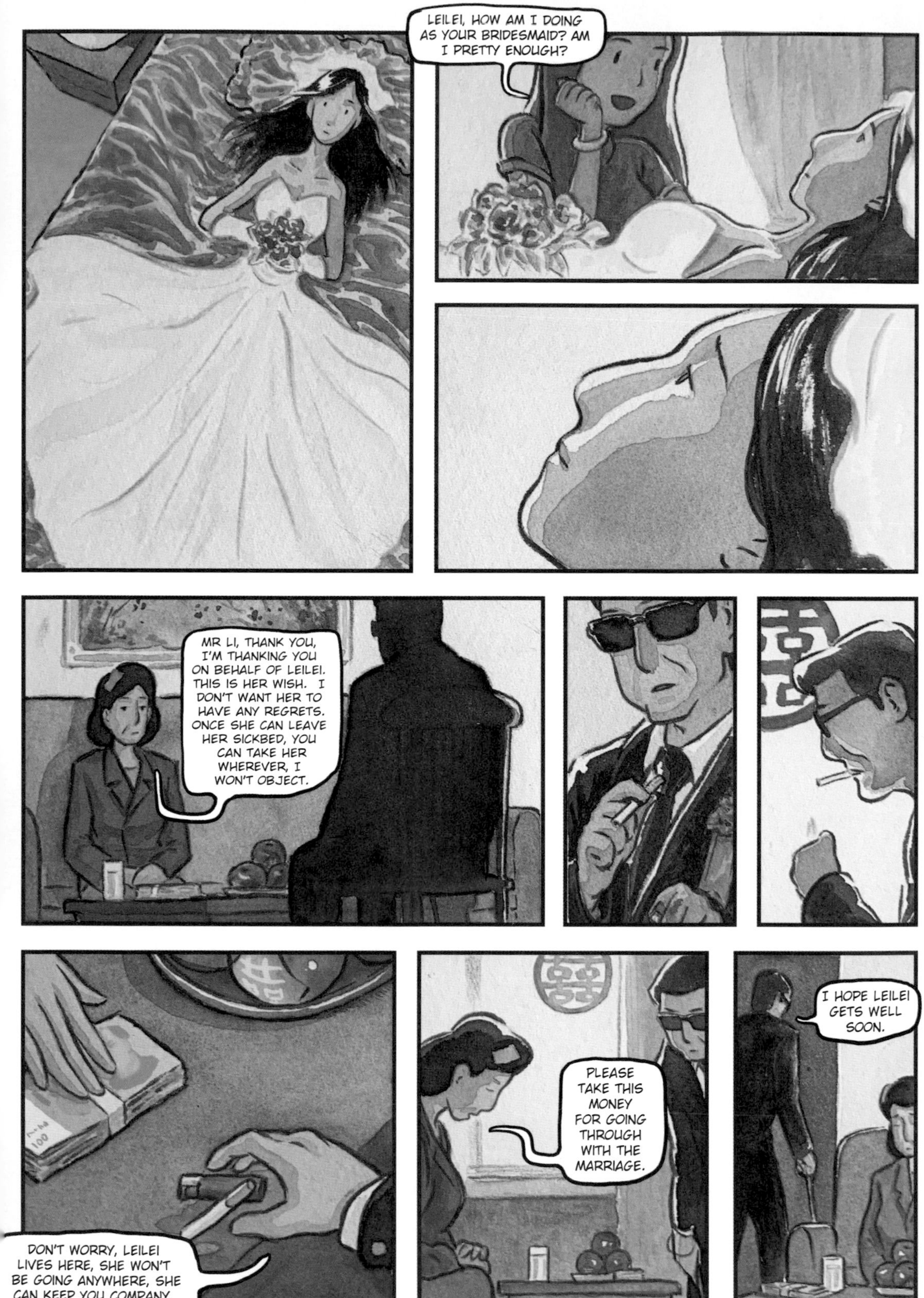
LEILEI, HOW AM I DOING AS YOUR BRIDESMAID? AM I PRETTY ENOUGH?
MR LI, THANK YOU, I'M THANKING YOU ON BEHALF OF LEILEI. THIS IS HER WISH. I DON'T WANT HER TO HAVE ANY REGRETS. ONCE SHE CAN LEAVE HER SICKBED, YOU CAN TAKE HER WHEREVER, I WON'T OBJECT.
DON'T WORRY, LEILEI LIVES HERE, SHE WON'T BE GOING ANYWHERE, SHE CAN KEEP YOU COMPANY.
PLEASE TAKE THIS MONEY FOR GOING THROUGH WITH THE MARRIAGE.
I HOPE LEILEI GETS WELL SOON.

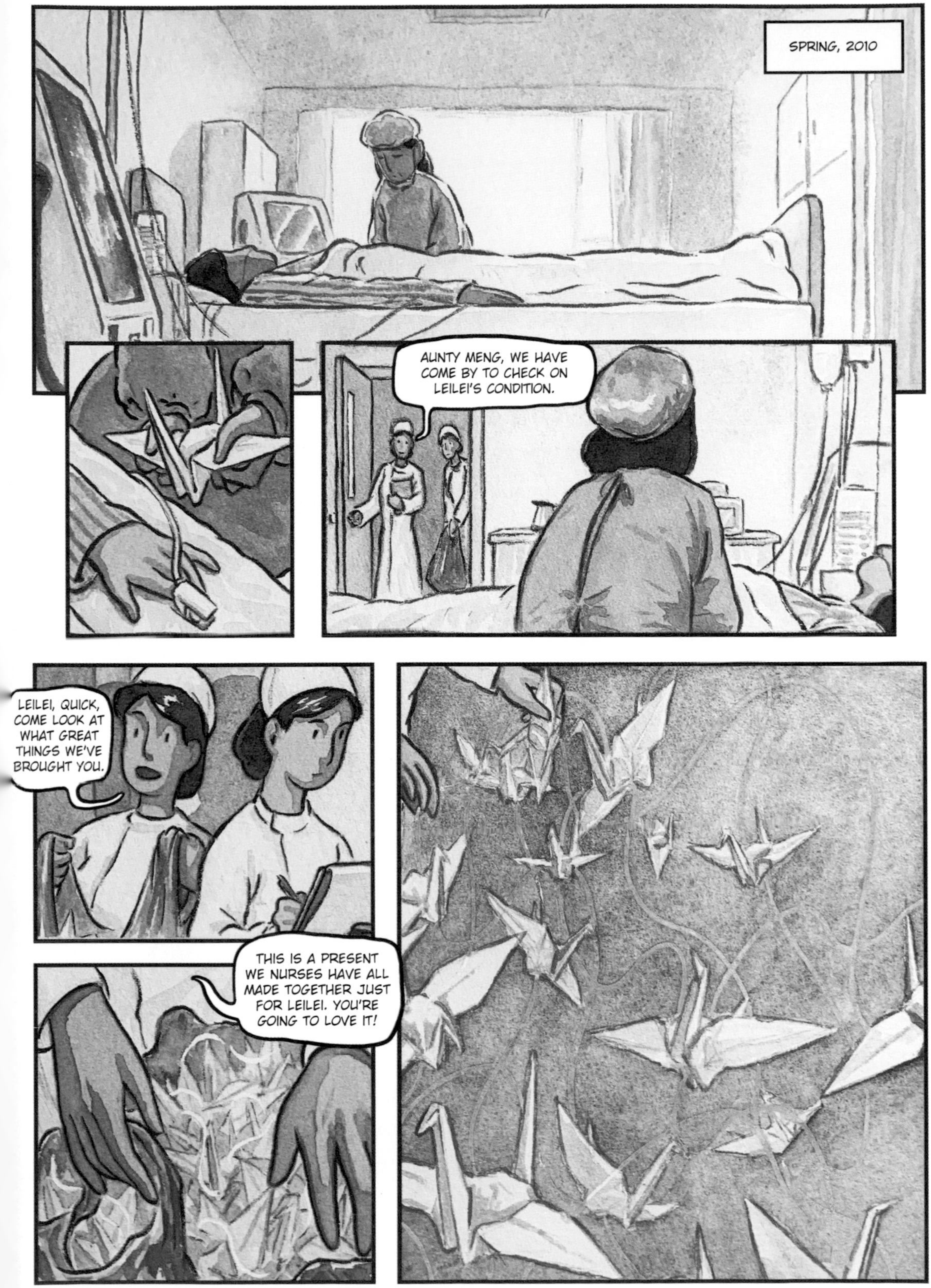
SPRING, 2010
AUNTY MENG, WE HAVE COME BY TO CHECK ON LEILEI'S CONDITION.
LEILEI, QUICK, COME LOOK AT WHAT GREAT THINGS WE'VE BROUGHT YOU.
THIS IS A PRESENT WE NURSES HAVE ALL MADE TOGETHER JUST FOR LEILEI. YOU'RE GOING TO LOVE IT!

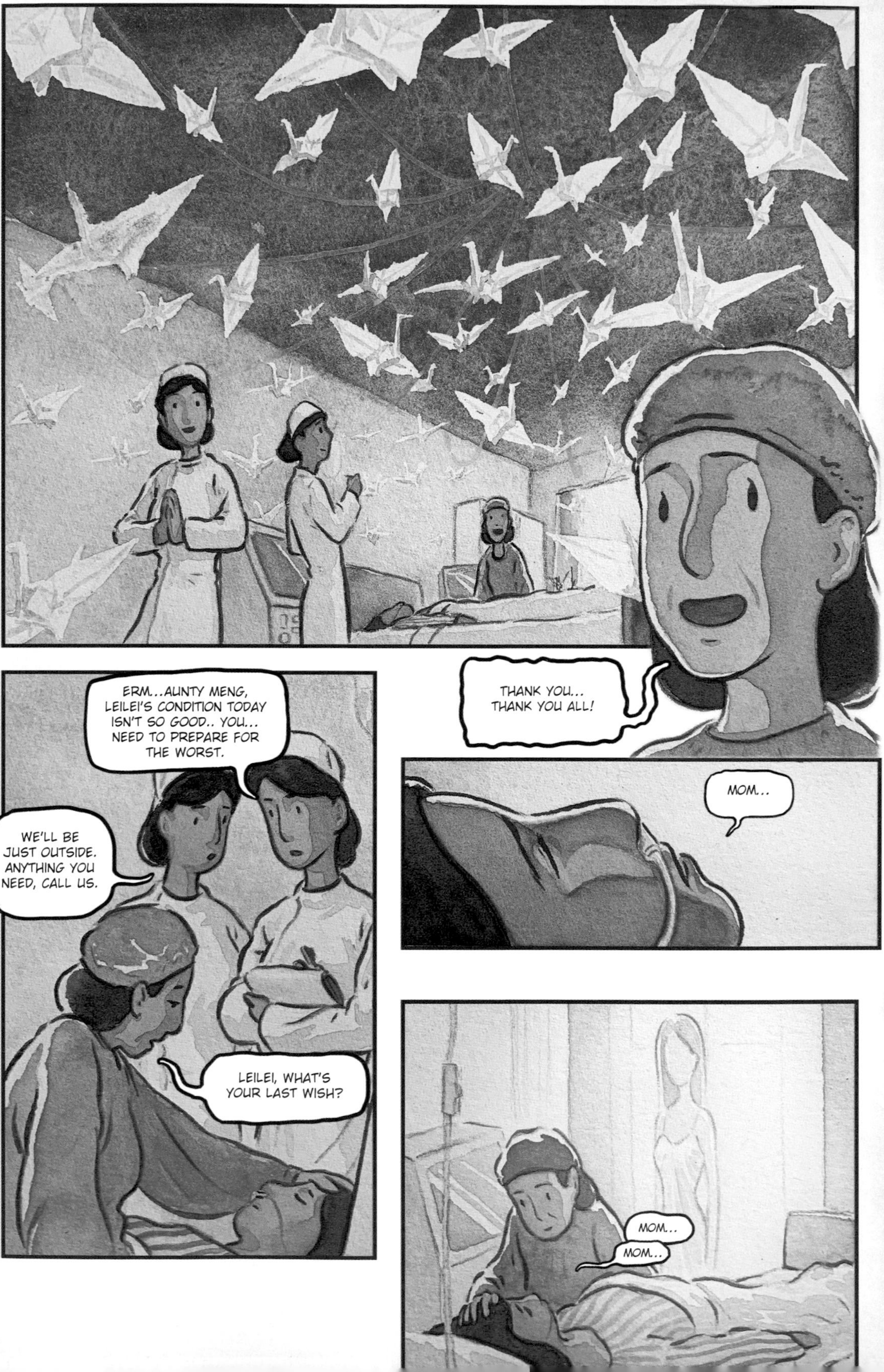
THANK YOU... THANK YOU ALL!
ERM...AUNTY MENG, LEILEI'S CONDITION TODAY ISN'T SO GOOD.. YOU... NEED TO PREPARE FOR THE WORST.
WE'LL BE JUST OUTSIDE. ANYTHING YOU NEED, CALL US.
LEILEI, WHAT'S YOUR LAST WISH?
MOM...
MOM...
MOM...

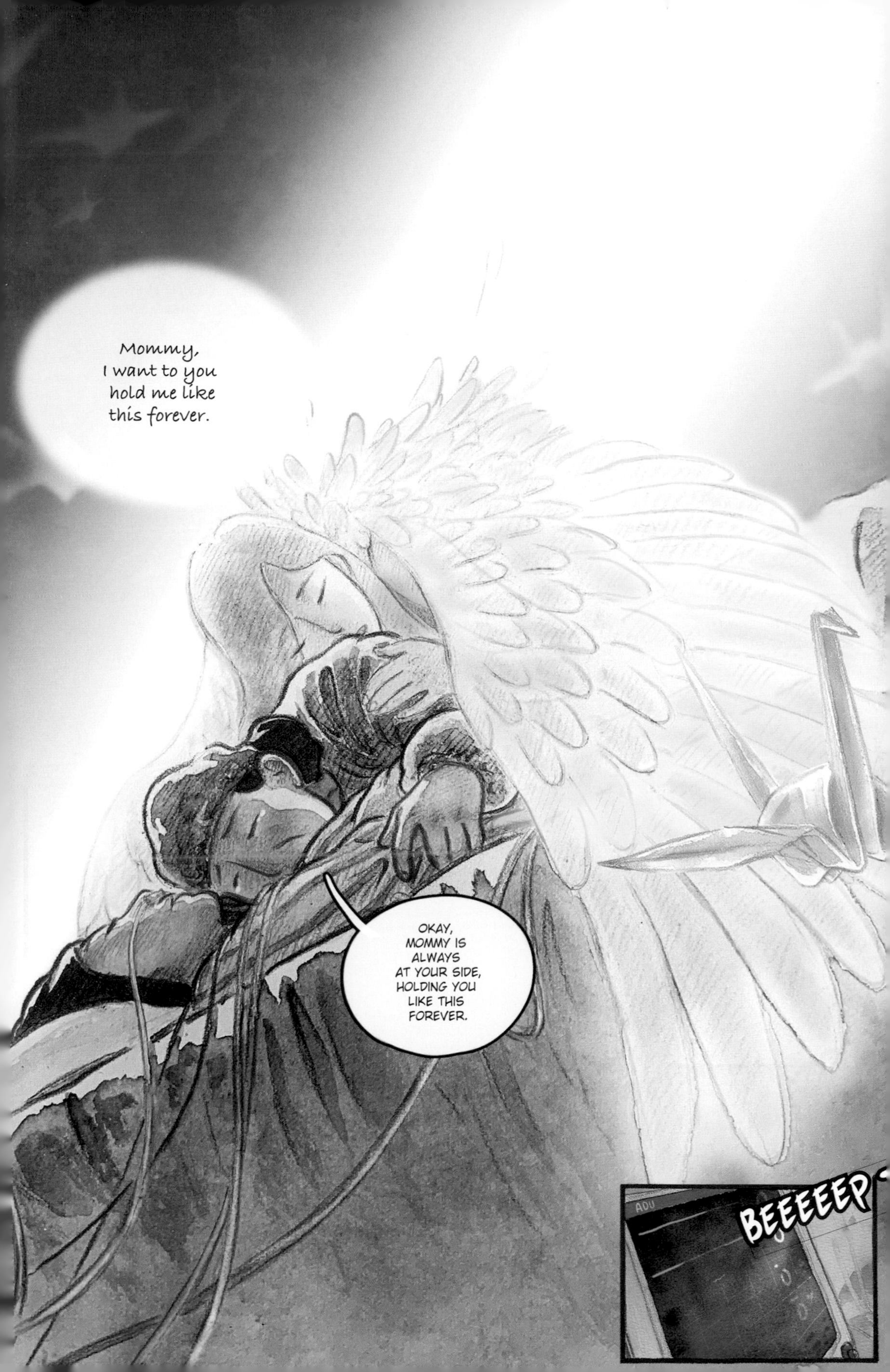
Mommy, I want to you hold me like this forever.
OKAY, MOMMY IS ALWAYS AT YOUR SIDE, HOLDING YOU LIKE THIS FOREVER.
BEEEEEP

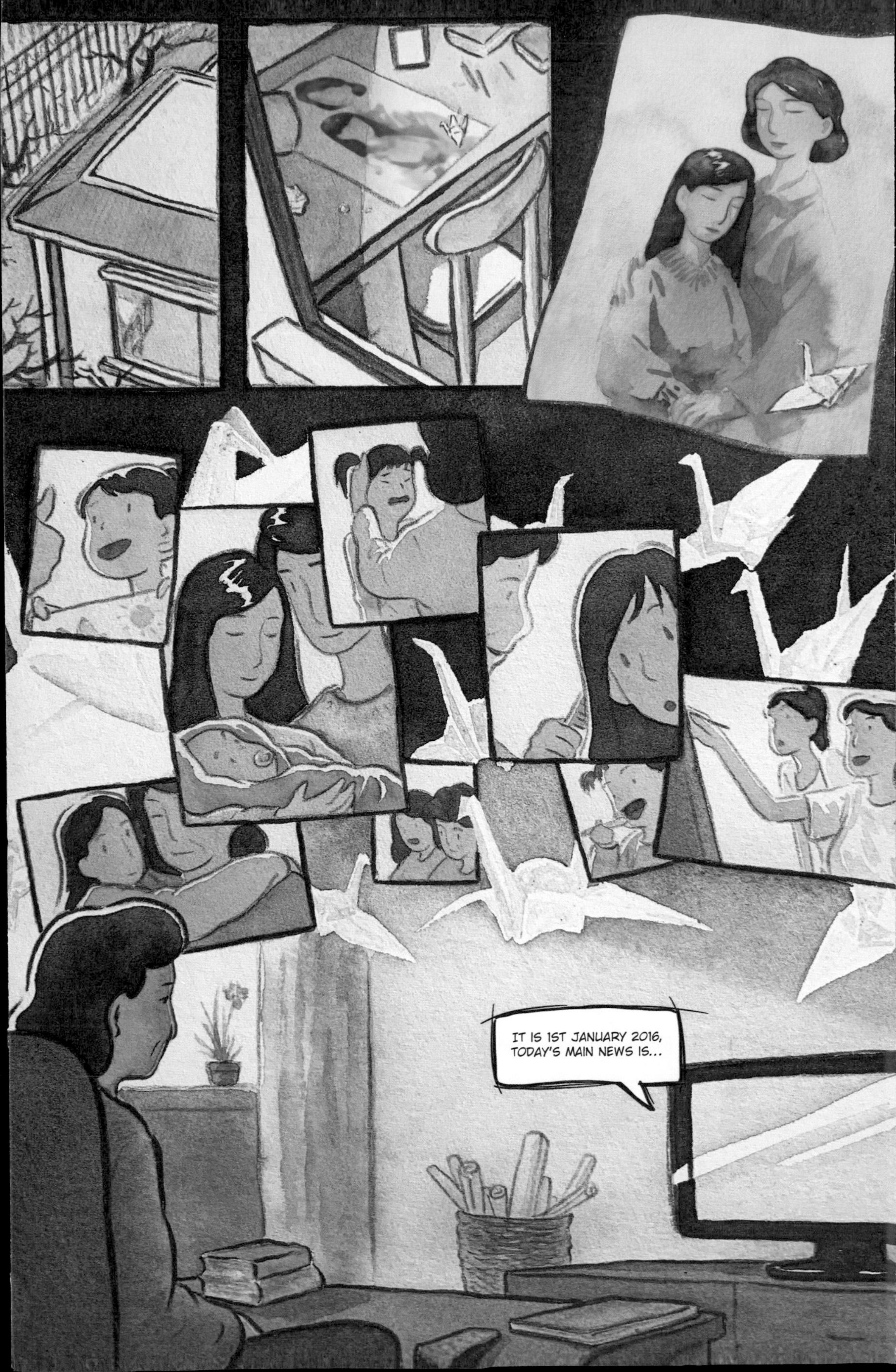
IT IS 1ST JANUARY 2016,
TODAY'S MAIN NEWS IS...

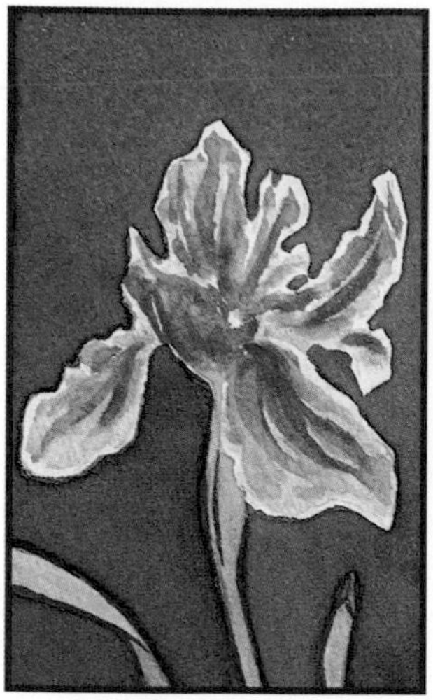

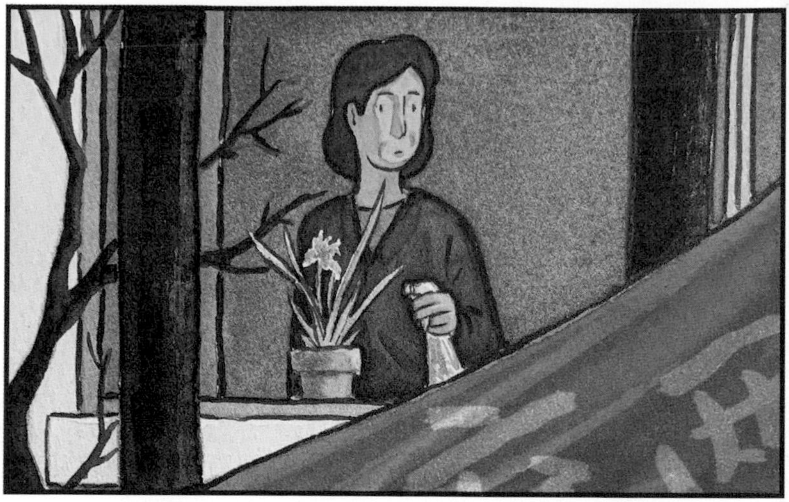

*PUT INTO PRACTICE THE NEW TWO CHILD POLICY

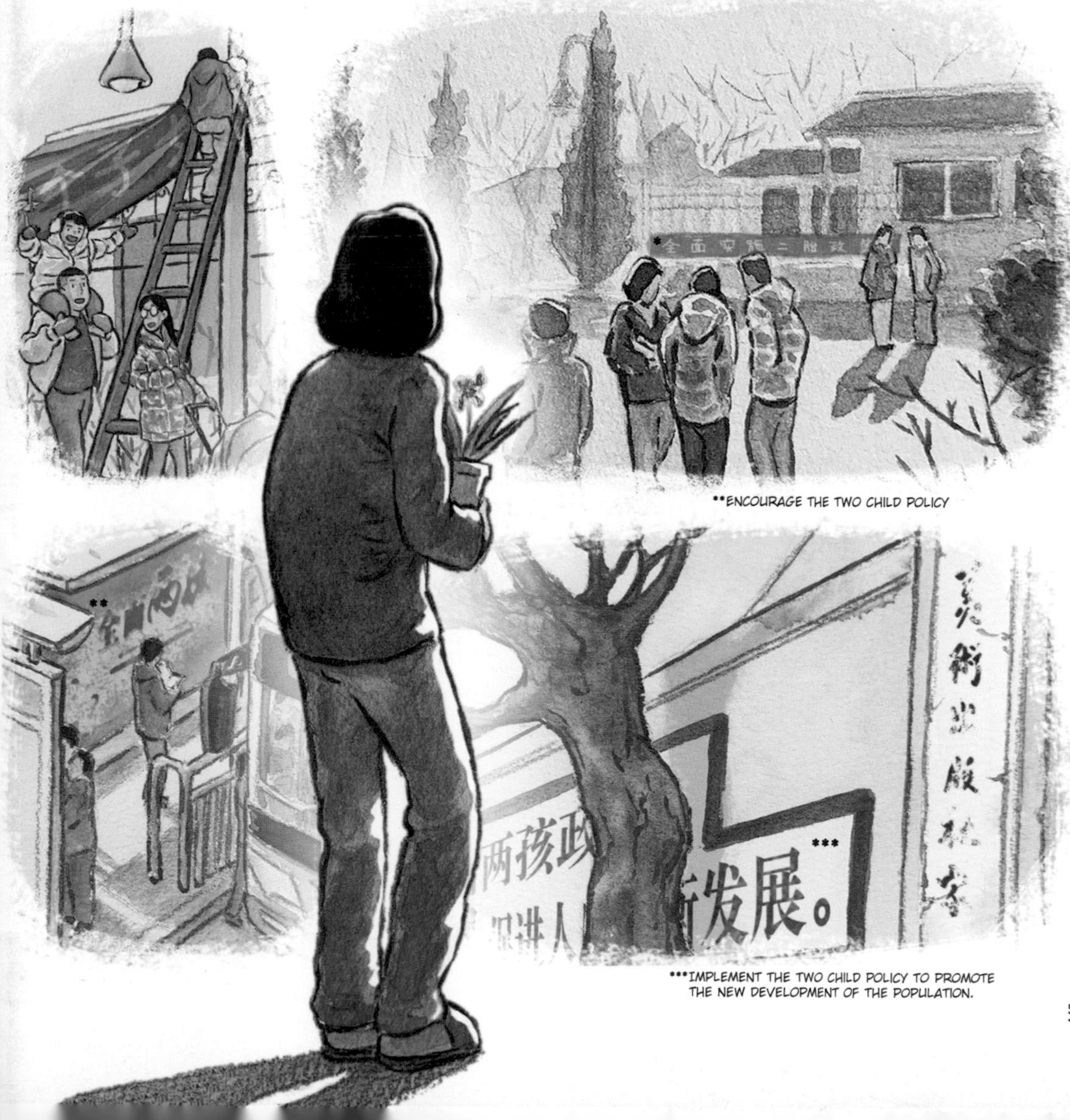
*全面实施二胎政
两孩政
新发展。

**ENCOURAGE THE TWO CHILD POLICY

***IMPLEMENT THE TWO CHILD POLICY TO PROMOTE THE NEW DEVELOPMENT OF THE POPULATION.

完。

Talk a little bit about my feelings

《**My Only Child**》这本书要在英国出版了，我努力尝试着让自己放松下来，尽量以平和的心态写下以下的感言。

The book "My Only Child" will be published in English. I try to relax myself and write the following testimonials with the calm mind.

自上世纪 70 年代至 2015 年的中国，因为人多国穷等原因，中国实行了长达 36 年的独生子女政策，即：一个家庭只能有一个子女。这个政策伴随着 70 后、80、90 后，甚至 00 后几代人的成长，使得我们这几代人、几代家庭都有着丰富且难以磨灭的记忆。

From the 1970s to 2015, China has implemented the one-child policy for 36 years, which means that a family can only have one child. This policy is accompanied by the growth of the generations born in the 70s, 80s, 90s, and even the 00s, making our generations and many families have lots of indelible memories.

在众多独生子女家庭中，由于身边没有和自己争宠、争利的兄弟姐妹，大多数的孩子都是伴随着孤独生活在相对优越或相对独立的环境里，很多父母都为了这仅有的一个孩子倾注了极大的心血，不余遗力地为自己的孩子在今后的生活中铺平一切道路。如果说，整个的家庭就像一个完整的世界的话，这个世界就属于这个唯一的孩子，看起来那么的幸福。

In many one-child families, because there are no siblings who compete with them for favor and profit, most of the children live in relatively superior or relatively independent environments, but they are very lonely. Many parents have devoted great efforts to their only child and spare no effort to pave the way for their children in the future life. If the whole family is like one person's world, so, this world belongs to the only child, it looks very happy.

但是，由于每个家庭只有一个子女，如果发生无法预知的变化，也会给无忧无虑的家庭带来灭顶之灾，甚至改变了很多人的生活和命运，这就是失独家庭。

However, since each family has only one child, if unpredictable changes occur, it will also bring serious disasters to the carefree family, and even change the lives and destinies of many people. This is the family loss the only child .

默默的故事因为篇幅所限，没有办法把我所知道的都讲出来，很遗憾。当默默离开后，她的父母不接任何电话也不见任何人，把自己锁在家里几个月。在长达 2 年多的时间里，他们没有再参加过任何家庭聚会。即使偶尔和家人见见面，但我们所有人再也没有在他们面前提过默默。当我和夫人隔了很久去看望他们时，眼前的一切和以前还是一样熟悉，但是缺少了往日的气息。小黑狗默默每天都趴在默默的床边，抱着默默的衣服睡觉。墙上的照片是默默抱着熊猫，照片上的默默笑得那么开心。

Because the story of MoMo is so short, it is impossible to tell everything I know. It's sad. When MoMo left, her parents did not answer any calls or meet anyone. They locked themselves at home for several months. In more than 2 years, they did not attend any family gatherings. Until to now, none of us have ever talked about MoMo in front of them again. When my wife and I visited them after a long time, everything in front of us was still as familiar as before, just lacked the breath of the past. The little black dog MoMo holding MoMo's clothes and sleeping next to MoMo's bed every day. The picture on the wall is MoMo holding a panda, MoMo in the picture smiles so happily.

默默的男朋友小李我们再也没有见过，如果他有了新的生活，我们不想再去勾起他对往事的回忆。如果他还沉浸在永远的痛苦中，我们更不愿意去反复的刺激他。

We have never seen MoMo's boyfriend, Xiao Li again. If he has a new life, we don't want to bring back his memories of the past. If he is still immersed in eternal pain, we don't want to constantly stimulate him again.

在故事的最后，这个政策已经改成了人们可以拥有二胎，2021 年的时候，国家又在鼓励生三胎。只是，对于这些家庭而言，这个政策的意义又何在呢？

At the end of the story, this policy has been changed, the people can have a second child. In 2021, the country is encouraging three children again. But, for this kind of family, does such policy has any meaning?

对那些失独家庭来说，那个家已经没有了，他们也随着家庭的消失失去了生活的意义。普天之下，哪个家庭不是把对孩子的爱、对孩子的希望倾注一生？对他们这一代的人来说，孩子就只有这一个，孩子就是全部的希望，是他们活下去的理由和动力。而如今，像这样的失独群体不在少数，而且越来越多。那种伤痛不会伴随着岁月减弱或消失，反而会越来越强烈。一个人的世界，真的没有想象的那么美好，反而可能成为伤痛的开始！

For those families who have lost their children, that home is no longer there. With the disappearance of the family, they also lose the meaning of life. In this world, every family hopes that the love for their children is eternal. For this generation of people, they have only one child in the life. The child is their all hope, and the child is the reason and motivation for their survival. Today, more and more groups have lost their only child. The pain will not fade or disappear with the years, but the feeling of pain will become stronger and stronger. One person's world is really not as beautiful as imagined, but it may become the beginning of pain!

最后，我要特别感谢 Julie Tait、Stephen Robson、Emma Massara、Amiram Reuveni and Kendal comic art festival，以及许许多多为了这本书所付出努力和心血的朋友们。因为你们，让这本具有纪实性的漫画书能够在英国出版，让更多的人了解了发生在我们身边的真实故事，也体会到了我们真实的感受，谢谢你们！

Finally, I would like to express my special thanks to Julie Tait, Stephen Robson, Emma Massara, Amiram Reuveni and Kendal comic art festival. As well as many friends who have worked hard and devoted themselves to this book. Because of you, let this documentary comic book be published in English. Let more people understand the real stories that happened around us, and also appreciate our true feelings, thank you!

Wang Ning
August 2021

Editor's Note:
These are the personal thoughts from the author Wang Ning written in both Chinese and English – his English. The words are so very personal I decided to leave them in tact except for a few very minor factual changes to the English.

Set up an emotional sanctuary for them

Children are the future of a country. They are also the continuation and hope of a family. The aim of every country is to have happy, prosperous families. Every country on earth is made up of countless families and the key to their happiness is the survival of the children.

"One couple, one child" was a national policy in China, formulated in the 1970s to meet the need of the country at that time. Thousands upon thousands of couples responded to the country's call, played their part and made their sacrifice. For various reasons, however, while reducing the number of births, many also suffered the pain of losing their only child, often unable to have another at their stage of life. They would endure tremendous struggles and suffering. This phenomenon is called "shi du". These "Lost Families" often affect the mental wellbeing of several families over generations. Some of the children were young when they became ill and their parents placed all their hope on a cure. They gave all they had to prolong the life of their child, but in the end they still lost them. Some of the children grew up and became adults, but due to unfortunate circumstances, the parents could only look on helplessly as their only child passed away. Through their suffering, they are gradually growing old and the only thing left is the cherished memories of their child. Some of the children were abducted and lost. Parents frantically searched everywhere for them, waiting anxiously for a miracle to happen. More moving still, are those parents who found themselves some solace. They adopted a child who had lost their parents, rekindling their love as well as giving those children the warmth of a family.

There are many more touching, heartrending stories about "shi du" families. We come from that era and far too many stories actually happened around us. Therefore, we had the idea of developing these moving stories into the form of a comic book. We hope they will be a window to understanding their experiences. We also want to set up a place where they can share their troubles and talk about their emotions.

Although months and years pass, slowly soothing their grief, the scar is still there. If only those children who died too soon could know our intentions, and could come to this 'emotional sanctuary' we have made for them and hear their parents' cherished memories of them!

Chinese Editor Wang Saili
28.04.2020
In 1995 she began as editor-in-chief of comic magazines and worked on developing comic artists. Later she taught comic creation at Beijing Film Academy, Central Academy of Fine Arts School and other universities.